How to Start and Succeed as an Artist

Daniel Grant

ALLWORTH PRESS
NEW YORK

Published by Allworth Press
An imprint of Allworth Communications
10 East 23rd Street, New York, NY 10010

Cover design by Douglas Designs, New York, NY

Book design by Sharp Des!gns, Holt, MI

ISBN: 1-880559-83-8

Library of Congress Catalog Card Number: 97-72217

Printed in Canada

■

Contents

Introduction

*D*URING THE 1960S AND 1970S, IT WAS commonly said in the higher echelons of the art world that "painting is dead." "I'm merely making the last painting which anyone can make," Ad Reinhardt said in a 1966 interview about one of his many black-on-black paintings. Formalist tendencies brought to their extreme had made traditional painting—with its emphasis on brushwork, the mix of colors and the idea of the picture as a window to the world—seem tedious and irrelevant, and many painters themselves began to look to other media, such as photography, film, video and performance, that weren't so weighed down by history. The idea that painting was a pleasure in its own right didn't seem relevant.

Formalist canon is but one of the many ways in which artists have been given to understand that their efforts are not required. The realist painter Fairfield Porter was told by critic Clement Greenberg that "You can't paint like that anymore." At least the reason for Porter's low regard in the art world was made explicit to him. Greenberg's view that the train of art moves only one way on one track and Reinhardt's opinion that his painting was where the train comes to a stop reflect a hierarchical system in which only relatively few artists, holding certain rarified beliefs, could be considered worth looking at—all others are anachronistic daubers.

The "pluralism" of the 1970s and postmodern eclecticism of the 1980s and 1990s have enlarged the scope of permissible styles, media and subject matter, yet it is easy for artists to find themselves wide of art world acceptance. Of course, artists need to maintain an awareness of new ideas and styles in their field by attending exhibitions and by reading critiques, essays and books—less to be told what to do or how to do it than to keep their own art fresh by periodically challenging their own work.

What distinguishes art from almost every other pursuit—vocation or avocation—is that the credentials of the artist are of no particular importance for its creation. Certainly, art schools will rarely hire teachers without Masters of Fine Art degrees, but the only degrees earned by Henri Matisse and Wassily Kandinsky were in the law. Matisse was 21, a clerk in a law office in 1890, when he took his first art class, and Kandinsky was 30 in 1896 when he moved to Munich, Germany, in order to study painting, leaving behind the post of professor of law at the University of Dorpat in Russia that had just been offered to him.

Artists are people who have defined themselves as such; those who believe in their own artwork have as much right to call themselves artists as the most celebrated figures whose works are displayed in galleries and museums. Art's greatest strength is that it is not the sole domain of specialists and technicians, that it follows no laws or doctrines. In fact, most art movements since impressionism have made a point of defying "rules" and traditions. Art will remain alive as long as there are people interested in making it.

There are no right and wrong ways to develop one's artistic skills, only approaches that may be better suited to certain artists than others. While some people prefer to go it alone, others may join an art club or society, for example, in order to meet fellow artists working in the same medium with whom to talk about art or socialize. Yet other artists choose to make those kinds of associations in an art class, joining a society primarily in order to exhibit with an established group. There are societies and classes for every purpose.

As much as artists are producers, they also are consumers—of art materials, art societies and other groups, of art classes and workshops, of services to the field and of books like this one—who need to be aware of the choices available to them as well as the benefits and (potential) drawbacks of each.

By its nature, art is a very private activity; yet, because art is a form of expression and communication, it is also by nature intended to be made public. It is in works of art that we are able to discover what an artist has been feeling and thinking, and it is through the process of creating that an artist is generally able to find a "voice." In developing one's artistic potential, one is able to make this voice more clear and distinct, better equipped to put a wider range of ideas into visual form. Certainly, the more adept or mature an artist becomes, the more prepared he or she is to present artwork to the outside world.

❧

CHAPTER 1

■

Developing One's Skills with Others

ART, LIKE EVERYTHING ELSE, TAKES
practice. For many nonprofessionals, that frequently involves taking
classes, working in a studio alongside other students engaged in their
own or a common project under the supervision of an experienced
teacher.

Art Classes

Before the Second World War, choices for art classes were either
extremely limited or nonexistent for most people, which was the main
reason that those seriously interested in studying art were faced with
the decision of moving to some major city (such as Chicago, New York,
or Paris) in order to obtain high-level instruction. Nowadays, with
professional artists teaching in art departments at colleges and
universities around the country and the emergence of regional art
markets, the opportunities have increased exponentially. One can take
art classes through adult education programs at high schools and
community (or senior citizen) centers, from artists in their studios and
at arts centers, at museums, art associations, and degree-granting
institutions.

Adult education programs tend to be the least intensive, providing
basic information for beginners, while classes offered at arts centers and
museums allow more time to work in a studio with more rigorous
standards set by peers as well as the instructor. Community college,
college, and university art classes, which frequently are open to
nondegree-seeking students when not filled by regular students, offer

the largest blocks of studio time. These latter classes are often taught with greater formality than those at high schools and arts centers and may include specific assignments, homework and serious critiques.

This hierarchy doesn't always hold true, however, as many of the same instructors at the college level also teach at museums, arts centers and in adult education programs. As a survey of the variety of art classes offered in the Boca Raton–West Palm Beach area of Florida reveals, the teachers may alter their approach and requirements depending upon the venue, but not always.

"My classes are definitely more relaxed when I'm teaching at the museum than at the university," said Rick Yasko, a drawing instructor at both Florida Atlantic University in Boca Raton, Florida, and the Boca Raton Museum of Art. "I'm more demanding of students in the university because I am supposed to be providing an academic training for students who are going on to graduate programs in art or to find a job and need a professional-looking portfolio. At the museum, there are no grades and if I give an assignment it usually can be completed by the time the class is over."

A number of his students at the museum also take his courses at the university on a nondegree basis. The nondegree people, he has found, are "sometimes more dedicated to their art than the regular students, because they're not interested in a grade or a degree." As it is not uncommon for these students to take the same course again and again, Yasko tries "to gear things differently each time the course is given, in order to let them try new media"—such as silverpoint and pastels—"and new ideas about drawing."

Other differences between taking a class at the university and at the museum are the cost and the amount of time involved. Florida Atlantic University charges $51.66 per credit to Florida residents for its three- or four-credit 14-week classes ($189.61 per credit to non-Florida residents). The Boca Raton Museum of Art, on the other hand, requires $95 for its once-a-week (for 6 weeks) class. Again, the differences may not be so sharp since, according to the museum's art school registrar, Lois Prochlik, "we have a number of people who take two or three classes. They spend the whole day here."

If classes at a museum are more relaxed than at a university or college, those taught at arts centers are often even more easy-going. "An art center is a more family-like institution," said Barbara Wasserman, a Boca Raton painter who teaches at both the Boca Raton Museum of Art and at the Armory Art Center in West Palm Beach. "Universities can sometimes treat you like a number, and museums are more focused on the needs of the museum than on painting students.

An art center, on the other hand, is focused on its students because the students are its reason for being."

Eight-week, three-hour classes at the Armory Art Center, which was set up in 1987 after the Norton Gallery of Art in West Palm Beach closed its teaching facility, cost $120. With the overlap of a number of instructors at both the Armory Art Center and the Boca Raton Museum and the fact that many of the students take classes at both, the level of teaching between the two institutions is not significantly different. However, several of the teachers indicated that more classes at the museum have specific assignments, such as painting from a model or learning color values, than at the art center, which has more of a do-your-own-thing approach.

Wasserman noted, for instance, that some of the students in her classes at the Armory paint in a highly realistic style while "others are very abstract. The challenge for me is to be able to work with each one of them, geared to their interests and to their level of skill." Another instructor at the Armory, watercolorist Lynn Thurmond, also teaches at the private Everglades Club in West Palm Beach, where the range of skill and devotion to developing one's craft among students is wider. "There are some people at the Everglades Club who are very serious about their work and really want me to give them any advice I can," she stated. "There are other people who just have the time to do something, and art is relaxing and a sociable experience. A lot of them don't want as much guidance and instruction and are pretty adamant about having their way about it. There's nothing wrong with that but at the Armory almost everyone wants to get their money's worth out of me."

Other than these kinds of art classes, one may locate adult education or night school programs, classes offered by artist associations and workshops offered at an artist's own studio. These frequently are less expensive because students do not have to pay as much for overhead expenses (rent, utilities, security, custodial services), and frequently go further along the road of informality.

There are various sources of information on art classes, starting with a local or state arts agency, since many institutions offering art instruction apply for governmental funding. High schools and community centers, arts centers and organizations, museums and colleges all may provide classes or refer inquirers to those that do. R.R. Bowker's *American Art Directory*, which costs $151.95 but is available at many public libraries, lists art schools and college art departments as well as art associations around the United States (by state and city) and the world.

Those wanting to take a class should decide in advance what they are looking for, such as a class exclusively for beginners or one with a mix of different levels of skill. Adult education classes, which may be taught by high school art instructors or someone in the community, generally last two hours a weeknight for six to eight weeks, while those offered by colleges may meet for four-hour stretches lasting an entire semester. Some classes have live models, others don't. Some classes provide specific activities or assignments, while others allow students to work on whatever they choose. Some schools have fixed time periods for classes, others allow those wishing to take a class to walk in anytime. Some teachers take a very activist role, assuming their students want considerable instruction and even homework, and others may just wander around students' work areas from time to time offering only the slightest commentary. Some teachers emphasize detailed critiques of student work, while others prefer to work on the level of suggestion. Some teachers may spend the entire class working on their own projects, while letting students with questions approach them, and some classes do without instructors completely.

Usually, it is the presence of a particular teacher that makes more of a difference than the specific school, and potential students might want to sit in on a class to see if they like what other students are doing and what the teacher is saying. This may be especially useful when one is taking a class at a college, as the content of the course may be difficult to comprehend by reading the language used in the syllabus but easier to understand in practice. At other times, the instruction may seem too basic or not rigorous enough. Robert Hertz, who currently teaches drawing and portraiture at both the Armory Art Center and the Boca Raton Museum of Art, remembered an art class he sat in on, in which the instructor "showed you a picture and asked you to copy it. After you had completed the assignment, he looked at it and said, 'Very nice.'"

It is not uncommon for students who have enjoyed an artist's instruction at a class to also study with the artist at his or her studio. "If you find a good instructor," Rick Yasko, who has held occasional one-day workshops at his studio (charging between $25 and $50 per person), said, "you follow them around continuously." It may or may not matter to certain students that their instructor is a full-time artist who happens to teach, as opposed to a full-time teacher who also creates art. Yasko, for instance, teaches not only at Florida Atlantic University and the Boca Raton Museum of Art but at Barry University (at Miami Shores), Broward Community College in Davey and Palm Beach Community College. Art instructors are always expected to be artists first, but teaching positions are generally so rare and so poorly paid that artists must get two, three or four jobs in order to support themselves and their art, which they no longer have much time to pursue. All that running around may, for some, also prove detrimental to their art and lessen their interest in teaching.

"The difference between me and someone who only teaches for a living is enthusiasm," said Sharon Koskoff, a self-supporting artist in Delray Beach, Florida, who also teaches painting and drawing at the Armory Art Center. "I never feel that I'm really working unless I'm creating art, so I can bring some of that enthusiasm to my students."

The Benefits of Taking an Art Workshop

There are a lot of ways to learn how to create art or improve one's artistic skills. Trial and error on one's own is the most common. Many people also look for help from other skilled artists, which increases the cost of that learning but may speed it up and give it new direction. Art schools, art classes, correspondence-school art courses, instructional videotapes, art instruction books and art workshops are among the main choices in this category.

Each type of instruction requires something a little different from the would-be student. Degree-granting art schools often require the greatest commitment of time and money; students leave these programs not only with studio art training but with in-depth knowledge of art history and theory. Art classes and correspondence art courses, on the other hand, require less time and money but cannot provide the intensity and individual attention of the art school experience. Instructional videotapes and art instruction books cost even less and make no specific demands on one's scheduling, but are the most impersonal.

Art workshops are something in-between. They provide an intense art experience, but for a relatively short period of time—three days or a week, maybe two—that may be easier for busy people to schedule; their cost ranges widely, from $200 to $2,800, depending upon the length of the workshop, the renown of the artist-teacher and whether or not one needs to travel to the workshop site, paying for accommodations and food as well as transportation.

A potential advantage of workshops over art classes is that, in a workshop, participants study with a professional working artist; not all art class instructors are full-time artists. Workshops also generally include demonstrations by the artist—art classes and schools rarely if ever do—which enables students to see every step in the creative process, from how to put paint on a palette and clean brushes afterward to how to capture a certain quality of light on a canvas.

Workshops come in all varieties. Some are oriented toward beginners, others are for those with some art-making experience, and still others are for people with considerable art training or even professional artists, and many accept a mix of all three. The workshops that accept potential students on a first-come-first-served basis are more likely to have students with a wide range of experience than those in which a selection based on one's level of skill takes place.

"I don't take beginners at all," painter Ann Templeton said, noting that beginners require so much attention when they are starting out that she cannot assist other students equally. "I prefer intermediate and advanced students, and I try to make that clear in the brochure I send out." Other artist-workshop teachers, on the other hand, aim for beginners "because you don't have to unlearn them of bad habits that more experienced students may have developed over years," stated Carmen Layden, who runs Valdes Art Workshops in Santa Fe, New Mexico. The Valdes Art Workshops brochure indicates which artists are interested in beginners and intermediates, which prefer more advanced students and those who will accept a mix. A third approach is offered by husband-and-wife painters Jack Beal and Sondra Freckelton whose four summertime workshops on their farm in Oneonta, New York, are broken down into intermediate and advanced groupings.

In many workshops, full-time, self-supporting artists can be found among the students. They add a degree of seriousness of purpose for those less advanced, and afford themselves the opportunity to expand their thinking and techniques in directions they hadn't tried before or perhaps felt they couldn't move in on their own.

Some workshops focus on particular media, such as pastels, watercolors, oil paints, acrylics, printmaking, and sculpture, while others concentrate on specific subject matter—such as the figure, landscape, portraiture, or seascapes. Some artists hold workshops in their own studios, while others are hired by hotel owners and workshop sponsors at a university or vacation setting to teach over a five- or six-day period, and still other artists hold classes on cruise ships or lead groups to foreign countries in order to paint there.

Hundreds of these art workshops are offered each year, advertised in the classified sections of *American Artist* and *The Artist's Magazine* as well as other art publications, and knowing how to choose the right one can be daunting. Actually, the sheer volume of workshops is an indication in itself. As one looks over the promotional materials for a variety of workshops in different locations, many of the same instructors' names frequently come up. These artists are often invited back to the same workshop site year after year, and it is safe to assume that they have established a good reputation for their teaching, critiques, demonstrations and ability to get along with their students. It is the artists who are not as capable in those areas whose names drop out of sight after a period of time.

Almost all workshop teachers or sponsors will answer questions over the telephone and, perhaps more useful, mail a brochure or some other information about the artist that shows his or her work (seeing examples of artwork will help the more experienced prospective student determine the artist's own level of quality) and may also indicate how the workshop will be conducted. Not all brochures are equally informative. Artists' own brochures are more likely to use color reproductions of their work and provide some sense of their artistic approach, for instance, whereas the material provided by hotel owner/workshop sponsors is more frequently in black and white and more explicit about the accommodations and area attractions than what happens during the workshop.

The brochure for workshops at Pine Mountain Studio in Arlington, Vermont, for example, is four black-and-white pages, with reproductions of instructors' paintings next to biographical information about the individual artists that frequently run several paragraphs or more. Potential participants read that "Each of the five days of the Workshop, we will meet at the Studio at 8:30 A.M. and, depending on your Instructor and the weather, have a lecture demonstration or depart for the painting site . . . Usually the Instructor gives a painting demonstration, then gives individual instruction as you paint . . . We will meet no later than 4 P.M. for a critique each day."

A number of the same artists who lead workshops have also written art-instruction books or created videocassettes of their methods that provide a sense of their approach to teaching. For instance, portrait artist Daniel Greene, who leads approximately 20 week-long workshops a year, is the author of two books, *Pastel* and *The Art of Pastel,* and has two videos of himself at work on a portrait. Zoltan Szabo and Frank Webb, who both hold watercolor workshops, are represented by instructional videocassettes and eight books (six for Szabo, two for Webb). Barbara Nechis, Jeanne Dobie and Ann Templeton as well as many other workshop instructors can be previewed through their videocassettes, which are either distributed by artist video companies or by the artists themselves. Timothy Clark, who has conducted workshops in the United States, Hawaii, and Europe, hosted a public-television series entitled *Focus on Watercolors,* and he published a book with the same title. A small investment in a book or videocassette may help one decide whether or not to make the larger investment in a week-long workshop. In addition, many artists either have written for art magazines or have been profiled in them. There is a lot of information available about those who lead workshops, and prospective students shouldn't be shy about asking.

The majority of workshop participants are women, middle-aged and older. Chris Unwin, a watercolorist who organizes cruise-ship workshops and sometimes leads them herself, noted that "male artists attract more men to workshops. Frank Webb, for instance, attracted an incredibly high percentage of men to his workshop, probably a third." Between one-quarter and one-half of the workshops of certain prominent artists are attended by people who have been there before, and prospective students can ask for references from the artist of past students. From these people (who are likely to speak favorably about the artist and the workshop), one can inquire about the kind of individual attention each student receives, whether or not there are demonstrations and critiques (and what these demonstrations and critiques consist of), the number of models used (or other kinds of assignments given), the level of ability of most workshop participants, the amount of studio space, the number of students in the group, how participants interact inside and outside of class, and whether the week felt like a vacation or serious, intense study. Word-of-mouth is usually the best guide one way or another.

There are a number of areas for which prospective students may do troubleshooting. Some workshop instructors lecture too long, providing more information and advice than students can hold at one time, and, by the time participants are allowed to start working, they have lost some of their energy. Some instructors seem to be "on an ego trip," Chris Unwin said. "They'll say, 'Anyone who wants to paint may do so but I'll be over here painting for anyone who wants to watch.' Well, who wouldn't watch the artist instead of painting oneself, but that defeats the purpose of the workshop."

All of the students in a given workshop deserve and expect individual attention, and some may attempt to dominate the workshop leader's time, but good instructors know how to give everyone equal time and consideration, taking each student at his or her own level. Everyone in the class also expects that critiques and comments on their work will come from the instructor, for whom students signed up in the first place, and may resent instead hearing the teacher ask the other workshop participants for their opinions. There is also the question of personal style. Some instructors are naturally enthusiastic, encouraging students to get excited about their work, while others are more relaxed and low-key in their approach. There are followers of both types of instructors and all the various types in-between, more often depending upon what ideas and techniques the artist has to teach.

Of course, not everyone cares as much about the artist-teacher's own work and how the workshop is structured as they do about the opportunity for a vacation-with-art. "Actually, I don't like the way Gerald Brommer paints, but he's a very nice person and a good teacher," said Floridian Marjorie Johnson who has taken watercolor and sketching workshops with Brommer in Maui, Hawaii, and Oaxaca, Mexico, that were arranged by Artists Workshop Tours Agency of Chula Vista, California. Johnson and her husband both took these trips (she painted while he pursued sightseeing) because "we both have always wanted to go to these places." She added that the two of them haven't just gone on their own because "I might not have found the same spots to paint in. It might not be as comfortable to just paint by myself, and I like the company. There is a lot of camaraderie."

For other students, the skill of the teacher is of paramount importance. Peter Seltzer of Bethlehem, Connecticut, who claimed to have always been interested in art but never pursued it, stated that, back in 1984, "the owner of an art shop was showing me someone's drawings; it was someone whose work I had seen before, and I noticed an enormous improvement in that person's work. I commented about that change, and the shop owner mentioned that this person had studied with Daniel Greene. I spent five summers studying with Dan after that."

Seltzer, who owned and ran an ice-cream business until 1983, said that "I walked into Dan's class doing stick figures and walked out doing credible figures. He turned my life around in a relatively short period of time, and he's the only person I've ever studied with." Since 1987, Seltzer has been a self-supporting painter of landscapes and figures, with gallery representation in New York City and Connecticut.

The intensity of the workshop experience is frequently left to the participant to decide. Some students who have traveled a distance to an area they've never seen before may choose to paint in the morning and sightsee during the afternoon, rejoining the group in the evening for a meal and a critique by the instructor. "Some of our beginners may get carried away by being on a cruise—they decide that they want to go scuba diving," Chris Unwin said. "We encourage that by scheduling free time." Bernice Taplitz, who lives on Long Island, New York, and has taken painting workshops with several different instructors, noted the vacation atmosphere of these events, pointing out that "you may not learn anything but enjoy the weekend."

Other workshops demand full-time attention to one's artwork, which may mean traveling to an attractive place but spending the entire time staring at a model or learning about color, composition, design, and values. "I work the hell out of them," Jack Beal stated. "No one plays here. I've asked some of the students what other workshops are like, and a number of them have said, 'No one has ever worked me this hard.' That's the way I want it."

The Benefits of Teaching an Art Workshop

Wolf Kahn teaches painting workshops because "I have a didactic vein. I really love to teach." Janet Fish, on the other hand, will teach a workshop "in a place I don't know so well. I get paid to see somewhere new," while Tony Couch primarily teaches "to make a buck or two." Traditionally, teaching has been the fallback work of artists, affording them a steady income until their art sells and allows them independence. But, as Kahn, Fish and Couch all could live comfortably from the sale of their paintings, one may ask why they choose to teach at all and why at art workshops.

Not every artist who teaches does so out of financial need, however, and not every teaching situation is the same. There are art classes at community centers and museums as well as at public schools, colleges and universities, but the art workshop experience tends to be of a different nature for the teacher. For one thing, workshops are short-term affairs, generally taking place on a weekend or during the weekday and often in vacation settings. Unlike teaching at a school, there are no faculty meetings to attend, and the money one may earn at a workshop is likely to exceed what an adjunct college-level teacher is paid for an entire semester.

Janet Fish, who has also taught at art schools, noted that workshop participants are frequently more eager to learn and make use of the small amount of time. "These people have paid for it and committed valuable time to the workshop," she said, "and so they may be more open to the experience. In a college, students may be taking a class for credit and are not always so happy to be there." Participants in a workshop are also more likely to be older (retired and widowed, in many instances) than those enrolled in art schools; they have more knowledge of the world and more money, both of which may make them attractive to some artists. "I've had it with kids," Wolf Kahn said. "They are so filled with self-importance that you can't talk with them. I like adults because they have had more life experiences, and they can understand and appreciate what I'm doing."

The appreciation comes from the fact that, in most cases, people pick a workshop based on the teacher, and they look for artists whose work they admire. As a result, workshops are often a warm and welcoming moment for the artists who lead them. They also may be quite lucrative moments. Artists usually earn between $300 and $450 per day, even as much as $5,000 for the week, and their travel, accommodations and food expenses may or may not be paid for by the workshop sponsor. In addition, workshop participants will often buy the demonstration paintings (demos) that the artist-teacher creates in front of the students every day and other works that the artists bring. This is a clear benefit of teaching to older and more financially established admirers.

"I sell most or all of my demos at $450 each," Tony Couch said. "The same size work in a gallery would sell for $2,000 or so. I usually bring other completed works from my studio to the workshops and sell them for $1,000 apiece—that's what I'd get from the dealer minus the commission anyway." Couch also has published three books and four videocassettes of art instruction, and brings 10 copies of each to the workshops, on the average selling half the videos and three-quarters of the books. The extra earnings are in the thousands of dollars, perhaps exceeding the workshop fee he is paid. Multiplied by the 15 workshops Couch regularly teaches annually, it becomes a substantial amount of money.

"I sell during the workshops without ever having to frame or mat the things," said painter Frank Webb, who teaches between 20 and 24 workshops per year. "At a workshop, you are ultimately directing attention to your own work, because you are telling people and showing them what has worked for you. Whenever I am teaching a workshop, everything I say goes. You can't have that at an art school."

Not every artist is able to sell as much during workshops, and workshop participants do not necessarily become buyers of the artists' work afterwards. Those who enjoyed seeing the artist create a demo and receiving instruction from that person are more likely to sign up for another workshop with the artist rather than become a collector. One reason for this is that workshops (and demos) cost in the hundreds of dollars, while the framed and finished pieces are priced in the thousands. "I'm a comparatively high-priced artist," Jack Beal said, "and my work is bought by wealthy people who live in large apartments in New York City. I get very few wealthy people in my workshops."

Not all artists are able to earn as much as Tony Couch from teaching workshops. Artists are usually paid a certain amount—between $150 and $200 per student—and a low turnout means less money for them. Artists who set up their own workshops without third-party sponsors may have a variety of costs that eat away at the potential profits. Chris Unwin said that "I charged $300 per student for a workshop I led in Taos [New Mexico], and I got 16 students, but there are a lot of expenses. There are the rooms, the food and the cost of a party for everybody. The party itself costs $700–$800." Jack Beal noted that his largest problems are last-minute cancellations and the amount of time spent planning and talking to people on the telephone in advance. "You burn the candle at both ends trying to teach workshops and paint," he said. "In order to run a workshop so as to make some money, you have to put off painting, which also earns money."

In addition, not all workshop participants and sponsors want to hire artists who regard workshops as an opportunity to sell their work. Many prefer artists who focus on teaching and helping each student learn new skills. "I personally like the teachers who paint more than the painters who teach," said Eliot Dalton, director of Hudson River Valley Art Workshops in Greenville, New York. "The people who take our workshops want these teachers more than the artists who are accomplished at marketing, who come looking to sell demos, videos and other paintings."

Teaching has its own potential benefits for artists, helping to clarify their own ideas in order to express them to others and seeing how students solve problems in ways that may be of value at some point to the artists themselves. "In trying to formulate design principles for my students," Frank Webb said, "I sharpen them for myself." Few workshop artists, however, describe significant feedback on their own work from students or inspiration for new work that was generated by a workshop. A potential drawback to leading a workshop is that the mainstream art world may look at teaching amateurs as not the work of serious professionals. "In my field, if you're known as a teacher, that's the kiss of death," Wolf Kahn said. "If you're known as a workshop teacher, that's even worse." Jack Beal also noted that "teaching workshops has diminished my stature in the New York art world. I don't talk about the workshops with other artists or with anyone else."

Art Tours

Some people travel to create works of art, others journey to see them. Group tours specifically oriented around cultural and artistic sights have become increasingly popular over the past two decades. People take trips abroad very seriously, frequently seeking the structure of an established itinerary and expert guides. Looking at art, in museums and art galleries as well as in art books, is one of the unstated secrets of learning to make art, because seeing what other artists have done and how they did it is as important as almost anything an art teacher can impart. A knowledgeable guide to a museum collection, for instance, may help one better see what an artist has done, and this has led to the growth of special-interest travel programs that focus on art and architecture.

For years, travel companies have offered "packages" to tourists for vacations to areas of artistic interest that include, among the usual bed-and-board amenities, sightseeing with local guides. More recently, the number of companies offering such programs has grown, as have the opportunities for day trips and other educational excursions on these tours. In addition, many major museums, organizations and alumni associations across the country have gotten into the act by offering "art tours." Many museums also organize day trips, for their members and nonmembers alike, to visit a museum in another city where an exhibition of particular interest or importance is taking place. The number and variety of art tours is impressive and, if a package doesn't already exist, a group may create its own. New York University's Psychology Department, for instance, has offered a two-week group dynamics course in Italy in which, according to Professor Paul Humphries who has led the tour, "the members of the group look at the art and then look at each other."

With all the offerings, representing a wide range of inclusive features and educational involvement, a potential traveler may become confused. Some travel companies' brochures of art tours show a famous painting on the cover, but inside the pictures and descriptions are largely concerned with meals and accommodations. Some brochure copy teases with bits of historical information, but the actual tour itself (or parts of it) is unguided, and the traveler must learn elsewhere what the brochure was referring to. Some programs sound as though one will be graded at the end of them, because they are taught by professors who assign extensive reading lists and give lectures before and during the trip, leaving precious little time for strolling on one's own. Travelers should have a good idea of what they want out of a trip, and choose accordingly.

The price of the tour program may help clarify the issue to a degree. Institutional programs—those set up by a museum or alumni association—generally cost considerably more than those offered by commercial tour operators, for a variety of reasons. The $2,500 price that Harvard University has charged for its 11-day tour of the former Soviet Union's art treasures includes a $300 tax-deductible contribution to the school's Fogg Art Museum, but it does not include membership to the Fogg ($35), which makes one eligible for the trip. The Metropolitan Museum of Art in New York City, the Smithsonian Institution in Washington, D.C., the Art Institute of Chicago and the Los Angeles County Museum of Art, to name a few, also include contributions of $200 apiece as part of the overall prices of the trips they sponsor for their members.

Museum and alumni-sponsored trips generally hold get-togethers in advance for the participants (and, possibly, a preliminary lecture) and include a professor or expert in the particular area who will lead the group for the entire time. This allows a greater continuity of perspective throughout the trip, according to Billie Foreman, a travel agent with Mercury Travel in St. Paul, Minnesota, who has arranged many such trips for schools. "Having the same person the entire way helps travelers relate different situations, different museums. It also gives people a better, more relaxed feeling that someone is taking care of them," she said. She added that "the feeling of belonging to a group helps relieve a lot of anxiety for people. It can be frightening to walk down a street in a strange city. Where to go for dinner can be a problem. Institutional tour programs generally take care of everything."

These kinds of tour packages often have a strong direction and purpose established by whomever is leading them. Guidebooks, history and architectural texts, even fiction or poetry may be assigned by the leader to be read prior to the start of the trip, and lectures may be given throughout. Richard Wallace, an art historian at Wellesley College who has conducted tours for alumnae, stated that the European trips he leads are not just fun and games. "I set the tone and conduct a fairly rigorous, academic program. I expect participants to read the assigned material and ask informed questions."

With a commercial tour program, group leadership is often more nebulous, and it is less possible to preconceive the intellectual atmosphere that may dominate as that depends on who signs up for it. In many instances, the travel company contracts with local guides and experts who will take tourists to specific sites of cultural and historical interest (for instance, an Egyptologist from the University of Cairo meets up with Abercrombie & Kent's tour groups for sightseeing in Egypt, and "white hunters who are knowledgeable of the bush area" lead parties traveling in Ethiopia and Kenya). While having a number of different guides may make one's experience of the culture a little more disjointed, locals may provide the kind of insider information—for example, good places to eat or shop—that an American professor could not.

Commercial travel companies are not alumni associations and do not assume that everyone has been to college. The educational component of these trips is less extensive, possibly more anecdotal. They place travelers at the scene of art without hitting them over the head with facts and opinions. Less is required of the traveler, and it is acceptable to wander off.

The other major differences between the institutional and commercial art tour programs are the quality of the hotels and the number of meals provided as well as the number of people in a tour group and how long the group will stay in a particular place. Institutional programs make the assumption—which, in many ways, is quite reasonable since travelers paid considerably more than commercial program tourists—that their group is accustomed to the better things and requires the best hotels wherever it goes. They also provide at least two meals a day. The number of people on a given program is usually limited to 20 or 30 and, due to the educational nature of the expedition, there is less traveling around and more intensive sightseeing than on commercial packages.

Commercial company brochures describe accommodations as "first class" or "superior" and, sometimes, just "adequate"—much further down the travelese pecking order from "deluxe," which the institutions offer—and there are usually fewer meals. One of the ways commercial tour operators can offer less expensive rates is by mass bookings, and some groups have as many as 60 people in them. This can pose a problem, for instance, if the group is to be transported by bus through scenic areas. What if someone doesn't get a seat by a window? What if all the important sights are on the right side of the bus? In addition, commercial tour programs often entail a fair amount of traveling around, which allows people to see more things although possibly in less depth.

They do, however, assume that their travelers are relatively independent and leave more time for personal exploration than do most institutional programs. For the commercial companies, group activities are researched and planned, but optional. Some travelers like to have a group to fall back on but are well enough versed in the history and art not to need instruction, finding these packages far less expensive than making all the bookings themselves.

From King Tut's sarcophagus to the Vatican's art collection to the finds from recent Aztec excavations, it is no longer uncommon to hear that some of the world's greatest cultural treasures are soon to be jetted over to a museum near you. Plenty of people, however, are interested enough in the rare objects to travel to foreign countries and witness them in their own setting. The gung-ho types will just book a flight and go, but others look for the security and intellectual rigor to be found in a tour group. There are a lot of different programs from which to choose, and it takes research but also (and more importantly) a personal sense of what one is looking for. With a wide spectrum of art tours on the market, something will be suitable. And with people of similar interests and (possibly) background, a traveler will not feel so much a stranger in a strange land but part of a cultural experience which, because it is shared, may give it all the more meaning.

&

CHAPTER 2

Learning to Make Art Alone

AT NO TIME IN HISTORY HAVE THERE been as many people interested in learning to make art and as many other people willing and able to teach them. The ways in which this teaching may take place have also grown, encompassing schools (both formal and informal, such as in an artist's studio), recreational art classes (in a variety of settings), correspondence-school courses in art, watching a paint-along program on television, reading an art instruction text and viewing an art instruction videocassette. The preceding chapter examined some of the methods by which one may improve one's artistic skills and appreciation in a group setting. Here, methods of instruction that may be pursued alone, such as at home, are discussed.

Correspondence Art Courses

Art classes and art schools provide a structured environment for learning and developing skills, but they may require more time each week than a potential student has to spare; they may be far removed from the student, especially if that person lives in a remote area and the tuition can be considerable. Art workshops are short-term versions (lasting between a day and a week) of the classes and schools, costing less but still usually involving travel.

For many people, learning to draw or paint at home is the only (and best) solution. The choices for them are correspondence courses, in which lesson plans are sent to one's address and completed assignments are returned to the school for a critique by an experienced artist-teacher, or instructional videos. The videos, which generally are between one and two hours long, show an artist making a drawing, mixing paint, preparing a canvas and creating an image..

A home-study course, many graduates of these programs claim, teaches independent thinking because one is away from the direct influences of instructors and fellow students. "A correspondence course fulfills the needs of those people who cannot attend a regular residence school," said Yolanda Agheli, general manager of the Hemphill Schools in Los Angeles, which offers art lessons by mail to Spanish-speaking people around the country. "They may work at night or work at two jobs or have children who keep them at home. It's hard to make time for yourself."

These courses may also be a younger person's first exposure to art. Lee Anne Miller, former dean of the art school at Cooper Union in New York City, and commercial illustrator Robert Heindel took lessons from the Art Instruction Schools (in Minneapolis, Minnesota) and Famous Artists School (in Westport, Connecticut), respectively, when she was 13 and he 16 years old. Both the Famous Artists School and the North Light School in Cincinnati, Ohio, however, have found that their students tend to be older, retired and predominantly female. "The kids are gone, and they have time to try their hand at art," said Charles Berger, director of instruction at North Light School. "They still may not want to do much traveling, and they also want to learn the absolute fundamentals, which you may not get at many art schools and classes because they tend to assume you know a lot of that by now."

Correspondence-course schools frequently set certain time limits for the completion of their lesson programs in order to receive a certificate or diploma (which only indicate that the student has finished the program and are usually not accepted toward actual degree programs in colleges or universities), but these time allotments are generous. The fees for these programs of home study range from $330 to $1,500, depending upon how many lessons are included. The art course offered by International Correspondence Schools in Scranton, Pennsylvania (subscribed to by more than 5,100 students every year), is a five-lesson program costing $399, whereas the Art Instruction School's $1,495 fundamentals course is planned as a two-year program. For their money, students are provided with textbooks (that describe and provide illustrations for every step in the process of drawing and painting) and, except for North Light School, most or all of the art materials one needs to complete the assignments. The schools pay for the shipping of these items.

Correspondence schools generally provide workbooks that contain lesson plans for students. The difference between these step-by-step workbooks and general art instruction books that one could purchase in a bookstore or art shop has less to do with the information provided (although the workbooks are likely to have a more abbreviated presentation) than the somewhat more impersonal style of writing. Anyone who buys Tony Couch's *Watercolors: You Can Do It!* is probably as much interested in how Tony Couch does it as how the reader can learn to become a watercolorist him- or herself, and one approaches this book looking for Couch's particular methods and secrets.

The workbooks, more than art instructional guides, also aim to approximate what one learns in a regular art class (if one were attending an art school) as well as the way a student is taught. Famous Artists School's *How to Draw the Human Figure* workbook begins with a section on the materials used (pencils, pastels, charcoal, drawing board, eraser, paper) and soon has one drawing, at first gestures, then configuring the body as a series of cylinders, moving on to contour drawing and later an analysis of anatomy. Photographs of male and female models in various poses, partially or completely nude, are also included in the workbook.

Students pay the postage for completed assignments sent back to the schools to be evaluated. The art instructors who look over each student's work may be on staff or on call, but students cannot be assured of having the same teacher twice. "Students benefit from a variety of opinions," Don Jardine, director of education at Art Instruction Schools, said. "They get the expertise of each instructor." Those evaluations or critiques vary in the degree of personal attention. Some may be fully handwritten, while others are preprinted sheets with various boxes (such as "Needs work in color" or "Needs work in line") checked off with far fewer individual comments noted.

As some students are less interested in purchasing an instructional video or attending a large art class precisely because of the lack of feedback and individual attention, this may be a great point of consumer interest for them. Charles Berger noted that prospective students should "ask the schools you are interested in for a copy of the kinds of things you get in critiques. If you end up taking the course and you get something that doesn't correspond with what you were told or shown, you have a cause for complaint."

Another concern that potential students should keep in mind is whether or not the school's particular lesson plan fits their goals. Most of these schools began with a commercial art emphasis, focusing on cartooning, advertising design, illustration and other purely marketable skills, and some of their current courses still carry that flavor. That may not appeal to every prospective student. Don Jardine noted that sales representatives for the Art Instruction Schools tell people in their presentations, "you can be successful. You can earn a living at something you would ordinarily do for fun," while Howell Dodd, director of education at Famous Artists School, stated that "we don't push moneymaking in our promotion as we once did."

While home art study from a correspondence school does not lead to, or provide credits for, a college degree, a couple of liberal arts colleges—Bard College at Annandale-on-Hudson, New York, and the Vermont College of Norwich University in Montpelier, Vermont— permit Masters of Fine Arts students to work at home for most of the year with only limited residencies on their respective campuses. Bard College requires two-month summer residencies while the Vermont College only asks students to come to the campus for the first nine days of each semester in its two-year MFA program. Students use those nine days to develop a plan for their home study with faculty members. The college then contracts with art teachers who are local to the students to allow five studio visits during the semester. Home study, however, doesn't entail paying less tuition to either school than students who live on campus, as both charge close to $4,000 per semester.

Correspondence art courses once were far more popular than they are today. There are only a handful these days, including a Cartoonerama program (with a mailing address in Branford, Connecticut) geared specifically to comic art. (See Appendix, "Correspondence Art Instruction Schools.") In its heyday, during the 1950s and 1960s, Famous Artists School had 40,000 enrolled students; now, it has fewer than a thousand who take lessons from the school on a pay-as-you-go basis. The largest schools of this sort now are Art Instruction Schools and International Correspondence Schools. A number of other schools have closed.

The reasons for the decline are manifold. There are more opportunities nowadays for art instruction in classrooms, with adult education programs at high schools, community colleges and large universities, even in the most rural locations of the country. In addition, the videocassettes sold by individual artists and video production companies provide quite graphic depictions of everything from the most basic problems of which tool to use and how to mix colors to technical problems of portraiture and landscape painting. The cost for these videos is also less than for full correspondence courses. One correspondence school, in fact, the Alexander School of Art in San Diego, was purchased and became the Lela Harty School of Art in San Diego, which predominantly sells videocassette instruction.

"The books that a correspondence school sends out can tell you all the same things, and even more, that are on a video, but it's still on a printed page," said Charles Reid, a painter who had first studied art through the Famous Artists School but now teaches art with three videotapes that are distributed by Artists' Video Productions of Westport, Connecticut. "Even if the picture in the book is in color, you still don't see the thing actually being done as with a video."

Correspondence art courses, which are usually advertised in art magazines such as *American Artist* and *The Artist's Magazine,* still make sense to a number of people. The local art instructor may not be to every student's taste; timing and distance still can be troublesome with art classes. Videos, of course, cannot comment on one's work or answer specific questions.

Art Instruction Books and Videocassettes

Deciding whether or not to learn art-making (or to improve one's artistic skills) through reading or watching is a matter of personal choice, depending upon how the individual best learns. "Reading books and attending workshops are great aids to learning; they're the most direct route to your goal," Tony Couch writes in his book *Watercolor: You Can Do It!* However, Couch's teaching is also available on several videocassettes. Presumably, he believes that videos are at least a relatively direct route.

Frequently, the same artists are represented by both books and videocassettes that feature their work and method; for people who are interested in the particular artist, it may be wise to collect both because either one or the other will be lacking something. Reading about how an artist works is never as good as seeing that person at work, and a 50- or 60-minute video can only provide so much information. In Charles Reid's "Flowers in Watercolor," for instance, one hears the artist discussing his technique, but one also watches in silence as Reid mixes colors and applies his brush to paper. Reid is also author of six art instruction books, and in *Painting by Design,* one learns how to approach a subject analytically, largely as an abstract form: "It's my aim to get you to see any subject you choose as a set of very definite shapes composed of color, light, and shadow. Forget what your subject represents. . . . Concentrate instead on what it *is,* a piece of a puzzle or part of a pattern that's meant to be arranged in some compelling way with other shapes."

There may be good reason for purchasing both books and videocassettes. Teaching (in any field of endeavor) usually involves explaining how something is done and then demonstrating it. Books tend to be preferable for explanations, while videos clearly show how the artwork is made. If one cannot afford to purchase both the video and the book, however, the decision depends on which method may prove most instructive to the potential buyer. Of course, books that are priced generally between $10 and $30 tend to cost less than videocassettes, which usually are priced between $25 and $70.

"I always tell people that if they have enough money for just one thing, get the book," Tony Couch said. "A book has more information, and it covers everything. The video is more limited; it looks at only one part of what you have in the book. I think some people can learn from just a book, while I doubt anyone can start painting by just watching a video." On the other hand, Daniel Greene, the author of *The Art of Pastel* and *Pastel,* who is represented in several videos on creating a portrait (among which are "Oil—Bernard" and "Pastel—Erika"), "definitely recommends starting off with a video, especially if you're a beginner, and later following up with the purchase of a book. With a video, you're privy to the process, seeing the image come to life, while listening to the explanation that is simultaneous with seeing the image develop. With a book, you lose the immediacy and have to visualize everything in your head." He added that colors are often truer on the video because, "if they're off, you can always fine-tune your TV, but if they're off in the book—as they frequently are—you have no way of knowing and you can't do anything about it anyway."

Frank Webb, author of *Watercolor Energies* and *Webb on Watercolor* and the subject of a video, also believes that videocassettes are preferable for beginners. "Books presuppose a certain acquaintance with art terms, while videos assume absolutely nothing," he said. He added that the written text is "sequential," moving logically from one idea to the next, while "film has an all-at-once quality in which one can apprehend across the field. You have the sound, the gestures in video; it's equal to being in the artist's studio."

As many of the same artist-authors also have produced videos or hold workshops, there is frequently a significant amount of overlapping information from one teaching approach to the next. Johnnie Mason Liliedahl's workshop in Baton Rouge, Louisiana, for instance, costs $350, which includes a 160-page, seven-lesson *Oil Painting Seminar Manual* and six days of her teaching. One may order the manual separately, however, for $250, which, according to the artist's brochure, "is written with complete, detailed instructions so that it may be used without the benefit of in-class instruction." For those solely interested in learning Liliedahl's technique, the extra $100 plus the cost of accommodations, food and transportation to Baton Rouge to take part in the workshop may not be worth the expense.

One never can be exactly sure what to expect from any specific type of art instruction—book or videocassette—until it has been tried. A particular teacher may not be rigorous enough or a book too wordy, the video image too grainy or the correspondence school instructor not personal enough for one's individual tastes. However, there are usually ways to cut one's losses if a specific program doesn't work out. Schools frequently allow students to drop courses with just minimal penalties, and the sponsors of art classes usually require payment only for the classes one has attended.

With art instruction books and videocassettes, however, the situation is a bit more complicated. One cannot "sit in on" a video as one can at an art class or school, and most art instruction books are not available in libraries for browsing. Some books, of course, are sold in bookstores and art supply shops, and one may thumb through or study them as long as the store manager or sales help will tolerate it. Of course, there are also television art instruction programs, such as those offered by the late Bob Ross, Michael Ringer and Gary Jenkins, which cost the viewer nothing and offer the opportunity to determine whether or not one could learn to paint by watching TV.

More commonly, those who are interested in learning or developing their artistic skills in art find out about art instruction books and videocassettes through advertisements in the back pages of art magazines, where the cost of advertising limits the amount of information about them. What's more, most art instruction books and videos have similar titles—*Make Your Watercolors Sing* and *Making Color Sing* (published by North Light Books and Watson-Guptill, respectively)—that make ferreting out differences somewhat difficult.

How does one find out about and choose among them? There are many questions that prospective buyers should ask. Does the book feature a variety of illustrations (by a number of different artists or by one artist?) or just a few pictures and a lot of text? Is there enough information in the video for repeated playings? Is the writing clear, the author's philosophy a help rather than a hindrance? Are the chapters set up as self-contained lessons or is the book divided according to various themes? Does the video offer step-by-step instruction on selecting a subject, choosing colors and mixing them, how to use brushes and other materials, bulding up layers and, finally, creating an image, or does it more specifically highlight a particular artist at work? Is the book or video geared to the level of the student?

There is a book or video for every aspiring artist, but each person must determine what he or she wants or needs, then formulate questions for the publishers of these materials. Most publishers, video production companies or artists selling their books and videocassettes will provide a brochure or some written information about their products, which may include critical reviews in art magazines, testimonials from satisfied customers, a biography of the author or artist and a sample illustration as well as some idea of what is featured in the book or video. Many of these same companies and artists will also answer questions over the telephone (some have toll-free numbers, while others return calls left on their answering machines).

Prospective buyers would want to know the type of medium used and whether the book or video is intended for beginners or artists with intermediate or advanced skills. Authors and artists generally have a specific reader in mind when they create an instructional book or videocassette, and that is usually made clear in the title, in the introduction or somewhere early on. John Blockley's *Getting Started in Watercolour* tells the reader clearly that this is a book for a beginner, as does the first paragraph in the first chapter: "Watercolour painting is basically a process of making colour washes. The painter mixes paint with water and brushes it onto the paper to form a wash of colour. The liquidity of the medium provides the main characteristics of watercolour painting."

Similarly, Manly Banister's *Practical Lithographic Printmaking* announces in its first paragraph that "This is a book for the beginning lithographer. . . . You are not expected to know anything at all about lithography, so instruction has been simplified down to step-by-step details that are made even more plain with photographs and drawings."

On the other hand, a book such as Hazel Harrison's *The Oil Painter's Solution Book*, with its focus on such problems as how to capture the texture of objects and how to mix colors with white without losing the whiteness, presumes a greater familiarity with painting and would be more appropriate for the intermediate or advanced student. John Howard Sanden's portraiture videos, "John Singer Sargent's *Lady Agnew*" (two cassettes, three hours of instruction, $134.95) and "John Singer Sargent's *Head of an Arab*" (one cassette, $69.95), which show the process of recreating a famous artist's technique and style, are also geared to the advanced student.

Equally, a book such as Gary Olsen's *Getting Started in Computer Graphics*, of which one-third is devoted to how to use a computer and select the correct hardware and software, aims at the novice, while L. G. Thorell and W. J. Smith's *Using Computer Color Effectively* is written for a far more sophisticated audience. The first sentence reads "If the premise that user interface is theater is true, then color is a major stage prop." In addition, the illustrations in the Thorell-Smith book suggest that their presumed reader is more interested in visual enhancement of images for scientific or commercial uses than in making works of art.

When the specific level of reader or viewer is not indicated, the book or video is probably intended for the more experienced artist. Instructional material for the beginner may focus on inspirational themes, such as developing one's creative instincts and how to see the world, moving on to various activities in drawing or painting. Other books and videos for the novice aim to provide a basic grounding in how to draw or paint, how to select one's subject, medium and tools as well as providing ways to critique one's own work.

Probably more for the beginning artist, Applewood Art in Cedaredge, Colorado, offers not books or videos but audiotapes with inspirational messages, proclaiming "I am a creative person. . . ."; "I am an open channel for creative energy. . . ."; "I believe in myself, my ideas, and my creations." A choice of three types of background music is also available—upbeat, marching rhythms, something called "waltz type music," and nature sounds.

However, programs for intermediate or more advanced painters may examine such technical problems as how to pose models or set up lighting. Some instructional programs for experienced artists focus on how the Old Masters worked or examine the techniques of non-Western artists, such as Chinese brush painters. Dover Publications specializes in publishing books that have long been out of print by noted artists and teachers of the past, including *The Elements of Drawing* by John Ruskin, *Gist of Art* by John Sloan, *The Anatomy of the Horse* by George Stubbs and *Anatomy for Artists* by Reginald Marsh. Other books and videos for the more advanced artist may explore how to refine one's working methods or how certain well-known artists, such as David Hockney and Philip Pearlstein, approach their subjects and create their paintings.

Prospective buyers, especially those who are gaining their first serious exposure to art-making, would certainly want to know whether or not there is a description of the tools used (airbrush, brushes, palette knives, pencils, for instance) and discussion and definition of such concerns as shape, space, edges, contrast, color temperature, color mixing, color intensity, perspective, composition, content, foreground and background, texture, line, grids, surface and how they all relate to each other. Book buyers of all levels of skill and experience would also be interested in knowing if different styles are represented (abstract, impressionist, realist, for example) as well as a variety of subjects (water, landscape, the figure) and ways of working (from a photograph, a model, in the studio, outdoors).

With a videocassette, one expects to see the particular artist at work and only that artist's finished work. Irving Shapiro's "Mountain Stream" video, for instance, presents the artist painting a section of a Colorado stream rushing past boulders and fallen trees while he describes how he composed the image, chose the colors, and resolved technical matters. Similarly, in Barbara Nechis's eponymous videocassette, viewers hear the watercolorist describe how she prepares the paper, chooses the colors to use and the importance of painting in her life as she creates, first, a group of trees and then a bouquet of flowers.

On the other hand, some videos attempt to show how different artists may approach the same pictorial subject. Lela Harty's four-videocassette, eight-lesson course features Ms. Harty's Monet-like impressionistic style of painting while she instructs students whose own work is in some instances more tightly realistic. Other artists' videos are filmed excerpts from particular workshops they have held. Presumably, the questions and difficulties that the workshop students have mirror those of the buyers of these videos.

In general, art instruction books offer a wider range of artistic styles and choices, but not always. Bert Dodson's *Keys to Drawing* provides examples of how to sketch certain designs that, one may suppose, are by the author himself, yet there are also drawings by Edgar Degas, Richard Haas, Kathe Kollwitz, Henri Matisse and Vincent van Gogh to offer a sense of variety. *Oil Painting: A Direct Approach* by Joyce Pike, on the other hand, contains examples solely by the author, befitting her chatty text that is concerned with how she approaches certain subjects.

Some videos also come with workbooks and other written materials in order to recapitulate what is on the tape, while some drawing books include pencil kits in order to help the artist get started. Caroline Buchanan's video on drawing for the beginner, "The Uncertain Artist," comes with two pens and a five-by-eight-inch sheet of paper containing additional hints, such as "rewind the tape and do it again" and "get a sketchbook and carry it with you at all times. Stop to draw the things that interest you."

No promotional brochure or selected reviews can answer all of one's questions, and other concerns may only be discovered after the book or video is purchased. Are the color reproductions in the book of a suitably high quality, and does the artist in the video appear comfortable in front of a camera? Books should provide a detailed discussion of the topics or artistic problems at hand while, in a video, the commentary should be subordinate to the image—no one wants an hour of a talking head.

There may be other problems that a student of art has with the manner of teaching in the book or video that have nothing to do with technical deficiencies in the product. One's ability to learn from any given teacher is quite personal, and it is no different when the teacher is a book or videocassette. However, as opposed to a teacher in an art class with whom the "chemistry" doesn't quite work, one cannot simply leave and not pay for any more, as books and videos must be purchased in advance. A final question to ask the publisher, video production company, distributor or artist is about the return policy.

There are no federal (or state) mandates that customers have to be completely satisfied with products they purchase. The Federal Trade Commission or state attorney general may bring action on false claims ("Guaranteed to Teach Anyone to Paint a Million-Dollar, Museum-Quality Masterpiece in One Week") or misrepresentations in advertisements. However, many claims that seem misleading, such as "Learn How to Paint," are not specific enough to warrant state or federal inquiry if a customer is not satisfied. According to Bonnie Janson, an attorney for the Federal Trade Commission, "it would be extremely difficult to win a complaint if you didn't learn to paint, because it's a subjective problem—you may be stupid. In this realm, any claim may be true or not true, because we're dealing with judgment and ability. Who can say which are the correct tips to learning how to paint?"

There are also inherent limitations in learning solely through books or videocassettes that should be taken into account. One advertisement for a $29.95 video from the Quinten Gregory Studio in Boise, Idaho, for example, claims to show "How professional artists paint to sell! How to create your own scenes, use the value scale and avoid amateurish habits. The keys to professional work with drawing, oil, and watercolor demos. One hour." That is a rather tall order for a sixty-minute presentation, regardless of how experienced the student may be, and buyers who take the advertisement at face value may find themselves set up for failure. Expectations need to be appropriately lowered, befitting the manner and length of instruction. A better reason for purchasing this video than discovering how "professional artists" paint is that one is familiar with the work of Quinten Gregory or interested in painting in a similar manner.

Potential buyers should be equally aware that not everything can be taught in a book or videocassette. Had someone thought to make a film of the highly influential artist and teacher Hans Hofmann instructing his students and selling it to other artists, the result might have proven an exercise in futility. Hofmann's importance to a generation of artists is traced to the interactive, personal give-and-take that occurred in his class, which would not have translated well into an hour-long segment in which technique, color selection, choosing the right brushes and picking a subject all might have to be included.

Learning good techniques is important, but art is also a matter of self-discovery. Any lesson program, in a book or on a video, that only stresses technique—how to paint a tree or a cloud (in effect, visual clichés), how to blend colors or use a fan brush for certain effects—may be destructive to one's inherent originality. Potential book or video buyers would want the instruction to strengthen their technical skills while offering ways to more fully realize their individual talents.

Some companies do have return policies, but their provisions vary widely as each company makes its own rules, determining its own period of time for returns or refunds and for which reasons. The Lela Harty School of Art in San Diego, for instance, which markets a four-videocassette series of art instruction for $119.95, states in its printed brochure that the videos come with a "30-day money-back guarantee. . . . [S]imply return the course and the purchase price will be refunded with no questions asked." The American Artist Book Club also guarantees that "If you are not delighted with your . . . book, return it within 15 days, cancel your membership and owe nothing." North Light Books, another large publisher or art instruction texts, allows readers 10 days to decide.

Lela Harty noted that "maybe 5 percent of the people who have purchased the videocassettes have returned them. Some of them feel that they are beyond the course, which I don't feel is quite true, but I don't want anyone to be unhappy with the videos. Some of the people who have returned videos may have made copies of them, but I can't do much about that."

Many marketers of videocassettes fear the potential for illegal copies and, in order to protect themselves, have established return policies that are only exchange policies—they will exchange a defective video for one that is free of defects—without the possibility of a refund. Both Centerpoint Distribution in San Jose, California, and Artists' Video Productions in Bristol, Rhode Island, deal with customer complaints in this manner. Still, there is always the chance of customers arguing themselves into a different settlement. Dee Alexander, director of operations at Centerpoint Distribution, said that if someone who calls up is "really unhappy with a video he bought, we can make an exception and refund his money. That did happen twice." For her part, Joanna Foster, a partner at Artists' Video Productions, explained that a very unhappy customer was allowed to "exchange the video he had bought for another video in our series."

James Godwin Scott, a watercolorist who distributes his own series of videocassettes, provided a refund to one dissatisfied customer "who had a pretty flimsy excuse: He thought it was in oils. It is very difficult to discern whether or not someone has made a copy." In general, however, it is wisest to assume that, when a company or individual makes no specific mention of a return or refund policy, none probably exists. Efforts to satisfy customers with complaints may range quite widely, which is why finding out in advance as much as possible about the books or videocassettes offered is so important.

Some companies may not have a written policy about the products they offer, but will provide detailed information about their books or cassettes as well as offer a money-back guarantee over the telephone. As noted previously, some of them are quite happy to discuss their products with potential buyers by phone, allowing them to gauge the callers' level of understanding and answer specific questions. To be on the safe side, one should write down what is said about the particular book or videocassette as well as about the return or refund policy and the name of the person with whom one spoke. If any misrepresentation is made, such as the description of a money-back refund if one is unhappy for any reason, then one may make a formal complaint to one's state consumer protection office, the state attorney general or the Federal Trade Commission (one's state consumer protection office will likely advise which route to take).

One way in which those interested in trying out videocassettes, short of buying them, is through renting, from Art Video Library (P.O. Box 68AA, Ukiah, OR 97880, 503/427-3024) or Video Learning Library (5777 Azalea Drive, Grants Pass, OR 97526, 503/479-7140), for $6 per week (payable by credit card). Most public libraries, however, do not carry these videos.

Art instruction books, of course, are not the only sources for printed information and advice on how to create art. Magazines and journals for artists, such as *American Artist* and *The Artist's Magazine,* also contain technical columns, offering specific suggestions in a variety of media. These same publications also frequently review instructional books and videos in the field.

Any books or videocassettes referred to in this chapter are not chosen on the basis of personal preference but rather to illuminate particular points.

☙

Studio Practices

$\mathcal{G}$ETTING DOWN TO WORK AS AN ARTIST requires a studio in which to create. The more this space can be limited to art-making—as opposed to sharing the living room or kitchen—the better for maintaining one's artistic concentration, ensuring the health of other family members (especially children) and obtaining a studio insurance policy. Getting down to work also means having the right materials; knowing which are the right ones involves research and some trial and error.

Selecting Art Materials from Mail-Order Catalogs

These days, almost everything that can be marketed is sold through mail-order catalogs: appliances, books, clothing, food, flowers and plants, furniture, guns, "kit" cars and sailboats, sports equipment, tools and even artwork are offered by the hundreds of companies that sell items through catalogs. It should be no surprise, then, that art supplies may also be purchased from catalog companies, and for the same reasons that all of the other items are marketed through the mail. Many people live at a distance from the retail outlets that would have precisely the supplies they want, and local stores may not offer an abundant variety or competitive prices. In combination with the items that are sold in local shops, mail-order art supply companies offer artists a wide range of products, prices, and quality. Even the wait for the mail may be shortened, if one wishes to pay for overnight delivery.

Buying through the mail, however, may also cause artists a high degree of nervousness and uncertainty. Products that cannot be examined and tested, salespeople who cannot offer detailed information, brands that are unknown to the prospective buyer and items that will only be sold in large quantity can easily unsettle artists and hobbyists who must make their decisions based on short descriptions and (usually) black-and-white photographs in a catalog. Like the art market itself, buying art materials through the mail requires one part knowledge, one part faith.

Practically anything that a painter, printmaker, sculptor or commercial artist needs is available in the many art supply catalogs, from brushes, canvases, inks, paints, pigments, overhead projectors and papers to drafting tables, chisels, clays, easels, frames, mats and sketchbooks, and a lot more than that. Frequently, the products listed in these catalogs are well known and could be found (and, thereby, tested) at major art supply shops, such as Winsor & Newton paints. Other products, such as Daniel Smith Finest Oil Colors or Nova Color Artists' Acrylic Paint, bear the name of the mail-order company—they cannot be found elsewhere and tested, requiring potential buyers to read the catalog descriptions closely as well as ask for additional information. Highly detailed information may not be easily obtainable if the mail-order company is not the product's manufacturer. Many companies buy paints from manufacturers and affix their own proprietary names on them, similar to supermarket brands of food items. The art product may be quite good, selling at an attractive price, but the people working at the mail-order company are unlikely to have much information on the permanence, lightfastness, ingredients and precise color index number of pigment, for example.

There are, for example, more than a dozen Hansa Yellows on the market, varying from the very fugitive to the permanent, according to Mark David Gottsegen, chairman of the committee on artists' paints and related materials of the New Jersey–based American Society for Testing and Materials (ASTM). Without knowing the color index number, a buyer will not know how the pigment holds up in combination with other pigments or over time.

"You don't want to buy some paint based on the name Hunt's Red or Joe Blow's Roast Beef Red, because you don't really know what color you're getting," Gottsegen said. "If the mail-order company isn't the manufacturer, go to the manufacturer and ask them what's in it."

A buyer of watercolor paints and papers from mail-order companies himself, Gottsegen recommended that artists obtain the respective ASTM standard specifications for oil paints, acrylics and watercolors in order to have a precise description of pigments as well as the composition and durability of paints. (These specifications cost $10 apiece, and one should write to American Society for Testing and Materials, 100 Barr Harbor Drive, West Conshohocken, PA 19428, 610/ 832-9500.)

There aren't similar standards for other art supplies, and one must rely on obtaining good answers to questions. In addition to more personal preferences, for instance, sculptors and potters would want to know the firing color range and grog of clays as well as whether or not they are pre-pugged and wedged; painters would be interested in the type (bristle, sable or synthetic), softness, ability to maintain a point and length of hairs on brushes as well as the length of the handles; printmakers and watercolorists would need to know the acidity, quantity, rag content, size and sizing of papers. Daniel Smith (located in Seattle, Washington) attempts to ease potential paper buyers' concerns by offering sample packets of papers—an $8 sampler containing one sheet of every paper it sells in four-by-five size as well as a printmaking paper packet and a watercolor paper sampler in regular size sheets, priced between $30 and $40 for each.

Federal law since 1989 (the Labeling of Hazardous Art Materials Act) also requires all art product labels to include a conformance statement ("conforms to ASTM D-4236"), the name and address of the manufacturers or other responsible party and a telephone number at which further information about chronic toxicity can be answered, and to list the names of any chronically hazardous ingredients and appropriate hazard warnings. In fact, it is now illegal to sell any art material without these items on the label (see Safety in the Studio below). The federal Occupational Safety and Health Administration demands that manufacturers provide Material Safety Data Sheets for their products that contain oxides or quantities of toxic elements. The law requires that these sheets be made available to employers whose employees use the product. Although manufacturers and importers are not required (except in a few states) to supply these sheets to individual consumers, artists should only deal with companies that do supply them. Most reputable companies, which have nothing to hide, are willing to supply them. Artists might want to ask the mail-order companies to send those sheets in advance of purchasing a particular item and certainly when the product is bought.

Sometimes, more information can prove confusing. Dick Blick Company (located in Galesburg, Illinois), like many other companies, uses the "AP Nontoxic," "CP Nontoxic" and "Health Label" seals of the Boston-based Arts and Creative Materials Institute (ACMI) on the labels of its paints. Both "AP" and "CP" indicate that the Institute certifies the products are safe even for children ("AP" specifically refers to

. . . .

nontoxicity, while "CP" includes both nontoxicity and performance requirements), and "Health Label" signifies that the warning label on the product has been certified by an ACMI toxicologist and, if hazards are found, appropriate warnings are printed on the label. The same paints, however, may be sold by other mail-order companies but without the ACMI emblems to indicate their safety.

Daniel Smith, on the other hand, provides the lightfastness rating for many of the paints that company sells, paints that are also sold by other companies. One shouldn't assume, therefore, that the same paints are less toxic when purchased through Dick Blick or more durable when bought from Daniel Smith, only that Dick Blick considers product safety a stronger selling point in its promotion of these products than some other companies, while Daniel Smith emphasizes longevity. Customers would still want to buy at the best price, all other things being equal.

Obtaining detailed information on art supplies is never easy, either when purchasing from catalogs or even many art shops. "Art shop employees may be able to answer some questions about the safety of products since that has been a very publicized issue," Deborah Fanning, director of the Arts and Creative Materials Institute, stated. "They may not know much about the quality. Probably, however, art shop employees will know a little bit more about those things than the people who answer the telephones at mail-order companies but, in both cases, you might have to ask for the manager and hope that person knows something."

Customer service representatives are likely to have basic information about products and can answer some questions. If they don't have the immediate answer, the representatives will generally attempt to get the information from someone at the company or from the manufacturer, calling back the person who made the inquiry. Some mail-order suppliers provide ongoing training seminars for their representatives, which may consist of listening to a talk about certain products by salespeople of the manufacturers or watching a promotional video supplied by the manufacturer. Other companies hire people with art backgrounds for customer service jobs, who will still be provided some training, because they are likely to be asked lots of questions over time.

Problems are not unheard of between mail-order companies and their buyers, regardless of the kind of merchandise sold, such as receiving the wrong item, damaged goods or an incorrect credit card billing. Many companies have time limits on returns, which may vary greatly; others do not or require explanation. Frames by Mail (located in St. Louis, Missouri) will accept damaged returns within five days of receipt by the buyer, while Montoya/MAS International Inc.

(headquartered in West Palm Beach, Florida), which sells sculpture books, materials and tools, allows 30-day returns for any reason.

Other mail-order art supply companies simply refer to a "reasonable period of time" as acceptable for returns. According to a customer service employee at Arthur Brown in Maspeth, New York, the company has no time limits for returns of pens, providing that they haven't been used, although there may be a restocking fee for other items if returned within a "reasonable amount of time, for instance, not more than three months." The employee did not indicate the amount of the restocking fee. Tom Newton of The Mettle Company (based in Fanwood, New Jersey), which makes custom frames, indicated a more open-ended policy: "I like to keep my customers happy. If you have a problem, call and ask to talk to me and we'll see what's reasonable to do."

A number of companies make blanket statements of guaranteed satisfaction in their catalogs, promising to accept all returns—for whatever reason—in exchange for another item or one's money back. In order to save oneself and a mail-order company some headaches, it is wisest to obtain as much information as possible about the products that may be purchased in advance. Gilbert Edelson, administrative vice president of the Art Dealers Association of America, said that a buyer should "never purchase something without seeing at least a photograph of it." Refunds for returned items purchased by check, money order or credit card must be issued within seven business days, according to Federal Trade Commission regulations. Refunds usually do not include the cost of shipping and insuring the item returned.

However, if a buyer believes that he or she is a victim of mail fraud (being duped by a misleading or false advertisement made in a catalog) or consumer fraud (for instance, money is not refunded or some advertised "handmade" papers were actually created by machines), that person should complain to either: Federal Trade Commission (Pennsylvania Avenue at Sixth Street, N.W., Washington, D.C. 20580), which regulates sales through the mail; Postmaster General (475 L'Enfant Plaza, S.W., Washington, D.C. 20260), if the seller is out of state, who will investigate and turn over its findings to the U.S. Attorney who may indict; State Attorney General, if the seller is in the same state; or the Better Business Bureau (contact The Council of Better Business Bureaus Inc., 4200 Wilson Boulevard, Arlington, VA 22203 for the address of the nearest office) or local Department of Consumer Affairs, if the seller is in the same city. There are jurisdictional differences between them, and some have more power than others.

Many companies that sell products through the mail also belong to various associations, which one may contact in order to resolve disputes with their members as well as find out which companies are members in advance of making a purchase. Becoming a member of an association does not ensure the quality of an art product, but the organizations do maintain standards to which member companies must adhere. Among these organizations are the Advertising Mail Marketing Association (1333 F Street, N.W., Washington, D.C. 20004-1108), Direct Marketing Association (11 West 42 Street, New York, NY 10036-8096, or 1101 17 Street, N.W., Washington, D.C. 20036), National Art Education Association (1916 Association Drive, Reston, VA 22091-1590) and National Art Materials Trade Association (178 Lakeview Avenue, Clifton, NJ 07011).

Most catalogs are free, although some cost up to five dollars (that amount is refundable with one's actual order of art supplies). Despite the fact that these are mail-order companies, buyers increasingly place orders over the phone, sometimes with a fax. Some companies have toll-free numbers, while others require buyers to make long-distance calls, and yet others provide no telephone number at all, ensuring that business is wholly conducted through the mail. The price of the telephone call may not always help determine from which company to order products as Co-op Artists' Materials (headquartered in Atlanta, Georgia), for instance, has a toll-free number, yet the company requires a minimum purchase of $35 for telephone orders whereas there is no minimum for orders that are mailed in. Jerry's Artarama (located in New Hyde Park, New York), which also has a toll-free telephone number, requires a minimum order of $50 if by phone and $20 if by mail.

In general, prices for products in mail-order catalogs compare favorably with the same or similar items in smaller art supply stores, and they may be equal to or a bit higher than those items in larger stores of major cities. Sales taxes will not be applied unless one buys from a mail-order company in one's own state. Beyond the prices of the items in the catalogs are shipping and handling charges which, of course, will not exist for supplies bought directly at a store. Shipping costs are determined based on a percentage of the dollar value of the purchase, and one receives a better break with larger orders. It may also be impossible to purchase just a small amount of some item, in order to try it out, as companies often require orders in bulk. That bulk rate keeps the overall price low, but consumers may feel reluctant to buy a lot of a product they have not sampled.

Although Jerry's Artarama allows one to mail in orders of only $20, the company adds a $3 handling charge for orders under $50; shipping costs are between 8 and 10 percent of the total purchase, depending upon the state to which the products are being sent. There is an overall 5 percent discount for orders of $250 or more, with the requirement that each item purchased be under $100, and an 8 percent discount for orders over $800. Utrecht (headquartered in Brooklyn, New York) accepts no orders by mail or telephone of under $40, and its shipping charges vary based on the amount of the purchase. Orders of $40–$74.99 are assessed a 10 percent shipping charge; there is an 8 percent shipping charge for orders of $75–$249.99; above $250, the shipping costs are reduced to only 7 percent. In addition, Utrecht discounts orders over $75 by 5 percent, over $150 by 10 percent, over $250 by 15 percent and over $450 by 20 percent.

On the other hand, Co-op Artists' Materials and Daniel Smith both offer discounts but only on certain items, and these are listed with each product in the catalogue. Art Supply Warehouse (headquartered in Norwalk, Connecticut) offers no volume discounts—"Our prices are already discounted," a telephone representative for the company stated—but the $4 handling charge is eliminated for purchases of $100 or more. One has to look for bargains, and it is wise to ask.

Montgomery Ward developed the mail-order business in the 1870s as a way of bringing store-quality supplies to people in outlying areas, but buying through the mail is no longer the exclusive domain of those in rural regions. Artists in suburbs and cities are currently the predominant buyers from art catalogs. The tremendous volume of art products on the market would overwhelm most stores but not necessarily a 500-page catalog. One cannot completely get away from relying on written or oral descriptions of products and old-fashioned trial and error, but artists who know what they need and can formulate the right questions minimize their risks.

Artists Who Make Art Supplies for Other Artists

Given the abundant offerings in art stores and mail-order art supply catalogs, most artists' supply needs are easily satisfied. What image to put on the canvas, paper or negative, or to shape into a sculpture, is the more immediate concern. Some artists, however, find that they cannot create the images they want because of something lacking in the materials they are using. Perhaps they cannot find the right color of pastel, or they want a thicker paper with more linen content, or the color of the paint loses its intensity when mixed with white, or they want to make art in a way that is currently not done, or the quality of the material has declined while the cost has increased.

Various artists experiment with their materials, making their own paper or mixing various substances in with their paints, for instance, some having more success than others. The venerable art supply manufacturer Winsor & Newton was founded in 1832 by two artists, William Winsor and Henry Charles Newton, who both had an interest in chemistry—Winsor was in charge of oil paints, while Newton handled watercolors. Even today, some painters have gone back to original sources in order to make their own paints, free of the fillers and additives that commercial manufacturers use to extend the life, decrease the drying time and increase the consistency of the pigments. A small but growing number of artists, who have become proficient in making their own materials in quantity, have created specialized lines of art supplies for other artists. Frequently, these supplies are less expensive by weight than those produced by large manufacturers, and the quality is as high or better.

"Years ago, there were two really good artist paints to buy, both made in Holland—Old Holland Paint and Bloxx," painter Bill Jensen said. "But then, Old Holland was sold to someone and old man Bloxx died, and the quality really fell off, in some cases below student grade. If Carl ever stopped making paint, I would have to get a paint machine and make it myself." That Carl is Carl Plansky, a painter who, since 1984, has operated Williamsburg Art Supply in Brooklyn, New York, and sells paint to many of the most renowned contemporary artists, including Jensen, Brice Marden, Joan Mitchell and Susan Rothenberg. There are more than 60 colors in Plansky's line of oil paints, which he calls "handmade oils," as opposed to paints created from a set recipe. "Any company with enough scientists can work out a formula," he stated. "They machine-grind the pigments, which may make them lose some luminosity, and then the pigments are treated with fillers and additives to give the paint shelf life and an even consistency. I keep experimenting: I work with every batch of raw pigment I receive to grind it to its maximum luminosity and soak it in oil for the right amount of time. I can also manufacture one pint of paint for what the big companies charge for a one-ounce tube, and I pass that savings on to my customers."

Many of the artists making art supplies for other artists refer to the "handmade" quality of their products, in contrast to the more generic nature of mass-produced items. Plansky noted that his paints are "the equivalent of health food." Stefan Watson, who started Watson Paper Company in Albuquerque, New Mexico, in 1979, producing handmade papers for artists, said that "if mass marketing had its way, everyone would use the same products. Who says that all paper has to be white, that it has only a standardized thickness?"

Keith Lebenzon of Portland, Oregon, a craftsman making calligraphy and watercolor brushes, claimed that the difference between his brushes and those manufactured by larger companies is that "mine are made by hand, which makes all the difference in the world. No two brushes are alike. Every one has a personality. People have told me that these brushes have changed their lives." Another difference between his brushes and those of his competitors, Lebenzon stated, is the use of hairs from the Roosevelt elk (which only lives in the Pacific Northwest and is on the national list of endangered species) and the silver fox for several models.

Artists involved in creating art materials for artists also frequently stress their aim of providing these products at affordable prices, recognizing that art is not a high-paying profession for most. "I look out for the needs of painters," said Robert Gamblin, a Portland, Oregon, painter who spent 10 years researching how to make paints before offering them for sale in 1980. "Painters need to have raw materials of high quality at affordable prices. I don't take economies inside the tube, such as adding fillers, but I will take them outside the tube. I have no distributors, no marketing people, no sales reps—that adds up to 22 percent to the cost of doing business."

Art Guerra, a painter who has operated Guerra Paint & Pigments in New York City since 1983, is another who claims to "look out for" artists. Selling over 250 dry pigments and water-based urethancs as well as a variety of antifoam, thickeners, dispersing, and texturizing agents (allowing artists to mix up their own acrylic paints to desired levels of strength and thickness), Guerra claims to charge "one-quarter of the price of the big manufacturers, and you're using better materials, too."

He considers himself "not only a business but an information source," offering prospective pigment buyers a booklet that lists (among other things) the exact color, durability, weatherability and alkali resistance of the pigments as well as what these terms mean.

Guerra also sells oil paints in jars that he creates as well as tubes of oil paint produced by William & Arthur of Brooklyn—Bill Rabinowitz and Art Graham, both of whom paint (although Rabinowitz is primarily a chemist) and both of whom worked for years at Grumbacher artist paints. Just like Bill Jensen, both Graham and Rabinowitz express disappointment at artist paint "companies that are taken over by people who are only in it for making money," Graham stated, "who don't really care whether they're selling oil paints or candy wrappers or gum. You need to have a moral position with regard to art materials, and you have to love the product, love making the product and love what the product is used for."

Whereas the high prices and diminishing quality of commercially available paints had originally pushed Robert Gamblin, Art Guerra, Carl Plansky, Art Graham and Bill Rabinowitz to make their own, Suzanna Starr and Ladd Foresline of Cochecton, New York, invented oil sticks in 1984 because, Starr said, "I wanted to draw rather than use a brush, but I also wanted the thing I drew with to feel more like oil paint. There was nothing like that on the market, so we created these oil sticks." At first, the two sold these sticks to artists who heard of them by word of mouth, bypassing retail stores, "but that proved impossible," Foresline stated. "We're artists—that's why we got into making these things in the first place—and not manufacturers. It's a lot of work to do all of this, and I think we both gained respect for manufacturers because of all the work involved." In 1991, Winsor & Newton bought the product, and the two artists have returned to their art as well as researching new art products.

In a similar vein, Diane Townsend began creating her own pastels in 1971 because she "couldn't find what I was looking for. The colors I observed in nature weren't made commercially, and I also didn't like the consistency of what I was buying. The colors and consistency seemed to get in my way." Many artists would assume that, if they had trouble with consistency, the problem is with them and their technique, but Townsend noted that "I'm arrogant and hardheaded. I secretly think I'm right and everybody else is wrong." Among her past and current customers are Chuck Close, Jim Dine and Elizabeth Murray ("They're great pastels," Murray said). Townsend currently produces pastels in 130 colors (three tones each, three sizes each) two or three days a week—they are sold through New York Central Art Supply in Manhattan—devoting the rest of the time to her art.

Other artists have come to make their own art materials, not because they wanted something new but, as a result of re-creating techniques that are centuries old and even forgotten. Eric and Roger Rieger, brothers and painters living in Denver, Colorado, founded Lapis Arts in 1987 in order to sell oil paints made in the same manner since the Italian Renaissance. "I couldn't get the glazing effects with the umbers I was buying," Eric Rieger said. "They were coming out very chalky, so I started mixing my own paints." He spent a number of years researching how paint was made, traveling in Europe to study with alchemists, and finally, in association with his brother, produced a line of oil paints that suited their purposes.

Richard Frumess of Rifton, New York, on the other hand, became interested in hot wax or encaustic painting, a technique that dates back to ancient Greece where it was a common process for both easel painters and muralists. Painting with wax—usually, white refined beeswax combined with dry pigments and some resin—is a somewhat cumbersome activity and was eventually supplanted by the use of tempera and oil painting. Interest in encaustic painting has revived over the past 200 years, in part due to the fact that it is "the most durable of all paint," Frumess said. "It won't rot or yellow with age as paint made with linseed oil does. I like painting with encaustics because of the enamel-like finish, the jewel-like effect. Texturally, you also get a large range of effects—you can build it up and carve into it."

He formed R&F Encaustics in 1982 (the only source of encaustic paints in the country), adding a line of oil sticks in 52 colors in 1990. "There is a lot to be said for artists making a product as opposed to a big company making it," Frumess stated. "Artists are basically making it for themselves, so it is a labor of love. Making encaustics is also very labor intensive and expensive, a process that big companies don't want to deal with because they want to mass-produce things quickly to make as big a profit as they can." The labor intensiveness, however, has proven to be a problem for him as "I haven't painted in a couple of years now because of the work of producing encaustics."

As noted above, more and more artists have come to make their own materials as well as experiment with the products they use. One cautionary note is that experimentation needs to be based on research and an understanding of the chemistry of substances that are combined. (A reliable source of information on what artist materials are made of and how artists may create their own is Ralph Mayer's *The Artist's Handbook*.) Art Graham noted that some artists "work up some homemade color, but they don't really know how to make paint. They get very strange ideas from their late-night readings and, if they don't do things right, it will fall right off the canvas."

As with anything else they might buy, artists should ask questions in advance in order to ensure that what they purchase meets their expectations. Howard Wolfe, executive director of the Clifton, New Jersey–based National Art Materials Trade Association, noted three areas of concern when buying paints. The first is consistent quality, that "within a certain tolerance, different tubes of the same paint will be exactly the same." The second is knowing to what standards the paints are manufactured, and whether or not they have been subjected to color- and lightfastness as well as permanency tests, such as those developed by the American Society of Testing and Materials. A third question is whether the people making the art supplies are actually creating them from scratch or if some or all of the product has been made by someone else. "Anyone can go to a major manufacturer of paints and say, 'I want you to make a line of paints that I'll sell under my name,'" Wolfe said. "When someone says he made his own paints, ask him where he got the binders, the resins, and the pigments."

Creating Artworks That Last

When artists create a new work, they expect that the piece will look for a long time as it did when first made. Works in poor shape not only lose some of their value, but may adversely affect the artist's reputation. This requires that the pieces are made with high-quality materials and treated with care during their lifetimes. Looking first at the materials, a growing amount of attention has been focused on graphic art prints. Because they are composed of organic materials, the inks and paper each expand and contract with levels of humidity as they absorb or release moisture. In high humidity, for instance, paper expands, causing a slight dimensional change. Printing ink, however, does not swell to the same degree and it cracks, permitting more moisture to enter and causing further cracking to take place later on. If this situation is not corrected, the bond between the ink and the paper will loosen, and ink will begin to flake off.

In some cases, both the paper and inks may have what conservators call an "inherent vice"—problems that will eventually cause them to break down at an early age. The paper may darken or the colors might change or fade or crack. "The problem is you don't know what you're getting," said Mark David Gottsegen. "The label on a can of printers ink won't tell you much more than the name of the color, and the people who work in print studios usually don't know much about the inks they are using."

Many printers inks are either water or soy based, which also may not be apparent from the label on the can, and their colors are either made from mineral pigments or vegetable dyes. Soy, which is intended to be used in commercial printing where the longevity of the final product is not a consideration, tends to yellow more than linseed oil (a common ingredient in artists oil paints and some printers inks), and it takes longer to dry than water-based inks. That latter problem is often solved by the manufacturers adding dryers to the mix, but that additive sometimes causes cracking. The optimal vehicle for printers inks is bodied or burnt plate oil, a polymerized linseed oil that does not yellow, although that generally costs more than the soy- or water-based inks. As labels may not tell the whole story, one should inquire what the medium is for the ink being used or sold.

The problem of the compatibility of inks, especially those produced by different manufacturers, may arise due to varying drying times and the vehicle. As with any liquids applied to paper, printers inks make the print sheet buckle slightly, and the paper will flatten as it dries. If the drying time of one ink is longer than another on the same print, however, the sheet may not resume its flat surface at the same time, resulting in quilted areas on the paper. Obviously, water- and oil-based inks will not combine at all. Mixing soy- and linseed oil–based inks "may affect the coating, how it adheres to the paper, and the durability of the print, in terms of cracking," said Ronald Harmon, chemist for Daniel Smith, the Seattle-based manufacturer and supplier of artists materials. "Let's just say that soy and linseed oils don't act synergistically."

Mineral pigments are less likely to change color or fade (as they are chemically inactive) than those created from far less expensive vegetable dyes. However, mineral paints are not available in every color, and one may have to settle for the more fugitive vegetable dyes. The water-based dyes in ink-jet printers, which are used in computer-generated artwork, are the most likely to fade quickly, often within three to five years. Pigments cannot be ground so finely as to fit through the small holes through which the ink jets spray colors onto the paper, and the very bright dyes that are used do not have a good lightfastness record.

As opposed to the manufacturers of artists paints, the majority of fine art printing ink makers do not subscribe to the voluntary fading (or lightfastness) standards of the American Society of Testing and Materials. The society has recommended four lightfastness tests —two outdoor (one in the heat and humidity of Florida, one in a hot, dry, high-altitude environment such as Arizona) and two indoor (one in fluorescent light, another in xenon light). Pigment manufacturers are supposed to apply one indoor and one outdoor test, averaging the results to determine the degree of lightfastness. Joy Turner Luke, who chairs of the society's committee on artists paints and related materials, noted that ink manufacturers do conduct lightfastness tests, "but not the same rigorous tests that ASTM recommends. The pigments may not be exposed to the same amount of energy or for as long a period of time, and as a result the manufacturers come up with higher lightfastness ratings than we think is accurate." The cost of testing is a main reason that companies do not do it, Harmon noted, as manufacturers must either pay for an independent laboratory to evaluate the inks or purchase expensive machines to test on-site.

Reliable and informed information is at a premium in this area. Even a company as well regarded as Daniel Smith frequently does not list the pigments on the label, requiring buyers to write for a separate technical sheet that notes the pigments used and the ink's overall lightfastness. "It's difficult to find ink suppliers that meet our specifications," said Cathie Humphries, chief operating officer and sales manager at Color-Q, the Dayton, Ohio, printer that guarantees a 70-year life expectancy for limited-edition prints. "There is less than a handful of ink manufacturers that we feel comfortable with, because of the way they test and the accuracy of their tests." Added to this, relatively few printers test the products they use for fading or durability, according to Bill Meyer, quality-control supervisor at Munson Printing in Red Wing, Minnesota. "They just take their supplier's word."

In the end, printers say that they buy from reputable suppliers of inks, and ink manufacturers claim that they buy from reputable suppliers of pigments, leaving artists with words that have ambiguous meanings. "'Fade resistant' is a term that begs interpretation," Meyer said. "A manufacturer says that the product is fade-resistant, compared to other inks the company markets using the same colors, such as for a magazine. It's just that you expect a fine art print to last far longer than a magazine."

An artist may test an ink's durability by applying ink to paper, cutting the paper in half and putting one part in a southern exposure window for a few weeks or months and the other part in dark drawer. Fading is accelerated in high heat, such as during the summer. At the end of the test period, the two halves should be compared to determine the degree of fading. According to Leslie Paisley, paper conservator at the Williamstown Regional Conservation Center in Massachusetts, "two weeks is equivalent to a year in someone's home or in a museum under continuous exhibition."

She also noted that artists sometimes sign and number their prints with an ink that runs. Artists should test the pens they use by signing "a piece of paper, letting it sit for a minute, then adding a drop of water to see if it runs," Paisley said, "and they should also test for fading. Felt-tip pens fade very quickly, and ballpoint pens are solvent sensitive, which can be a problem when the work is cleaned. Pencils are OK; the only problem with them is smudging." She added that artists should look for run-proof, pH-neutral pens.

No less important than the paint is the paper, which is made from wood pulp, cotton, linen or some combination of these. Just as with paints, paper should be tested, using the window-and-drawer method or even baked in an oven to artifically age it. The main signs of trouble with an artist's paper are discoloration or overall darkening as well as embrittlement, which are often the result of acids in the paper breaking down the cellulose polymers that hold the paper fibers together and make them flexible.

There are various ways in which acidity becomes a part of, or can attack, paper. Unrefined wood pulp is high in acidity and will cause yellowing in a short period of time (most newspapers are 80 percent unrefined wood pulp). Other internal problems that may damage the paper are chlorine from the bleach that wasn't completely rinsed out of the paper when it was washed, sizing agents (used to give paper its absorbency and surface character) that leave behind metallic (that rust) or organic (that form fungus) particles and brighteners (that make the paper look very white) that may also leave chemical compounds behind.

Air pollution (acidic gases) is another cause of paper deterioration as is contact with poor quality framing and matting materials (acids in these discolor the paper where they come into contact). Of course, spills of coffee, oil, tea or water may also lead to deterioraton and staining. It is advisable for artists to maintain a clean workplace and collectors to protect pieces from young children or their own clumsiness. Paisley noted that artists need to "store their paper in a dark, acid-free environment; they should never leave their paper outdoors. I've seen instances of artists buying very good paper but by the time they're ready to use it, the paper is all discolored from having absorbed too many acids from the environment."

Another problem affecting all works on paper is destruction by insects and rodents. As insecticides may damage the paper, conservators generally advise collectors to store works on paper away from places where these pests may gain access. Works on paper also react negatively to high humidity. The paper itself, as all wood, tends to expand in humidity, which often results in wrinkling and discoloration. This discoloring is called "foxing," which is due to copper or iron ions in the presence of mold or bacterial growth.

After the artists have done their part, it is up to the collectors to maintain the artworks in good condition. In general, artists should be forthcoming in advising would-be buyers on how to display and care for their works, as that builds trust and confidence. (Dealers, on the other hand, are reluctant to discuss the kinds of care the objects they are selling will need as they worry about scaring potential buyers away.) Buyers are apt to blame the artist if a piece fades, even if the fault was their own neglect, and they should be made aware that knowing how to care for objects in one's home is no less important than understanding what to buy and for how much.

Most museums these days have high-tech temperature and humidity monitoring systems controlling the interior environment. That kind of control is less possible where people live, periodically opening and closing the windows in the spring and fall, turning on the heat or air-conditioning in the winter or summer, but care can be taken to minimize the problems that a changing environment may cause precious objects.

There are some easy, practical ways that conservators recommend to avoid problems. Art should be kept at a distance from doors and windows, and humidifiers are advisable when the air-conditioning or heat is on. Pictures should not be hung above a fireplace, which naturally draws in dirt and dust, nor on an exterior wall of a house as the cool air of the outside and the warmer air inside may provide some form of condensation on the art itself. Many people believe that they are showing off their art to advantage by putting it in frames to which a light in a brass holder is attached. However, the heat of the light acts to fade colors and may burn the canvas or paper itself.

An ideal relatively humidity for works of art is in the range of 40–60 percent, and this can be measured by a hygrometer which many hardware stores carry and costs as little as $25 for the most basic models. Homes in the Northeast tend to be dry and a little overheated during the winter, requiring a humidifier, while the Southeast is more frequently damp and in need of a dehumidifier. Humidity controls should be installed in rooms where important (that is, objects of sentimental or real financial value) pieces are displayed or stored. After humidity, light is the major scourge of art, emitting damaging ultraviolet rays. Fluorescent lights also give off ultraviolet rays. Regular lightbulbs, or incandescent light, are the least harmful as they largely emit heat that is easily diffused in a room. "Objects are made up of molecules," one art conservator explained, "and light energy may cause molecules to separate. When that happens, it releases acidity, which is a product of the reactions, and that eats away at the canvas and paint, causing fading." To be safe, most conservators suggest placing paintings, drawings and prints away from wall areas that will receive strong direct sunlight as well as away from lamps.

Margaret Holben Ellis, consulting conservator at the Metropolitan Museum of Art in New York City, stated that the galleries in museums devoted to works on paper are usually lit to scientific measurements of between five and eight foot-candles. To determine whether or not one's own rooms are brighter than that, she recommended using a photographic meter, which is built into many 35mm cameras. Setting the ASA scale to 100 and the f-stop at 5.6, the indicated shutter speed will be equal to the number of foot-candles. If that number exceeds eight, the room should be dimmed or the artwork moved elsewhere. Keeping the light dim may make some rooms more difficult to read in without some redecorating—moving the art to walls at a distance from the lamps, for instance.

In addition, ultraviolet filters might be placed over the windows, or ultraviolet Plexiglas in front of the work itself, to shield it from the most harmful effects of the light. There are also ultraviolet coatings that one can apply to windows, retarding the most severe effects of strong sunlight, as well as certain types of accordion-shaped blinds that allow a certain amount of light and heat to enter a room while reflecting high heat. Hardware and home decorating stores will have many of these products. If not, call a local museum to find out where to get them.

Almost all works on paper that are displayed on a wall should have a protective glass in front, although the work should never touch the glass itself but be separated from it by an acid-free mat. The backing for a work must also be acid-free, not cheap cardboard and not wood. Paper can easily absorb resins, pollutants and acids from its backing and mat. Ultraviolet Plexiglas is the best kind of protective glass in almost all cases, although it does have a slightly yellowish tinge that may affect the appearance of a work to a degree (regular glass often has a slightly greenish tinge). The only time never to use Plexiglas is for a pastel drawing. Plexiglas has a static charge that acts like a magnet to draw dirt and dust to it. Pastels, which have a chalky consistency, can be problematic as the glass would tend to pull the medium off the paper.

Another area of concern is when artists begin experimenting on their own without studying the chemistry or physical properties of the materials in use. Early in his career, Spanish artist Antoni Tàpies loaded up his oil paints with sand and other gritty material in order to give his paintings a sculptural quality on the canvas. The idea was fine, except the canvas couldn't support all the weight and the medium simply fell off time and again. As one of Tàpies' former dealers noted, "it would just fall on the floor. You sweep it up with a broom and send it back to Tàpies who would put it back together again."

The maintenance problems of most contemporary works are not as extreme, but much of the most important art created since the end of World War II contains extensive experimentation, not only with style but with media. A number of the abstract expressionists, for instance, sought to heighten the emotional effects of their work by mixing dirt, metals, sand, wax and other materials with their paints, resulting in paintings that contain inherent vices.

Willem de Kooning, for instance, sometimes mixed safflower oil and other substances with his paints. "De Kooning wanted to make his medium buttery and sensuous," Margaret Watherston, a conservator for the Whitney Museum of American Art, said. "I'm not going to criticize his intention, but it does make it difficult for the paint layer to dry. That results in later problems for conservators."

Mexican muralist David Alfaro Siqueiros and French cubist Fernand Léger both created difficulties for later conservators by painting on burlap, while Marc Chagall made designs on bed sheets. Franz Kline, another abstract expressionist who was perennially short on cash, occasionally worked on celatex board—a low-grade paper pulp. A large number of Andrew Wyeth paintings have developed problems with flaking because the artist made mistakes mixing gesso and egg tempera. Robert Rauschenberg "didn't take any particular pains with a lot of his earlier pieces. He just stuck things on with glue," his biographer, Calvin Tomkins, said. "At that time, he felt that the work itself is ephemeral and that it's the process that is important. I don't think he feels exactly that way now. He has a lot of people working for him now who make sure things are put together right."

The Romans had a saying that art is long and life is short, but sometimes the art doesn't hold up enough. Those who wish to treat art as an investment probably won't keep particular pieces very many years, and the conservation problems won't be all that important to them. For those who expect their art to be with them for a while, the question of whether a work of art is or isn't properly made, existing for posterity or for the moment of creation is very important. It is part of a larger debate among artists, collectors, conservators and dealers, and it will undoubtedly remain until humankind decides that art has lived long enough and chooses to destroy it.

Safety in the Studio

No news to those involved in it, creating art is challenging, rewarding and fun. The materials used in making art, however, can also be harmful to one's health, affecting all of the major bodily organs, if one's work habits are sloppy or if basic precautions are not taken. The concern with safe art materials dates back to 1940, when members of the Crayon, Water Color and Craft Institute engaged a toxicologist to review product formulas for harmful ingredients. By 1946, a voluntary commercial standard was developed in conjunction with the National Bureau of Standards of the U.S. Department of Commerce, concerning wax and pressed crayons as well as semimoist and dry watercolors, liquid and powder tempera, several varieties of chalks, pastel crayons and modeling clays.

By 1960, finger paints were added to the list and there was a change in the standard for toxicity. The 1946 standard stated that the included products ". . . shall not contain lead, arsenic or other toxic materials in excess of 0.05 percent," but that was changed in 1960 to read ". . . are certified to contain no known toxic materials in sufficient quantities to be injurious to the human body." Not everyone was convinced by these somewhat loose (and voluntary) standards. In 1981, a study conducted by industrial hygienist Michael McCann, and Barry A. Miller and Aaron Blair of the National Cancer Institute found that visual artists had higher rates of bladder, brain and kidney cancer as well as leukemia than the general population. That study was based on reports of the causes of death of 1,598 professional artists. Subsequent studies have only added to the general sense of concern.

Some of the most common toxic materials found in arts and crafts materials are listed in the chart below.

Toxic Materials in Arts and Crafts Materials

CHEMICAL	ART MATERIAL MAJOR ADVERSE EFFECTS
Ammonia	Found in most acrylic paints Irritates the skin, eyes, and lungs
Antimony	Pigments, patinas, solders, glass, plastics Anemia, kidney, liver, and reproductive damage
Arsenic	Lead enamels and glass Skin, kidney and nerve damage, cancer
Asbestos	Some talcs and French chalks Lung scarring and cancer
Barium	Metals, glazes, glass, pigments Muscle spasms, heart irregularities
Cadmium	Pigment, glass and glaze colorant, solders Kidney, liver and reproductive damage, cancer
Chromium	Pigment, glass and glaze colorant, metals Skin and respiratory irritation, allergies, cancer
Cobalt	Pigment, glass and glaze colorant, metals Asthma, skin allergies, heart damage, respitation
Formaldehyde	Most acrylic paints, plywood Irritates skin, eyes, and lungs, allergies, cancer
Hexane	Rubber cement and some spray products Nerve damage
Lead	Art paints, enamels, glazes, solders Nerve, kidney, reproductive damage, birth defects

Manganese	Glass and ceramic colorants, pigments, metals
	Nervous system damage, reproductive effects
Mercury	Lustre glazes, pigments, photochemicals
	Nervous system damage, reproductive effects
Uranium Oxide	Ceramic, glass, and enamel colorant
	Kidney damage, radioactive carcinogen

Fortunately, information on which potentially harmful ingredients are contained in art materials and how to work with them safely is increasingly available, but one needs to know where to look. The first place is the product itself. The Labeling of Hazardous Art Materials Act, which went into effect in 1989, requires that art material ingredients that are known chronic hazards be listed on the label with appropriate hazard warnings. Artists should be aware, however, that many pigments and other art material ingredients have never been studied for chronic toxicity. These can still be labeled nontoxic, even when they are related to known toxic chemicals. Caution is still needed when one is working with art materials. This enables buyers to make safer choices and, if artists understand the hazards of particular chemicals, they can use the warning to identify the contents. For example, a yellow material labeled with warnings about cancer and kidney damage is likely to contain a cadmium pigment. A material labeled with warnings about reproductive damage, birth defects, nerve, brain, or kidney damage may contain lead. (Unlike ordinary consumer paints, artists' paints are still permitted to contain lead.)

Manufacturers of products containing toxic elements are also bound by state and federal "right to know" laws to fill out Material Safety Data Sheets, which are provided to those in employer–employee relationships. Artists may write to manufacturers for these data sheets, although in many states the manufacturers and distributors are not required to provide them to individual consumers. Most responsible manufacturers, however, will supply this information. A second source of information on what is in art materials and how they should be properly used are several private and public agencies concerned with these and other related issues, and one can receive written material and advice over the telephone. Among the agencies are:

Occupational Safety and Health Administration
U.S. Department of Labor
200 Constitution Ave., N.W., Room N3101, Washington, D.C. 20210
(202) 523-8151 (information); (202) 523-0055 (publications)

Centers for Disease Control
1600 Clifton Road, N.E., Atlanta, GA 30333
(404) 639-3311

Arts, Crafts and Theater Safety
181 Thompson Street, No. 23, New York, NY 10012
(212) 777-0062
http://www.caseweb.com/acts

Arts and Creative Materials Institute
100 Boylston Street, Boston, MA 02116
(617) 426-6400
http://www.creative-industries.com

Center for Safety in the Arts, Inc.
2124 Broadway, P.O. Box 310, New York, NY 10023
(212) 366-6900, ext. 333
http://www.artswire.org:70/1/csa; e-mail: *csa@artswire.org*

In general, the largest problem for artists, both hobbyists and professionals, is that the majority of them pursue their art in their homes rather than in a studio located elsewhere. Dusts from clays and pastels, solvents in turpentine and aerosol spray paints, lead found in stained glass and ceramic glazes and a variety of other toxic substances may become a permanent part of their home environment, affecting everyone who lives there. Airborne contaminants may enter the lungs, while other harmful elements are able to penetrate the pores of the skin or be ingested orally when on one's hands (which touch the mouth) as well as when toxic materials settle on food. In a separate studio, the health risks are confined to the individual who is involved in the art project for the few hours a day that the room is used, whereas in one's house—especially in a kitchen or living room—there may be people around all the time.

The danger is greatest for young children as they have a higher metabolic rate than adults and will absorb toxic substances more quickly into their bodies. In addition, as childrens' lungs and body defenses have not completely formed, they are more susceptible to disease that may damage them permanently. Often when a child is born, the room previously designated as the studio will be converted to a nursery, and the parents begin working on their arts and crafts projects in more well-trafficked rooms, such as the kitchen or living room. There is then a greater probability of contamination through the air or skin as well as the chance for a serious accident, such as a child drinking from a former milk container that the parent is now using to store turpentine, pottery glaze or other hazardous substance. The potential risks are great.

Parents are generally advised to segregate their art activities in rooms that have a special outside entrance and that are locked to prevent small children from entering, such as a garage or outbuilding. Work tables and floors should be wet mopped regularly. Ordinary household and shop vacuums ought not to be used since their filters will pass the small toxic dust particles back into the air. Sweeping is even more hazardous, for this will cause dust to become airborne. Running water should be available in the studio. Floors should be sealed to facilitate easy cleaning, and spills must be wiped up immediately. Separate clothing and shoes should be worn and left in the studio in order to avoid carrying and tracking contaminants into the house.

Dusts and debris should be disposed of in accordance with local, state and federal disposal laws; one can find out what is required by calling the local sanitation, environmental protection, or public works department. These laws vary widely, depending on the type of waste treatment in one's community. Pouring solvents down the drain is against environmental laws everywhere as well as a danger to the artist and his or her family. Solvents in drains and sewers tend to evaporate, producing flammable vapors that may cause explosions.

Many communities have a toxic chemical disposal service that will accept waste solvents and other toxic waste created by households and hobbyists (defined for this purpose as people who do not make money from their work). Professional artists may be required to hire hazardous waste disposal companies to pick up their toxic refuse. Usually, ordinary waste from consumer art paints and materials can be double bagged and placed in the regular trash. Lead metal scraps, on the other hand, can be recycled. Again, one should call local authorities for advice on disposal of art materials, as the fines for violating the laws can be quite high.

Monona Rossol, an industrial hygienist and president of the nonprofit organization Arts, Crafts and Theater Safety in New York City, recommends that studios be properly ventilated. The ventilation should be tailored to fit the type of work done in the studio. For example, all kilns need to be vented, and there are several commercial systems that can be purchased for them. More complex equipment may require an engineer to design a proper system. One simple system she recommends for many individual studios requires windows at opposite ends of the room. The window at one end is filled with an exhaust fan, and at the other it is opened to provide air to replace that which is exhausted by the fan. This system should not be used in studios where dusts are created, although it is acceptable for painting and other arts activities that produce small amounts of solvent vapors. Check local codes to find out if this system is permitted in your area.

The concern over potentially hazardous ingredients found in many art supplies has led to new laws (as noted above) as well as efforts by manufacturers to reformulate their products in order to exclude the most toxic elements. There are also a growing number of alternatives and substitutes for the more dangerous materials, such as talc-free, premixed clay (in place of clay in dry form), water-based inks and paints (instead of solvent-based inks and aerosol sprays), vegetable dyes (rather than fiber-reactive or commercial dyes) and wax crayons or oil pastels (in place of dusty pastels and chalks). Artists, especially those with children, should contact the various private and public agencies about safe materials to use.

The Home Studio

When the architect Charles Gwathmey designed a two-story house in Southampton, New York for his father, the renowned painter Robert Gwathmey, half of the downstairs was the artist's studio. "Painting was such a big part of his life," the architect said, "not just his work, that it didn't seem right to separate where he lived and where he worked."

Consigning such a large portion of one's living space to art-making may not satisfy every family. However, where the studio should be—at home or somewhere else—is a question that most artists (professional and hobbyist alike) have to confront. For some, the distractions of home require that they pursue their art elsewhere, perhaps renting a studio downtown. "I had a studio in the attic once," said painter Gregory Gillespie. "It was cramped, cold, dirty; it had poor light, and you could hear everything going on in the house. Now, my studio isn't far from the house, maybe 100 yards, but it is a significant psychological distance."

Others, however, find that working at home makes the most sense. The reasons may be young children at home, the cost of renting a studio elsewhere or just the inconvenience of traveling. "For a while, I rented a studio in a factory building in Boston," said Jane Smaldone, a painter who lives and now makes art at home in Roslyndale, Massachusetts. "I like working at night, but I didn't feel safe going there at night, especially since I didn't have a car and took public transit."

She arrived at a solution by converting the attic of their house into a studio, at a cost of between $4,000 and $5,000, not including her husband's labor. Considering the fact that the rent for her downtown studio was $400 per month, the cost of the conversion (the largest expense of which was supplying heat to the room) was recouped in one year.

What artists need in a studio is as individual as the artists themselves, and converting a room into a studio will likely be as elaborate or simple as the artists are able to afford. Traditionally, artists require a window (preferably with a northern exposure, as that offers a relatively unvarying source of light during daylight hours) and a sink (for cleanup). The cost of adding a sink frequently convinces artists to do without additional plumbing and take their brushes to an existing bathroom. An attic or bedroom that receives little natural light may be helped by skylights, which cost between $200 and $300 (not including labor for installation), although many artists may prefer to have greater control over the light in their studios, using lamps or floodlights. Artists with jobs or small children, who are only able to work on their art at night or early morning, may especially rely on artificial light.

Garages, spare bedrooms, basements and attics, sometimes kitchens and living rooms, may be taken over by the artist of the family when home studio space is required. Each has its advantages and drawbacks. In a kitchen, everything would have to be cleaned up thoroughly after each art-making session before any food touches the same kitchen surfaces, and art could only be created between meals. In such a public room, there is also a problem of privacy, as many artists would not want everyone passing through to see (and comment upon) the latest work in progress. When a studio is sited in a well-traveled area, the likelihood of passers-by getting paint on their clothes also increases substantially. Basements and attics have less traffic, but moisture in one and cold in the other as well as a lack of light in both might prove challenging without extensive remodeling.

For instance, Josie Lawrence, a painter in Hanover, Massachusetts, who works at the Kennedy Library in Boston, uses a space heater for warmth in the attic of her house that she uses as a studio. "The cold makes oil paints harder and less pliable," she said, "and I have to put the heater on for a while in order to soften up the paints before I can go up to work."

David Deutsch, a painter who spends half the year in Boca Raton, Florida, and the other half in Manhasset, New York, has encountered mild problems in both of his home studios. In Florida, the studio is the garage, and the natural light is sufficient when he keeps the garage door open during the day. When he has tried to paint at night, however, "I have to turn on artificial lights, which attracts bugs, and there are just so many of them down here that I can't stand it and give up," he said. In Long Island, the studio is a guest bedroom on the second floor, and the solvents he uses for his oil paints creates an odor that pervades the entire upstairs of the house. "I use odorless solvents, but my wife says there still is a smell."

Certain kinds of artwork, such as printmaking (which uses strong, toxic solvents) and sculpture (which often employs noisy, heavy machinery and creates extensive amounts of dust) may simply prove incompatible with a private home or neighborhood. Ventilation systems, exhaust fans and even permission from the municipality to use certain kinds of equipment in a residential community may be required (see Safety in the Studio above).

The benefits of having a studio at home are also the hazards. Susan Baker, a painter in North Truro, Massachusetts, noted that having a studio in the front room of her house means that she is "there when things happen. I can answer the telephone and watch my son. Having a studio somewhere else sounds like a pain to me." On the other hand, Beverly Ferguson-Deevy, a pastel artist in Plainville, Massachusetts, whose studio is the family garage, said that "sometimes, I can be getting pretty deep into my work, and hours go by—I don't even notice. All of a sudden, I hear a tiny 'Mommy' from one of my children, and a whole train of thought is blown away. Everything goes blank, like when the computer crashes, and I'll have to start again another day."

Young children are a common reason that many artists (especially women artists) prefer to work at home, yet they need to be instructed that mom's (or dad's) art studio is not their studio. "My children do not enter my studio, under pain of death," Ferguson-Deevy said. "All in all, they've been pretty good at respecting that rule."

The artist-parent, too, must learn to tune out household noises in order to concentrate. Smaldone, who has a one-and-a-half-year-old daughter, hired a babysitter for 16 hours a week in order that she may work undisturbed in her studio. "Sometimes, I hear the baby scream-ing," she noted. "Basically, I have just trained myself to ignore it."

Similarly, Jon Imber, a painter who lives with his family in a loft (a wall divides the living space from the studio) in Somerville, Massachusetts, stated that he loves not having to travel to work and to be able to work all the time, if he wants. "I set up my life so that I can work where I live," he said, "but now that I have a family, I'm not sure it's such a good thing. It's very distracting when you can hear your own kid, or your wife, on the other side of the wall. There is a wall but, psychologically, it's as though the wall isn't there."

A studio is not just one more room in the house but a space in which one is allowed to be messy, and it may never be entirely cleaned. A different set of standards apply to a studio than for the rest of the house, and sometimes there are different clothes. David Deutsch noted that one problem he has with an at home studio is that occasionally "I forget to take off my painting shoes and track paint through the house." Other artists find that they do not take their own time in the studio as seriously when they are working at home, preferring to make art somewhere else. "I like to go to work, like other people," said John Shahn, a sculptor who lives in Roosevelt, New Jersey, and rents a studio space in the same town. Jody Mussoff, an artist in Riverdale, Maryland, who works in the library at the Hirshhorn Museum in Washington, D.C., noted that when doing her art at home she is "always conscious of something that needs to be done around the house. I can hear the bathroom calling, 'Clean me, clean me.'"

"The problem of having a studio in your home is having a studio in your home," said Edwin Ahlstrom, a painter in Monrovia, Maryland, who teaches art at Montgomery College in Rockville. "With a studio somewhere else, you may only get two or three times a week, but you will pick up where you left off and it's your time completely, without the constant pull of whatever is going on inside the home."

An additional problem cited by a number of painters whose studios are in their homes is that, by working at home, they become isolated, not meeting other artists who can offer informed ideas, or even camaraderie.

Jennifer Gilbert, a Boston art dealer, noted that the where-to-have-the-studio issue is a "two-sided coin, but you often find that women like the idea of a studio at home, because the studio gives credibility to the work they do at home, while men in general prefer a studio away from home and accept a studio at home only as a matter of keeping costs down." Some artists find that the best way to make art at home is to build an addition to their house that becomes the studio. Ahlstrom, who has used his home basement ("it can be distracting when you hear the kids are running around upstairs") as a studio and rented space in office buildings ("traveling back and forth late at night is not ideal"), created a $20,000 addition to his house for a 22-by-28-foot studio with a 12-foot ceiling. He wanted the large space, in part because he shares the studio with his wife, Judith, a portrait painter, and also because "you need to be able to step back, 15 feet or so, to see your work at a distance."

Judy Shahn, a painter in South Truro, Massachusetts, whose 24-by-26-foot studio was built attached to her house in 1978, found that in the days when her studio was in a small, upstairs bedroom, her work had gotten smaller and smaller. After the addition, the scale of her paintings grew significantly. For her, the primary benefit of working at home is that "it is wonderful to start working in the morning, before you even get dressed. It's frustrating not to be able to get to work when you're snowed in and your studio is somewhere else."

On a smaller scale, a 12-by-12-foot studio with a cement floor, metal siding, high ceiling, picture window and a skylight was built in 1992 for Jody Mussoff by her partner. She, too, had the experience of setting up a studio in her apartment ("one half would be the studio and the other half would be everything else, and the smell of oil paints and solvents pervaded everything") and renting space in factory buildings ("it was a funky neighborhood that could be dangerous at night"). "In some ways, it's the best of both worlds," she said. "It's handy to be at home, and it's not a big outing to go to the studio. But, when I'm in my studio, I can't hear the phone or see that the bathroom needs to be cleaned, so I can really concentrate on my work."

Studio Insurance

A lot of things may happen to an artist in a lifetime—big-time commissions, rave reviews, a museum retrospective. They may also become incapacitated, see their work damaged or lost through fire and theft, or get sued for millions of dollars by someone who tripped over the scaffolding in their studio. One cannot insure great success in a career, but artists—from the least well-known to the most established— may insure against some of the worst hazards.

Various insurance companies have what they call "studio insurance" or "artist floaters" that offer levels of protection of the physical premises of the studio as well as the tools, materials, furniture and artwork (commissioned or not, completed or unfinished) therein. In addition, artists may purchase transit insurance (when objects are being shipped to a gallery or art fair, for example), general liability coverage (for someone hurt moving the artwork, for instance, or a visitor injured in the studio), worker's compensation (for the artist's employees) and disability insurance (if the artist becomes unable to work).

Not every artist requires every type of insurance coverage. Conceptual artist Sol Lewitt, whose works have an international market, spends "tens of thousands of dollars a year" on various types of insurance, according to his business manager, Susanna Singer. Sculptor Glenna Goodacre pays $8,000 in yearly insurance premiums, which doesn't include worker's compensation. However, policies exist for those in need, regardless of their stature in the art world, and at far more affordable prices.

"All artists have something to lose if there is a fire in their studio, even if they've hardly ever sold any works," said Tony Newman, vice president of American Phoenix Corporation, which provides studio and other related types of insurance policies for members of the Chicago Artists' Coalition, American Crafts Council and several other crafts organizations, with annual premiums starting at $250.

Regular homeowner policies would likely cover damage to a studio in one's house if the artist is a hobbyist (although the existence of a studio and its contents should be noted on the policy), but artists who are able to earn any money from selling their work might want to consider special studio insurance. "As soon as you've sold a work, you have a market," Robert Salmon, vice president of Allen Insurance Associates, stated, and that market gives value to unsold pieces sitting in a studio. Artists who have reason to view themselves as more than hobbyists (whose artwork is solely intended for personal enjoyment) will find that homeowner policies regularly exclude commercial activity, such as an art studio, from their coverage.

There is no rule of thumb to determining how much in premiums buys how much insurance protection. Different carriers require certain minimum premiums (Flather & Perkins's is $250, Huntington Block's is $500, Chubbs' is $1,000, Allen Insurance Associates' is $2,500), and costs are determined based on where one lives, the amount of the coverage and of the deductible (usually between $500 and $5,000), the existence of a 24-hour central station alarm system, where the studio is located (in the artist's house, in the woods, near a fire hydrant, in the downtown section of a city) and its construction (wood, metal, brick), how inherently subject to damage the art is (glass and ceramics are high-risk items, bronze sculpture far less so) and what kinds of insurance protection are required. Except with studio insurance offered to groups, coverage is usually tailored to the circumstances of the individual artist.

It is not uncommon for artists to buy a certain maximum amount of insurance coverage that is less than the full value of their art and studio as a way to keep the premium lower, with the hope that no fire, for instance, would result in a total loss. Bill Christenberry, a Washington, D.C., painter, photographer and sculptor, has a $75,000 policy for his studio and the artwork in it, even though there is several hundred thousand dollars worth of art there and the studio itself would cost $100,000 or so to replace. He pays $1,200 in premiums for this coverage from the Fireman's Fund "because that's all we can afford," his wife, Sandra, said. "We have three children, and two of them are of college age. We just have to hope that no damage or theft occurs that's more than $75,000 worth." Other artists, such as Corpus Christi, Texas, sculptor Kent Ullberg and Northampton, Massachusetts, painter Scott Pryor, have coverage for their studios but not for the work in them because "it's rare that I have more than one work in the studio at any one time. When a work is finished, I frame it up and send it out to one of my galleries," Pryor stated.

The studios of both Bill Christenberry and Kent Ullberg have been burglarized, which included the theft of artwork. At the time, Christenberry had no studio insurance at all, suffering a total loss. Ullberg later installed a central station alarm system for his studio, resulting in a small savings on the overall insurance premium. However, damage, especially for works in transit, is a far greater problem than theft. Because of the higher probability of loss, a policy solely for transit insurance is often the most difficult to obtain unless coverage for the artwork itself already exists.

Some insurance carriers require central station alarm systems, while others may lower the premium up to 15 percent for artists who install them. These alarm systems, however, may cost as much as $1,500 to put in and another $30 or $40 per month to monitor. Some artists choose to forego the alarm system as the expense may outweigh the discounted premium.

At times, artists may be required to purchase insurance, such as in a contract that a corporation or public art sponsor may use when making a sculpture commission, and this coverage usually is for general liability—for instance, a workman hurt moving or installing the piece as well as someone injured because of faulty construction or a material weakness. Most other types of insurance are optional. One kind of general liability protection that is available for commissioned work covers disputes between artist and buyer over what the piece should be or look like.

Insurance carriers are most willing to provide studio coverage for commissioned works, because the stated price of the work in the contract alleviates the need to hire appraisers and determine market values. These companies will also frequently accept claims for commissioned works that were not completed, paying the percentage of the insured value proportionate to the degree that the work was finished. Valuations and completed and unfinished artworks that have not been commissioned can become an area of contention between artists and the insurance companies. "We're very reluctant to under-write studio policies for artists because of the difficulty of valuing the things," said Dr. Dietrich Von Frank, senior vice president of Nordstern Insurance Company, which insures art dealers, museums and "one or two artists only." "The artists have to prove that their work has value and, if it hasn't sold or they haven't sold all that many works in their careers, that may be difficult."

The burden of proving that something of value was lost, and how much that loss is, falls on the artist. Insurance companies may write a policy for an artist for a certain level of coverage, take a premium based on what the artist says his or her art is worth, but not pay what the artist claims he or she has lost. Artists can help themselves in proving the value of their work by keeping good records of what they have sold, to whom and for how much as well as a list of all the pieces they have in their home or studio and the individual values they place on them. These records and lists, of course, should be placed somewhere else or in a fireproof safe.

If determining the value of completed works is complicated, unfinished pieces are more trouble still. "We don't do incomplete works," Robert Salmon said. "Was the work half-done, two-thirds? Is it all in your head but just not down on paper? What are we dealing with? With completed works, you insure more cleanly." Still, some of the larger insurers of artwork, such as Chubb and Huntington Block, will underwrite policies for unfinished works, determining the stage of completion through discussion between the agent and the artist and valuing the artwork on a prorated share. The Washington, D.C.–based National Artists Equity Association's fine arts insurance program with Northbrook Property and Casualty values "works in progress" at "cost of materials and labor but not to exceed $5,000 for any one work."

The valuations made by insurance carriers are usually "net values," that is, the market price of the work less the standard commission that the artist's dealer would have charged. Insurors will agree to pay the entire market value to those artists who commonly sell out of their studios without middlemen. There is a range of coverage areas for artists, but insurance carriers also include in their contracts a number of exclusions, some of which may be modified by purchasing additional coverage. Standard among these exclusions are inherent vices, dishonesty by the artist or his or her employees, wear and tear, gradual deterioration, rust, corrosion, dampness of atmosphere, wet or dry rot, mold, change in temperature, freezing, insects or vermin, water that backs up through a sewer or drain, loss of market (the artist's work becoming less sought-after), damage due to restoration by the artist, mysterious disappearances or inventory shortage, theft from unattended vehicles, earth movements (earthquakes, volcanic eruptions, landslides), floods, war, and nuclear disaster. Insurers may also set limits to the amount of liability they will accept for works damaged in transit or for any one item.

᭜

CHAPTER 4

Exhibiting One's Work

$\mathcal{M}$AKING ART OFFERS A VARIETY OF
personal rewards for the artist, from solving technical and formal
problems in the work to discovering areas of thought and wonder in
oneself and expressing them in a coherent manner. However, art is a
form of communication with the outside world, not simply an internal
monologue, and this communication best takes place when the work
is exhibited publicly. Eventually, all artists want to show their artwork
for reaction and comment.

Where to Exhibit

Selling artwork is one of the most difficult acts for artists, many of
whom dream of collectors who will "discover" them or dealers who will
take over the responsibility of marketing their work. Some artists will
often spend a great deal of money to buy space in who's who-type
directories or rent vanity galleries (see "Not Every Chance to Show
One's Work May Be Worth It" below) or create Internet "home pages"
or self-publish catalogs of their own work in the hope that these
substitutes for entering the world to sell their art will pay off. However
they may try, artists cannot escape the responsibility of creating their
own markets.

The first step in the process is showing one's artwork to the public.
Fortunately, there is a wide variety of sites suitable for an exhibition
in almost every town, of which a commercial art gallery is but one
possibility. Banks, restaurants and cafes, churches, art supply shops,
libraries, town halls, community centers, schools (public schools and

colleges) and office buildings are often hosts of art displays as the art does not cost them anything and may bring more people in. For the artist, especially one who has not had much experience in exhibiting artwork in the past, this kind of show creates the opportunity for comments, praise, suggestions, meeting other artists, and perhaps even a sale.

Nonprofit or alternative art spaces are also venues for lesser-known artists (or those whose art is outside of the mainstream) to display their work. A growing number of fine art museums have created exhibition series that spotlight the work of younger and regional artists. Charity auctions offer yet another way to put one's work before the public, this time in a setting that affords the artist a pat on the back. Artists attending a class or school are usually permitted to enter work for student shows, and those who are members of societies or clubs exhibit with these groups at their annual shows (see chapter 6).

Juried competitions and sidewalk shows (some juried, some not) are yet other possibilities for exhibiting one's work. There are reportedly 10,000–15,000 arts and crafts shows held somewhere around the United States each year, usually during the summer months in the North and during the winter in the Southern states. Many of the larger shows are listed in publications for artists (see Appendix).

Entering a competition generally entails sending away for an application that must be filled out and returned with one or more slides of one's artwork. As the slides are to represent one's work and career, they should be made with care. A high-quality 35mm camera should be used, set on a tripod (especially when shutter speed is below one-sixtieth of a second) to prevent accidental movement, placed parallel to the work (in order to reduce distortion and blurriness), with the photograph taken indoors in order to control the direction and distance of the light source. The type of film should be matched to the light source. One might also experiment with the light source (diffused or aimed directly on the object, perhaps bounced off a white wall) to determine how the work being photographed looks best. If it all seems overly complicated, hire a professional photographer (particularly one who specializes in this kind of work). That may be expensive, but it's worth it.

Framing and Matting One's Artwork

Art and beauty are often seen as synonymous, but knowing how to make a work of art look good is another matter entirely. For paintings and works on paper, the issue largely comes down to what kind of frame and mat to use. Good framing sells a work in the same way that clothes make the man, dealers insist. "Yes, you should only buy a work based on its pictorial merits," Beverly Hills, California art dealer Louis Newman said, "but if I only believed that, why have a decent-looking gallery in which to show it? Why have a nice logo on the gallery's stationery when I send the bill?"

Stephen Rosenberg, a New York City dealer, suggested that a frame, even one that is likely to be discarded by the collector, "shows how the work looks completed."

It would be easy to say that most contemporary painting seems to call for relatively simple, unadorned frames—New York City's Museum of Modern Art thinks this way, having recased a large portion of the works on display in thin, solid metal frames—but many works look quite good in fancier casings and sometimes the frame becomes an integral part of the artwork. Picasso sometimes placed his own paintings in seventeenth-century Dutch frames, which not only worked aesthetically but was also part of his overall concept of the piece as being within an artistic tradition. Joseph Cornell bought dime-store frames for some of his works, giving them a sort of mock elaborate quality, and it turned off some potential buyers.

Artists can clearly be quirky, which may or may not work to their benefit, but most prefer not to do anything that will harm the possibility of sales. There are no hard and fast rules to framing, but there are ways of playing it safe. Inappropriate frames—those which seem to clash inadvertently with the picture—may turn off the person looking at the art who, at best, will try to mentally edit out the frame. Many dealers claim that badly stretched and poorly framed paintings work against an artist seeking sales and representation. Not all pictures need frames all the time; generally, frames are most often required when the works are being moved around (corners and edges may otherwise get banged up) and when they are being put on display.

Diane Burko, a Philadelphia painter, said that sometimes she exhibits her work unframed—in order to emphasize the edges of the work in her allover style—and other times framed. "It depends on whether the work is going to be traveling," she noted. "If the pieces are just going to stay in the gallery, I may leave them unframed. If they are going to travel to other galleries or to another city, as some shows of mine have done, I generally put frames on them for protection."

Another reason to keep works unframed or not to spend much money on the matting and framing is that a potential buyer may like the picture but find that the casing doesn't go with the decor in his or her house. "Some people like to do the framing themselves and they may not like the mat and frame that the artist put on it," said Carol

Becraft, customer service manager at Westfall Framing, a mail-order frame company in Tallahassee, Florida. "It's better for artists to keep it simple and inexpensive."

Others, however, find that many pictures don't look complete without a frame and that an attractive frame can help sell the work. The prices of frames vary widely, based on whether or not the artist plans to fit a picture into an existing frame (costing as little as ten cents per inch), whether or not the frame has to be built to a special size and whether or not a frame shop will do the entire job of matting, framing and setting in a glass protector (costing hundreds of dollars). "It depends on where you're showing the work," Ronald Cohen, manager at MADD Frames in Philadelphia, which provides frames for a number of galleries in that city and Manhattan, stated. "The air of certain better galleries just seems to demand a high-quality frame while, probably, a nice frame doesn't matter so much at an outdoor art show."

If unsure how best to frame a particular work, one may want to ask one's dealer or a show organizer for some advice, if their good favor is important to the artist, or check with a museum curator. In the past, art dealers would automatically take charge of framing the pictures that were going on display but, nowadays, fewer gallery owners are willing to pick up that tab. Dealers, however, still may want some say even when they don't reimburse or only partially reimburse the artist for the frame.

Increasingly, the gallery look in frames is stark and clean, composed of thin pieces of hardwood (stained or varnished) or metal (black and silver or, rarely, with a gold color), and artists are generally leaning in that direction. One of the more simple types of framing that more and more artists use is a casing of four thin strips of lattice wood (one-quarter-inch thick) that are nailed into the stretcher with brads. Frequently, artists will also place four additional narrower strips of lattice wood between the outer perimeter of the picture and the strip frame. Those narrower strips are recessed (and sometimes painted black or another dark color) so that the painting seems to "float" within the frame; the distance between the picture and the strip frame keeps the artwork from looking visually compressed. Besides being inexpensive, the strip frames can easily be taken off by a collector who has something else in mind.

Joe Sweeney, an artist in Ardmore, Pennsylvania, who works in pastels and oils, stated that he frequently uses strip frames for his larger works because "strip framing is cheaper than a big frame and, in galleries, the paintings get pushed around and bashed a lot. If you spend $200 or $300 for a nice frame and it gets damaged by the gallery, you may have to frame it again when a buyer decides he wants it." For smaller pieces, however, he generally uses uncarved blond hardwood (ash and maple) frames—one-half inch or less for the face of the frame for the pastels and three inches or more for his larger oil landscapes. "If the buyer doesn't like the frame or wants to put on his own," Sweeney added, "I can always reuse the frame, because I generally do work in the same size."

In addition to protecting the artwork, the purpose of framing is to separate or isolate the piece from the world around it; the frame walls off the picture in order to distinguish a work of art from anything else. Frames, however, have rarely been wholly neutral and often reflect aesthetic concerns of their times, which is why older-style frames are thicker and made of heavily carved wood, while contemporary frames tend to be more minimal, using thinner wood or metal. Even those thin, minimal frames may differ from region to region. Many New York City and Los Angeles art dealers note that they prefer less ostentatious frames—silver or black metal—while other gallery owners in the Southeast and Southwest claim that their customers respond positively to gilt frames as well. "This is a decorator's heaven here," the gallery manager of the Tanton Gallery in West Palm Beach, Florida, said. "People seem to want gilt, or frames with beveled edges. They want the frames to stand out, too."

The style of a frame does reflect its time, yet it must also complement—rather than detract from—the pictorial image and not clash with the collector's overall decor. A conflict in any of these areas will lessen the impact of the art itself. Noting that "people forget what they're framing," Marian MacKinney, director of Portraits, Inc., in New York City, stated that artists are no less guilty than collectors of harming their creations with inappropriate frames. "Artists often don't know how to make their work look best, and some use large, ugly frames." She and other dealers recommend soliciting advice from reputable professional framers or from the dealers themselves, since they may understand a particular buyer's taste or may have seen where the buyer plans to hang the work.

There are many museum-quality framers around the country that artists, collectors, dealers and art museums use, each having their own specialties, such as antiqued or carved wood, gilt-edged, lacquered metal or something else. Artists who wish to purchase frames for their own work should visit a variety of galleries and museums, asking for the names, addresses and telephone numbers of framers from those whose frames seem most appealing (see "Sources for Matting and Framing Artwork" in Appendix).

Many artists and dealers are reluctant to spend a great deal of money on a frame, believing, as does Janine Thompson of the Archway Gallery in Houston, Texas, that "collectors know they're buying the art, not the frame. The customer is likely to reframe anyway, in order to match the living room." Simple, less expensive frames may be the best way to play it safe, but not all artists believe that. Fran Larson, a watercolorist in Arizona, purposefully buys "ugly frames or raw moldings from Mexico," which she carves and paints "in various colors that relate to the image. They have a distinctive look. At first, people were horrified, but I said to them, 'Calm down, you'll get used to it,' and slowly but surely they have." She added that "the frame is part of the picture," calling her framing technique "pushing decorativeness beyond decorativeness." Another artist who feels the same way is Tim Vanya of Webster, Texas, who creates life-size drawings of homeless people, which are sandwiched between two pieces of Plexiglas and encased in "raw wood, unfinished pine frames with exposed hardware"—the corner joints— "that simulate the crates that homeless people live in." His works are not placed flat against a wall but are hung suspended from the wall by a chain. This creates a shadow effect, which is also part of his overall statement about the homeless.

The question of how to present watercolors, drawings and other works on paper for exhibition can be more troublesome. Unless they are to be seen in a drawer, stored flat, they cannot be hung without a frame and, because paper is more fragile than canvas, this framing usually includes matting and glass. This three-part framing is often more expensive than what is minimally required of a canvas, and each of the three parts involves a decision about color. (Regular glass has a slightly green tinge, while ultraviolet Plexiglas is perceptibly yellow.)

The mat is another large area of concern. Used for the purpose of protecting and presenting the art, its width, depth (with double or triple matting) and tone may all affect how the work looks. Improperly matted pieces may also have an adverse impact on the look of the art by allowing the paper to buckle or become stained, lowering its value and requiring considerable restoration. The best mats are made from stiff paper boards—rag boards (composed of cotton fibers), buffered rag boards (cotton fibers to which calcium carbonate has been added) and conservation board (wood pulp that is chemically refined and treated with calcium carbonate)—that are acid-free, pH-neutral or alkaline (a pH of 7 or more). Acidic mat boards will damage the work on paper, first darkening the paper and later making it more brittle, subject to pieces tearing or falling off.

The mat separates the image from the glass or frame. Moisture on the glass could otherwise cause the paper to buckle and even become attached to the glass, while acids in a wood frame could infect the work on paper. In many cases, the mat is hinged to the backboard (the support directly underneath the artwork) with cloth or linen tape. Something as inexpensive as a utility knife can be used to cut a window in the mat board through which to view the artwork. The size of the window is a matter of opinion: Some artists and collectors prefer an "overlay mat" or "overmat," with the size of the window smaller than the total dimensions of the artwork; others choose to make the window larger than the borders of the art, allowing the work to seemingly "float." Art conservators at museums generally recommend an overmat, limiting the possibility that the work will escape through the window and lose the protection that the mat offers.

Double matting is another option, in which the artwork is treated almost as a book, and is suggested for pieces that are especially delicate or will be examined frequently. Two mat boards are cut with the same size window, both hinged by cloth tape to the backboard, and one opens the outer mat to view the work through the inner mat. Double mats provide extra protection against anything pressing against the image, particularly when in storage, and the outer mat also helps keep the inner mat clean.

The width of the mat around the image is also a subject of differing opinion. Three inches on all sides is common, but much narrower or wider mat borders are frequently seen as well. For some, very wide borders around a small image may provide a sense of great drama, a large curtain-raising build-up to the art, while others believe that a wide expanse of mat dwarfs the image to the point of making it almost disappear. While white or cream-colored mats are often thought of as the safest choices, some dealers suggest finding a neutral hue amidst all the colors in a watercolor for the mat. "Colored mats generally detract from the work," Louis Newman stated. "At a midrange distance or further, you tend to notice the mat more than the image, and that seems to emphasize the wrong thing."

An intriguing thought on the subject of framing watercolors was offered by Stephen Rosenberg who, noting the belief among collectors that "a work on paper should cost less than those on canvas, even when it takes just as much time to do the painting," suggested that watercolors be framed without the protective glass. "If you think of the work as a painting and not as a work on paper, don't use the traditional glass-covered frame, and you can charge as much as you would for a small canvas." Some juried art shows refuse glass-covered pictures because of the weight and potential for breakage. Artists should find out whether or not the shows they are entering have a glass policy and frame their works accordingly.

Should Framing Be Left to the Art Dealer?

"Artists shouldn't be in the framing business," one contemporary art dealer said, "and they aren't always the best judges of what kinds of frames to use." Still, most dealers and gallery owners require artists to bring in paintings and works on paper that are ready for presentation, and that usually means fully framed (framed, matted and glass-enclosed with works on paper). On occasion, a dealer will arrange for the framing but deduct that cost from whatever the artist is owed after a sale takes place.

Considering the fact that many collectors discard the frames anyway, purchasing ones that better match the decor in their homes, who should pay for the original frames? As one might expect, artists and dealers are of different minds on this question. Dealers usually believe that framing makes a work of art complete and is therefore the artist's responsibility, while some artists see framing as part of the domain of making a sale, which is why the dealer earns a commission. Dealers contend that an aesthetically appropriate custom-made frame dramatically influences a potential buyer's decision about purchasing a work of art, while many artists view expensive frames as superficial trappings. Buyers should only purchase works based on their pictorial merits, they feel.

"Emerging artists especially don't understand that presentation is everything. Some artists are so cheap that they won't pay for a real frame," Sue Viders, an artists' advisor in Denver, Colorado, stated, but the cost of framing can be prohibitively expensive, particularly for emerging artists whose market may be too limited to recoup these (and other) expenses. Marcia Lloyd, a Boston painter who is able to support herself from sales of her work, spent $4,000 to frame the paintings and works on paper in her most recent exhibit. "I had to put out the $4,000 up front," she said. "A lot of people who collect just assume that the gallery picks up the framing charge."

Lloyd used to make her own lattice wood (strip) frames but since 1983 has paid professionals to create more polished-looking framing. It seems to be worth the expense. "The more professional a work looks, the more likely that you can sell it for more money," she said, adding that her frames are neutral in color in order to appeal to a wide range of tastes and decor. "I have no way of knowing for sure, though, that using a professional framer has increased either my sales or my prices.

It's just a matter that the quality of the framing has increased with the prices." To cover the expense of framing, Lloyd stated that she has had to raise her prices, and her dealer—Boston's Portia Harcus of the Harcus Gallery—deducts that amount from the gross receipts before taking her commission.

Raising prices will not work for every artist because that might drive prospective buyers away. Michael Ingbar, a New York City dealer of contemporary art in the "emerging" category, said that a number of his artists "scour flea markets for frames." He doesn't recommend that they spend hundreds of dollars on new custom frames because, "if the framing is very expensive, it might put the work out of my clients' price range." As with Portia Harcus, the framing costs are not part of his commission.

For Memphis, Tennessee, painter Burton Callicott, the expense of framing—and he strongly believes that all works should be framed—is more one-sided, falling entirely on him. Callicott builds his own frames using architectural molding, the same material placed on doors and walls. He applies three coats of flat black oil-based paint, then rubs it with steel wool and gilds the top rim of the frame. The molding extends beyond the surface of the canvas in order to protect the picture's surface, "because I have done jurying for art shows in the past, and I know what happens behind the scenes. Paintings are stacked one against another, and the surface sometimes gets scratched and damaged." All of this care and know-how in the framing is Callicott's expense, without reimbursement from a dealer. What's more, he stated, "when a dealer thought that another kind of frame would be more suitable for a client, the dealer put a new frame on it and charged me" by taking that expense out of his earnings. "Galleries don't give you anything, and I think that's unfair."

The issue boils down to what a dealer owes (or believe he or she owes) an artist. Stephen Rosenberg pointed out that "dealers don't get their commissions from getting works framed and running errands. Dealers get their commissions from making sales and getting the artist's work known." His best offer is to split the cost of framing with the artist, which is still better than what the majority of artists receive.

In the past, dealers were more prone to assume the financial burden of framing, but the high costs of gallery rent, advertising, travel, salaries and other expenses associated with dealing in art have led to higher commissions and fewer free services for artists. Like juried competitions, most dealers now expect artists to bring them works ready for elegant presentation, the cost of which is not their concern.

However, a more old-fashioned approach can be found here and there. Louis Newman said that "I take my commissions for selling works, which involves marketing and presentation, and that includes framing. I pay the rent for the walls the paintings are hung on, and I pay for framing."

Crating and Shipping One's Artwork

Sending off slides of one's art for juried competitions or to art dealers is an important step, but it is only the first step in placing work before the public. The actual art objects must eventually be transported to the shows or galleries where they have been accepted, and this takes care on the part of the artist. Works of art are frequently a casualty of moving, especially when the hired movers don't have specific expertise in transporting art. "We've had people come to us who have used general movers in the past," said Bob McCracken, president of Richard Wright, Ltd., an art moving firm in Massachusetts. "They tell us stories: someone's foot went through their painting; things were dropped. General movers hire from pools, people who say they have moved things before."

Works of art require special handling as even a light bump can cause paint to fall off a canvas or permanently unbalance a sculpture. The glass covering a print or watercolor may shatter and tear the artwork underneath, or a frame may break and create a pull on the canvas. Transporting art even short distances can prove troublesome. "You can strap a painting into the back seat of your car and hope you don't hit any potholes along the way," said John Buchanan, registrar at the Metropolitan Museum of Art in New York City, "but there are a lot safer ways to do it." Those ways can also be considerably more expensive, and the Metropolitan Museum regularly spends over half a million dollars a year moving objects from one place to another. The cost is high because of the risks.

Federal Express, for instance, discourages people from using the company to ship artwork because of the high probability of some sort of damage. "Things with a high intrinsic value have a high breakage rate," a company spokesman said. There are, however, a number of sensible precautions one can take, some of which are quite inexpensive. One of the more painless things to do is remove the hanging devices from behind a painting—the screws and wires—and take the picture out of the frame. Both the canvas and frame may expand and contract under certain climatic conditions, brushing against each other which may knock off some paint. Museum conservators often recommend putting some felt or foam between the frame and canvas, then wrapping it all up in brown paper. This provides protection against dirt and dust as well as a cushion against a small bump. Disassembling a work for shipping, of course, is not always an option, as art shows frequently require artists to send in their pictures ready for hanging out of the crate. Frank Marcotti, national operations manager for U.S. Art Co., said that it is "common sense to pack and ship a painting upright, the way it is hung on the wall. If it is tipped on its side, the artwork may move, the canvas may be stretched and paint could pop off."

Movers typically wrap a painting in a buffered, acid-free glassine paper, then wrap it again with a bubble wrap and finally place the piece in a cardboard box that is at least three inches larger on all sides than the wrapped picture. Within that three-inch space, McCracken noted, one might put Styrofoam "plastic peanuts" or even cooked popcorn. "You can feed the popcorn to the birds afterwards," he said. "It's environmentally friendly." The cost of the packing, for a single thirty-by-forty-inch painting ranges from $35 to $45, Marcotti stated. Some art movers are also willing to simply pack artworks that will be trucked by more general home movers.

If the picture is covered by a sheet of glass, one might also choose to place a couple of strips of tape across it, securing the glass in one piece if it breaks rather than allowing it to shatter all over the work. To remove the tape, pull it back slowly along its own length so that it is almost doubled over itself—pulling it back at a right angle may cause the glass to break from the stress. The tape may leave a residue on the glass when it is later taken off, which can be tricky to remove, especially if it is ultraviolet Plexiglas whose glazing material may be damaged by the potent chemicals in some household cleansers, such as Fantastic and Formula 409. Those chemicals, by the way, also give off vapors that may damage the art. The tape residue should be removed with hexane or mineral spirits, dabbed on a cotton swab; nail polish remover is also usable, although not on ultraviolet Plexiglas. Razor blades may also be used to scrape off residue. A number of museums now cover the glass with clear contact paper, which quickly allows one to see what the work is and also lessens the problem of tape residue.

Works may also be cushioned in bubble wrap, which is available at many hardware stores, although the entire package should be wrapped again in brown paper because bubble wrap is difficult to tape down securely. An unfortunate problem with bubble wrap is that it tends to retain heat and moisture that may harm the art. Wood, for instance, may warp inside bubble wrap; paint may flake off or a metal sculpture may develop rust. One way to avoid this problem is not to pack or move on a rainy day, and it is possible to stipulate to movers that they should not come if the relative humidity is above 65 or below 40 percent, or when it is raining.

An alternative is to demand in writing that movers not store works left overnight on a loading dock where heat and humidity levels, not to mention dirt, are likely to be unregulated and the possibility of theft is quite real. It is possible to demand that the moving van itself have temperature and humidity controls (a practice of many larger art museums), although this is rather costly. In addition, one should resolve in advance with the mover the amount of insurance as well as instructions on how the art objects should be handled, and this should be in writing. Shipping one's creations can be traumatic, but decisions should not be avoided by letting whatever happens happen.

It is not uncommon that paintings and delicate works on paper are shipped in wooden crates. For almost any sculpture, this is mandatory, and crates can be constructed at a cost of between $100 and $1,500, depending on how careful one wishes to be. A crate is relatively easy to build. It is a simple pine box, reinforced with three-quarter-inch plywood and lined with waterproof paper and a layer of polyurethane foam. One must make sure that objects do not bang against the sides but are fitted snugly inside. Screws, rather than nails, should be used to attach the lid of the crate as hammering may prove quite jarring to the works inside that one is trying to protect. Many conservators also suggest coating the outside with oil paint as it adds an extra sealant to protect against rain. It is also advisable to place skids on the bottom of the crate, so that the prongs of a forklift are able to slide underneath easily, and some ornament on top so that the crate could not be shipped upside down.

The heavier the crate, the more expensive the shipping charge. A 250-pound sculpture, for instance, may require 1,200 pounds of crating material just to ship it safely. Certain other factors also determine the cost, such as where the shipment is going, the time of year, the amount of insurance one places on the objects and how they will be cared for along the way. Many artists and collectors ship valuable objects by air, as the storage cabins of most planes are pressurized and environmentally controlled to degrees that are not destructive to most works of art.

John Buchanan stated that "outside of the major urban areas, there are very few commercial movers who know anything about how to pack or move works of art. You really take your chances with some of them." He recommended calling museums to ask who has moved objects for them. There are a number of companies regularly used by most museums, and they are equipped to provide a certain level of insurance coverage for valuable pieces, although most collectors and museums get additional insurance elsewhere. The classified sections of a number of art magazines, such as *ARTnews* and *Art in America,* are also good places to look for companies that are equipped to handle art objects.

The more one ships works of art, the greater the likelihood of some damage taking place, but it can be minimized by providing certain kinds of care. Understanding the needs of one's art objects is the first requirement, and it may be the most important one for reducing the worry over whether or not these pieces arrive safe and sound at an art show or gallery.

Obtaining Gallery Representation

Increasingly, artists have taken the job of selling their artwork upon themselves, bringing their work to arts and crafts fairs, entering pieces in juried competitions, opening their studios for visitors, mailing full-color brochures to prospective buyers, even developing their own home pages on the Internet. Doing without middlemen (galleries and dealers), they gain greater contact with their collectors and keep their prices affordable (or, at least, forgo paying a gallery commission on sales). Still, most atists tend to measure their career achievements in terms of gallery representation. (The ability to claim that one's work is shown in a New York gallery—almost any gallery there—often outweighs the fact, in many artists' minds, that sales are rare and few or no one-person exhibits take place.)

The value of a gallery connection, however, even to artists who sell very little, is more than boasting rights. The existence of a third party— the art gallery owner or dealer—to speak on behalf of someone's artwork is a powerful psychological boost for both the artist and potential collector, as it suggests that the work has at least met with one expert's approval. A dealer's mailing list is likely to be larger than the artist's, which will bring in more (and different) people to view the work than if the artist created the show him- or herself. Art critics are also more apt to attend and write about an exhibit at a gallery than visit an artist's studio; as journalists, art writers describe news events (the show) that are available to their readership (a public space, such as a gallery).

Art dealers may well be interested in representing one's work, exhibiting it in group or one-person shows. The kind of dealer who will promote an artist's work, increasing the volume of sales, bringing in higher prices for individual pieces and placing the art in prestigious private or public collections, will generally want that artist to already

is very important, as galleries are unwilling to spend money to return something that was generally unsolicited to begin with, and they also resent the artist's failure to include it. Unless a dealer agrees to hold the material for the artist, it is best not to drop off the packet and say, "I'll be by Wednesday to pick it up." That creates a storage problem for the dealer and increases the possibility of the packet being lost.

The more contained this packet is the better, as a cumbersome package of loose clippings and other bits of information that are difficult to contain or to put into the return postage envelope make a poor first impression. Many art dealers receive between 10 and 30 of these packages a day; by necessity, they approach them hurriedly, and a messy presentation engenders an irritation with the artist, which is a poor way to begin a relationship.

As the world becomes more and more oriented toward the use of computers, there may be opportunities to put images of one's work (plus information on oneself as well as an artist's statement) on a CD-ROM, as some artists' advisors have suggested. However, the cost of a CD-ROM and the need for no more than 20 images might make this high-tech approach somewhat impractical. Artists with home pages might also inform dealers where their work may be found on the Web, yet placing slide or photographic images in front of someone may still be more efficient that hoping that the dealer proactively turns on a computer.

Other than slides and albums of color photographs, there are other ways of presenting one's work that may be considered. Color xerographic copies of photographs are often less expensive than making additional copies from the photographic negatives, and the quality may be good enough for the purpose—once again, find out what the recipient wants. Caroll Michels, an artists' advisor on Long Island, New York, recommends creating a brochure, with pictures of one's work and information about the artist, that may be sent along with a "cover letter that says, 'If you're interested, I will be happy to send slides.' You have to look at the initial outlay. The cost for each packet of slides and postage on the self-addressed stamped envelope is likely to be $15–$25, while a brochure may cost 85¢ a copy. With a brochure, you save money on those who aren't interested in your work."

The art world has traditionally been run on trust and handshakes, but no artist should leave his or her artwork with a gallery or dealer without making certain agreements, preferably in writing. These include a consignment agreement, listing which pieces are being left with the dealer, their prices and any discount in those prices that are agreed upon, the conditions under which any works could be loaned or leased and the dealer's commission. (Galleries typically take artwork on consignment, that is, they do not purchase the objects themselves but agree to act as the artist's agent in selling them.) The artist and dealer should also agree on how and when the artwork will be exhibited (in group or one-person shows, annually, or every other year), who pays for publicity, framing, crating, shipping and insuring the work.

The issues of bookkeeping and prompt payment are frequently troubling in the artist-dealer relationship. If the artist is selling throughout the year, the accounting should probably be monthly; at the very least, it should be quarterly. Artists should also carefully maintain their own records, knowing where their works are consigned or loaned as well as which pieces have sold and to whom. It is wise to see the sales receipt for any consigned work after it is sold in order to ensure that the dealer has not taken too high a commission or paid the consignor too little. The practice of keeping two sets of books is not unknown, and artists are wise to check every step of the way.

Many art galleries are notoriously poorly financed operations that often use today's sale to pay yesterday's debt, and many artists have had to find recourse in the courts when a dealer withheld money owed to them. Twenty-one states around the country—Arizona, Arkansas, California, Colorado, Connecticut, Florida, Georgia, Illinois, Iowa, Kentucky, Maryland, Massachusetts, Michigan, Minnesota, New Mexico, New York, Oregon, Pennsylvania, Texas, Washington, and Wisconsin—have enacted laws that protect an artist-consignor's works from being seized by creditors if the gallery should go bankrupt.

Even artists whose dealers are in other states than these have some protection from creditors seizing art on consignment in galleries. One recourse for artists is to file a UCC-1 form for works on consignment (available in the County Clerk's office, requiring a nominal filing cost), which stipulates that the artist has a prior lien on his or her own works in the event that the gallery has to declare bankruptcy. In the event that one's dealer disappears in the face of numerous creditors and leaves a warehouse full of art, the law permits artists who have filed the UCC-1 form to retrieve their work.

Of course, there may be a more innocuous reason why an artist isn't contacted after the gallery closes. For example, an artist may have moved without leaving a forwarding address. In general, any changes in the artist's situation or work should be made known to the dealer, as they may aid in sales or alleviate problems that result from miscommunication.

A Word About Web Sites

Sometimes, new technology seems the answer to old, nagging problems, in the way that irrigation systems helped overcome inconsistent weather patterns and soil erosion as well as produce more crops at lower consumer prices. In a century that has seen break-throughs in one field after another, there is a tendency to look to new technology as the answer in itself. The World Wide Web has offered individuals and businesses in all areas the ability to communicate with, and sell to, each other on a scale unheard of a generation ago. Artists looking to display their work to a huge audience—potentially millions of people, rather than the relative handful visiting the galleries in which their pictures are hung—increasingly have come to view the Web as a viable marketing tool.

Certainly, many art galleries have created their own home pages as a means of displaying works they represent to prospective buyers without the printing and mailing costs associated with publishing a catalog. Similarly, an artist's Web site may be a way of informing past and potential collectors of available work, upcoming exhibitions and related subjects of interest.

As yet, the jury is still out on the effectiveness of this approach for artists. Some artists (a small percentage) have reported making contacts with collectors and dealers, resulting in sales; others point not so much to actual sales but to useful connections with artists elsewhere who are exploring the Web and came upon their home page; yet others claim that their site has generated neither sales nor communication. Obviously, as all art is not equal, there are a variety of factors involved in why one artist may achieve success while another does not.

Already, there are millions of Web sites, with more being added every day. In this maze, it is important that any artist setting up a site make it as easy to find as possible. An Internet service provider will help to create a site but not publicize it. Artists should attempt to connect their Web sites with other, popular, relevant host sites or servers, such as those of arts groups and galleries (and the more the better), in order that browsers there may look into what the artists have to offer. Having a Web site will probably not alleviate the need to send out mailers to prospective buyers, if for no other reason because these people need to be told where the artist's site can be found.

One's "domain name"—*www.danielgrant.com*, for example—should be relatively short and easily remembered. Overly long routes to one's site (*www.server/artsorganization/art/writing/danielgrant/help*) creates opportunities for typing errors and gives prospective buyers an incentive to look for something easier. This domain name should be registered with InterNIC (*http://www.internic.net*), which costs $100 for two years. In addition, the domain name should belong to the artist rather than to any server since if the site is moved to another server, the artist will be able to take along the name.

Marketing Work During the Periods Between Shows

In the lives and careers of visual artists, exhibitions tend to be the highlights. These events focus attention on the artists and their work, creating opportunities for sales, praise, reviews, and even controversy. Their psychological value to artists is immense, allowing them to communicate with and be recognized by the world outside of their studios. Small wonder that the categories of one-person and group shows dominate most artists' résumés.

Shows, however, are short term, and there may be months or a year or more between one exhibit and the next. Few artists will earn a year's livelihood from one annual show, and they can only hope that visitors to this year's exhibition will remember them next year. Artists must come to see exhibits as but one element of their overall marketing efforts, which must carry forward during the long stretches of time in which there are no shows.

Exhibitions offer the chance not only to sell but to collect the names, addresses and telephone numbers of those people who express interest in an artist's work. That list is the difference between the short term and the ongoing, as artists may keep in contact with those potential buyers through personal correspondence ("I enjoyed meeting you, and hope that you would visit me at my studio . . .") or general mailers. A month or two "before Christmas is a particularly good time to send out note cards," Barbara Ernst Prey, a painter in Oyster Bay, New York, said. "A lot of people are looking for a gift idea for a spouse."

Some artists send out postcards—picture of artwork on one side, written information on the other—that describe some work (series of prints, major commission, new subject matter) that recently has been completed. Other artists mail "newsgrams" to their collector list, noting upcoming shows or describing highlights of the preceding year. Perhaps, an opportunity to see or buy the work is mentioned, such as a studio sale or a private showing for past buyers.

A collector list needs to be more than a series of names and addresses, according to Sue Viders, an artists' advisor in Denver, Colorado. "The biggest problem of people who exhibit their work is that they don't know who their audience is," she said. "Shows give you a chance to meet and collect information on the people who have some interest in your work." She added that a gallery sign-in book is valuable to learn the names and addresses of visitors, "but it is always better for the artist to be at the exhibition, to talk to visitors about their likes and dislikes. If someone buys a work, the artist should personally deliver it to the collector's home. You can see the type of home they have, the type of furniture they buy, the color scheme they use, whatever other art they own. Artists should keep as extensive a file as possible about anyone who has bought their work, and call or write these people if your work fits them or their house."

When they are meeting the public or potential buyers, many artists are accompanied by an assistant (perhaps a spouse or relative), who does the actual collecting of names and addresses and handles the exchange of money and other important but mundane tasks, freeing the artists to be charming and conversational. Inviting past or potential collectors to the intimate setting of an artist's studio allows the work to sell itself, and the artist need only answer questions or otherwise be polite in the face of nonartistic comments. Studio invitations also should be extended to art dealers, art consultants (who buy for corporations), art critics, other artists, museum officials and independent curators, as any one of them may become buyers or recommend the work to others.

Exhibitions place artists in the public eye, but the period between shows provides opportunities in which artists and their work may receive public notice. Teaching an art workshop or an adult education course, offering work at a charity auction, staging a demonstration of one's technique or painting a mural all may generate attention, perhaps some extra income and the chance to make some sales. Even non–art-related activities, such as volunteering for a United Way Fund Drive, is a way to meet company executives and other people with money who could be added to a mailing list and who may eventually turn into buyers of one's artwork.

If there are long periods between exhibitions, it might seem obvious for an artist to have more shows. Art dealers, however, cannot always squeeze another show into their schedules, and they may be reluctant to "arrange an out-of-town show, because the dealer has to split the commission with someone else," said painter Nancy Hagin. Exhibitions are usually thought of as affairs that are arranged by others, but artists may also create their own events. Hagin, along with fellow artists Janet Fish, Sondra Freckelton and Harriet Shorr, decided to each paint the same group of objects but in their own separate styles. At the end of this exercise, they decided to exhibit all their paintings in a combined show, which they arranged with an alternative art space in New York

City. "If a dealer won't generate some attention for your work," Hagin said, "you try to generate things on your own."

In a variation on the same theme, sculptor Elyn Zimmerman, who participates in two or three group shows per year and has one solo exhibit every other year, noted that "I try to put my work somewhere on loan, at colleges, museums or sculpture parks." She contacts these institutions herself, finding that many of them are interested in short- and long-term loans. Her reason for doing this is that "maybe two or three works sell from a show and the rest take more time to sell. Meanwhile, I've got all these big sculptures to store while I'm making others. If I can put my work on display where people can see it, it's better than my paying to store it. They have guards and insurance, so I don't have to pay for that, either. An added benefit is that I can bring people out there to look at it—that may result in a sale."

Alerting the Media to One's Artwork

Politicians call it "living off the land"—generating attention through newspaper or magazine articles about them rather than buying short radio or television spots for expensive commercials. They schedule press conferences or press walks, issue policy statements and appear on talk shows, all of which keeps their costs down and their visibility high. Artists also need to know how to get a free ride in the media, offering a publc demonstration, scheduling an art exhibit opening, teaching a class, opening one's studio to the public, or anything else that qualifies as news. Journalists rarely just write about an artist unless there is an event that calls for coverage. News and feature articles, interviews and reviews all keep an artist's name before the public even when sales of artwork are slow or nonexistent, and the media attention itself may result in sales later on as more people become aware of the artist.

The getting of that attention, therefore, becomes a major concern for artists, especially the creation of a press release. Two critical points are: to whom the release should be sent, and how to write the release. One does not just send off a release to a local newspaper and wait for a reporter to call. Relationships with critics and journalists should be ongoing whenever possible, creating an investment in one's career on the part of the particular media. This relationship may involve telephone calls or a meeting at a gallery as well as in one's studio.

Relationships with critics and reporters must also be flexible, as journalism is a nomadic profession where reporters move from one publication or station to another with some regularity. Journalists also migrate from job to job within their companies, moving from the features to the business pages, for instance, based on the serendipity of new editors or some new management concept. Mailing lists must be kept up-to-date, verified by telephone calls. Artists also must be prepared to like the next writer as much as the last one. "The New York artists I represent, who have become friendly with freelance art critics, are generally the most successful," said Jane Wesman, who heads a New York City–based public relations firm of the same name that specializes in artists and writers. "You need to cultivate the people who can be helpful in your career."

There are various ways to determine who is eligible for a release or press package—a press package includes a release, illustrations (slides, photographs or color copies), biography or résumé of the artist, artist statement (if relevant) and clippings of past articles about the artist's work or career (those with photographs of the artist and/ or his or her work are most likely to catch the eye of a journalist, who may not choose to read the entire article). One of the more expensive ways is by purchasing printed lists (or preprinted labels) of specific editors (such as, arts and entertainment editors or features editors) at newspapers and magazines nationwide from Burrelles (Media Labels Department, 75 East Northfield Road, Livingston, NJ 07039, 973/992-6600), which costs between $150 and $200 for 1,000 names. The same information and more is available in Burrelles's multivolume *Media Directory*, which includes newspapers (two volumes: $180), magazines (one volume: $180) and broadcast (one volume: $225— the entire four volumes (Media Directories Department) sells for $450, although these books may be available at certain libraries— college, public, and university.

A less expensive way is to read on a regular basis the publications in one's own region in order to determine who covers openings, who writes about art, who writes about women, who reports on education issues and who does personality profiles. In most newspapers and magazines, the pages devoted to the visual arts are very limited, and artists should look for other areas in the newspaper or magazine for coverage. Those other sections may have considerably more space and the same readership as the arts section. Wesman noted that artists should not confine themselves to art magazines in their press marketing efforts, perhaps sending press material to an airline or fashion magazine. "You want to broaden your audience to people who don't necessarily read art magazines, because those people may have money and interest, too."

Through telephone inquiry to a newspaper, one may learn who is the calendar editor (listings of upcoming events), as well as the arts and entertainment editor, features editor, living editor, home editor, magazine editor, Sunday editor, education editor—they assign the reporters. One should probably send press releases to different journalists and their editors even at the same newspaper, as it is unlikely that a single press release is passed on from one person to another. Usually, if the press release isn't absolutely pertinent to what the editor or reporter is doing, it is tossed out. Journalists also are inundated with press releases, which requires that the information they are sent be eye-catching, concise and followed up with additional releases and telephone calls. A somewhat cynical rule of thumb in marketing events to journalists is that, the second you hang up the telephone, they have forgotten the entire conversation. Second mailings should note that there had been a conversation with the journalist, with a clear and concise summary what the artist wants the journalist to do.

Magazines have a longer "lead" time than newspapers, and artists should prepare press releases and packages for them as much as six months in advance. With newspapers, six weeks is usually sufficient, unless there is a holiday tie-in, which may involve a special section and more time. In most cases, a press release should mimic a news article in a newspaper, with a headline in bold letters that tells journalists something quickly about the event and keeps them reading. "You could write, 'Jane Wesman to Talk about Art World at Conference,' which is all right if everyone knows who Jane Wesman is," she said. "Probably better is, 'World's Greatest Publicist Presents Inside Look at the Art World.'"

The press release should be in a newspaper's inverted pyramid style, with the most important news featured at the beginning and the less vital information at the end. Many smaller publications type news releases directly into the newspaper and, if there are any cuts to be made (usually for reasons of space), the editing is done from the bottom up. The most important information is what is happening (exhibition, demonstration, class), when (time and dates) and where (street address, floor number), noting the significance or uniqueness of the event (for instance, printed by photogravure, first time these works have been shown publicly, honoring a recently deceased parent or public figure). Depending upon the nature of the event, this initial lead could be followed up by more information about the artistic process, the cost of attending the class or demonstration or a quote by the artist or a third party (a critic or gallery director, perhaps) about the nature of the artwork.

The artist's previous experience (where exhibited or taught before) and educational background may have greater value to the local media if that show or class or schooling took place locally, and it might be placed higher in the press release; otherwise, this information should appear further down.

If the artwork is key to the story, as in an exhibition or demonstration, there should be an accompanying image, or more than one. Bombarded by a myriad of press releases, journalists need their information presented in the most time-efficient manner, and a good quality image—no snapshots—says more than a thousand words. Color copies (usually costing between 90¢ and $1 per copy) are one way to provide visual information to a journalist, but they usually are not a satisfactory illustration for a review or story, which may take place if the newspaper or magazine simply scans in the image from the copy by computer. For that reason, actual photographs or slides (costing, on the average, between 75¢ and $1.25 per slide) should accompany the copies. The number of visuals that are sent out, as well as the number of repeat mailings, is often dependent on the artist's budget, as press packages may be sent out to a number of journalists and editors.

Not Every Chance to Show One's Work May Be Worth It

Me? Invited to be in an art exhibit in Paris? That's what the advertisement seemed to say. Paris! Oo-la-la! Actually, anyone can be in it just by sending five paintings and a check for $800 to Paris's Centre Internationale d'Art Contemporain. Oh, well, it sounded good for a moment. What about an "Artist-Dream-Come-True show in famous SoHo NY Gallery"? That one asks me to send slides of my work, plus a $25 "processing fee," to Palace Pyramid Promotions, which isn't listed in the telephone directory and only has a box number address in Beverly Hills, California. Hmm. Maybe I should think twice about it.

Or I could be listed in a directory, such as *Artists of New England*, published by Mountain Productions, Inc., of Albuquerque, New Mexico, or the *Encyclopedia of Living Artists*, published by ArtNetwork in Penn Valley, California. Then, people will have heard of me. Well, maybe not. I would have to buy space in either book for a reproduction of my work and a brief biographical summary, just like an advertisement, costing $900 for a half page and $1,500 for a full page for *Artists of New England*, $398 for a half page and $598 for a full page in the *Encyclopedia of Living Artists*. Besides, there is hardly a library in the country that stocks these vanity publications.

A tour through the classified sections of major art magazines leads to a growing number of services offered to artists, generally involving exhibition opportunities and art directories. Once, art was the expensive part; now, it appears that promoting one's work may cost a small fortune. Just like anything else they might pay for, artists need to approach gallery shows, juried competitions and other career aids as consumers, asking hard questions and making informed choices.

One advertisement, for instance, announces "Have a show in SoHo. We take no commission, so any sales you make, you keep." A show in SoHo, however, doesn't mean in a known gallery or art space, as Manhattan Fine Art Storage has set aside two rooms off its storage areas for exhibits. A show in SoHo also doesn't mean for free, as those two rooms are for rent, costing either $56 or $75 a day, depending upon whether or not an artist has work stored at this facility. Artists who simply need somewhere to display their work, in order for potential buyers to see it in quantity, for instance, may consider this a reasonable amount to pay, but others who hope to have their art reviewed by newspaper or magazine critics or looked at by walk-in traffic are more likely to be disappointed.

The opportunity to claim that one's work has been exhibited in SoHo is very tempting, just as artists may be anxious to have their art shown in Paris, but vanity shows are not accorded any prestige in the art world. In fact, they tend to be looked down upon, indicating, not that a gallery believes in the artist's art but, that the artist had enough money to get his or her work displayed somewhere. Those who want to build up their credibility as artists by loading up a résumé with various shows of this sort may find that this is a very expensive and not particularly effective way to establish themselves or their work as good or marketable.

Another magazine advertisement reads: "Artists wanted to exhibit in our Georgetown, Washington, D.C., gallery, our dynamite Public Spaces program and our New York show." The Michael Stone Collection doesn't provide these services for free, however, charging $95 per month (twelve-month minimum) or $110 per month for those who only want to try it for six months in addition to a 30 percent commission on all sales. The Public Spaces program currently consists of exhibiting works in various offices (such as the national headquarters of the American Society of Interior Designers) in the Washington, D.C., area for up to six months. This certainly gives an artist's work considerable exposure, which may lead to sales. Many commercial art galleries also place work in corporate offices as well as in private homes for a period of time, but they usually charge the company a rental or leasing fee, and most of that money goes to the artist—artists generally don't pay to decorate corporate office walls.

Yet a third advertisement, this placed by the Chim Gregg Art Gallery in La Puente, California, calls for artists whose work is abstract and two-dimensional to apply for representation, submitting four slides of their work. However, interested artists are told to submit a check for $5 as a "jurying fee," which is unheard of in the gallery world. Art dealers and gallery owners look at slides for free; it is their job to seek out new talent, not a favor they are performing for artists. In a separate letter to interested artists, the Chim Gregg Art Gallery's director, Bobby-Lou Hargis, also states that "The Gallery owners only insure the works that belong to the gallery," and there is "a fee for services rendered, as the artists do not have to be here to help with Gallery sitting." Again, it is customary for galleries to provide insurance for all works, owned or consigned, on their premises, but highly unusual for artists to be required to pay a fee for gallery "sitting"—isn't being present in the gallery one of the main jobs of a dealer? This letter also notes that "The ARTISTS that we represent can advertise, using the Gallery name and address in their ads." For many artists, the ability to refer potential collectors to their gallery itself is worth various extra expenses; clearly, this is a service that the Chim Gregg Art Gallery believes is worth paying for.

Many of these advertised "opportunities," especially those offering a show in a SoHo gallery, appear to be aimed at artists who don't live in (and hardly, if ever, visit) New York City but see an exhibit there as a measure of achievement. Vanity art shows, like vanity publishing, however, carry no prestige. They may lead to sales, if the artists themselves find buyers and get them to come to the exhibit, but these kinds of shows are not stepping stones to better things.

National Artists Equity Association recommends that artists ask a series of questions of potential gallery owners before they provide any money. Among these are: Who are the owners of the gallery and what qualifications do they have to exhibit or sell art? Do they have contacts with collectors and critics as well as museum curatorial experience? When was the gallery started? Does it have a reputation in the local arts scene? Have exhibits there received critical attention in local or national media? Are the owners members of any dealers association? How is the gallery organized to make money—charging fees of artists or actually selling artwork on which it makes commissions—and does it have a reputation for selling? Artists Equity also recommends asking the gallery owners for names of other artists as references and obtaining detailed information on how the money paid to the gallery will be used, such as by examining a sample exhibition budget.

A great many advertisements for juried art competitions demand an up-front payment. Jurying or entry fees have long proven troublesome for artists. A variety of visual artists membership organizations, such as the Boston Visual Artists Union, the Chicago Artists Coalition and

Artists Equity, have advised their members not to participate in shows that require artists to send in money along with slides. Their view is that, just as writers don't pay editors to read their manuscripts and dancers and actors don't pay theater companies in order to audition, visual artists shouldn't have to pay someone to view slides of their work. This view has been endorsed by the New York State Council on the Arts, the Oregon Arts Commission and the Washington, D.C., Commission on the Arts and Humanities, which have adopted rules prohibiting these agencies from giving money to groups that charge artists entry fees. Peer review panels at the National Endowment for the Arts also turn away applications from groups that call for fees, although there is no official policy on this by the federal arts agency.

The organizations that charge these fees defend the practice, claiming that art shows are expensive to mount. However, a show sponsor's expenses should not be transferred to artists, which includes those who paid for someone to look at their slides but rejected them. Artists already have enough expenses in creating, framing, photographing, crating, shipping, and insuring their artwork without being told that they must pay for someone to look at their art. There are also other ways for show sponsors to recoup their costs (such as charging a commission on sales, charging admission to visitors, or publishing a catalog of the show that can be sold), which are fairer to participating artists. Whether or not artists refuse to take part in competitive juried shows that require entry fees, they should at least make their unhappiness with these fees known to the show sponsors. If enough artists complain, perhaps a change may eventually result.

Other show sponsors, such as those holding art fairs, sometimes require artists to submit a check for a "booth fee" with their slides and applications, and the amount may range from $40 to hundreds of dollars or more, depending upon the booth rental charge. This fee is given back if the artist is not accepted, but it may be months between the time when the application was sent in and the time the money is returned. The check the artist receives is often that of the show sponsor rather than his or her own, which means that the sponsor has been able to draw interest on this money instead of the artist. Once again, artists may wish to protest a situation in which they find themselves subsidizing people who claim to be aiding the arts.

Whenever there is a jurying system, artists should be informed who the judge(s) or juror(s) will be in advance of applying, as it is the prestige of those persons that give importance and validity to the event. If one also knows something about the juror—he is a dealer of mostly avant-garde art, she paints watercolor landscapes—that may help potential applicants assess the chances of having their work selected. It doesn't tell potential applicants much when Art Enterprizes of Lompoc, California, announces that its First Annual Art Competition will be "Juried by professional artists." Similarly, the "International Biennale" [sic], organized in Miami, Florida, for the Musée d'Art Moderne in Bordeaux, France, will have art chosen "by international selection committee appointed by museum director." For some artists, the possibility of having their work displayed abroad may outweigh not knowing who the jurors are, the existence of an entry fee ($20 for three slides, $5 for each additional slide submitted) and the unwillingness of the French museum to take responsibility "for loss or damage of any kind for any work." It is a difficult decision to make, but artists should at least know what they are facing.

The sponsors of many competitive exhibitions will develop a prospectus, outlining what the show is, where and when it will take place, how many artists are to be selected, the type of art (subject matter and media) that will be featured, the names of the jurors, the liability of the sponsor (in the event of damage, fire, loss or theft), how art is to be shipped, whether or not there will be prizes offered (and in which categories) and commissions on sale of artwork as well as any other charges. Artists should send for this information before submitting slides and any money to be in the exhibits. Similarly, artists should see in writing what kinds of arrangements galleries or other exhibition spaces that advertise for artists have in mind in advance of sending slides and, certainly, before shipping original work.

Not Every Honor Bestowed upon an Artist Is Worth It

When does an honor become an insult to an artist? Perhaps when the honor represents a sizable loss of income or a diminution of the artist's reputation. It may be an honor, for instance, when an artist's work is selected out of a juried show for a purchase award, as this offers recognition and hard cash for the artist. However, many show purchase awards are in the hundreds of dollars—sometimes as low as just $100— whereas the artists may price their work much higher. Artists may find themselves in the awkward position of drastically discounting their work or trying to push the award sponsor to kick in more money or simply declining the award, which may alienate a prospective buyer in the process.

It may be an honor when an artist is asked to donate a work to a charity auction, which again increases artistic exposure and enhances his or her reputation as a good citizen. However, current tax law only permits artists to deduct on their tax returns the cost of materials for artwork they donate to charitable institutions, as opposed to the full market value of the art that a collector may declare. Artists also may feel resentment over how little their work sells for at charity auctions—free dinners at restaurants tend to be more coveted, especially at mixed auctions, and that is often the price range for bidders at these affairs—and that they have somehow damaged their own market.

Artists must balance the interests of good publicity against a financial loss, and their decisions may change from one event to another. Joseph LaPierre of Palm Beach, Florida, turned down a $300 purchase award for a $700 painting at a show in Alabama, because "that award was sponsored by a major corporation, and they could have afforded the full price." However, he accepted another $300 purchase award at a show sponsored by the Art Guild of Ponce Inlet, Florida, "because that award was sponsored by a mom and pop business that put up the $300 as a way to help the cultural life of the community. With that kind of sponsor, I won't object to taking less."

In many smaller arts and crafts shows, purchase award sponsors are individuals or local businesses, who make their own selections rather than await the decision of a judge, and they usually look for artworks within the price range of their award. Local merchants pledge amounts ranging from $100 to $500 for purchase awards at the Roswell Fine Arts League National Show in Roswell, New Mexico, according to show chairman Richard Cibak, and these businessmen also pick the works for these awards. "It is often the case that the award may be considerably less than the market value of the work," he said, "and it is up to the sponsor of the award and the artist to negotiate a final price." It is likely that the chosen artists feel some pressure under the circumstances to cut their prices.

Purchase awards sponsored by museums are likely to be for larger dollar values, and there is also a résumé value in being able to claim that one's work is in the collection of some major institution. In 1981, Howard Terpning of Tucson, Arizona, won the Prix de West purchase award from the Cowboy Hall of Fame in Oklahoma, receiving an amount that was "several thousand dollars less than what I thought the painting was worth, but it was a significant honor to win and I didn't mind taking a little less." Subsequent events more than compensated for the loss of income, as Terpning won the 1990 Hubbard Art Award for Excellence, a purchase award worth $250,000 for the artist's entry (*Transferring the Medicine Shield*) that was otherwise priced at $185,000.

Worse than accepting less than a piece is worth is being asked to give one's work away. Some smaller arts and crafts shows also have door-prize raffles, at which the winners receive a work by the exhibiting artists. Grumbling results from the pressure on exhibitors to donate their work for these raffles, which cuts into potential sales and may give the entire event a carnival-like quality. Charity auctions equally may raise troubling concerns for artists, who want to be supportive of a good cause but may not have the ready cash to donate. "Very often, I'll do a painting for some worthy cause, which my dealer could sell for a good amount of money, but the worthy cause turns out not to be a very good marketer of artwork," said Robert Bateman, a painter in British Columbia, Canada. "I may help out some conservation group, but you find that environmentalists don't have any money and my work sells for very little. This becomes a blot on my escutcheon. If I put someone up the flagpole and I don't get much of a salute, it can be a little bit embarrassing and diminish my reputation."

The problem, many artists find, is that once they make a donation of artwork to one charity, they are inundated by requests from others. "I can nickle and dime my career away with all these good causes," Bateman noted. Similarly, sculptor Glenna Goodacre found that "you give to one group and you get 15 more requests the next week. People don't believe it when I tell them I don't have anything to give them." She and others pointed out that charity events are not sensitive to the tax disincentives for artists to give their work but see artists as having an inexhaustible supply of available merchandise. Also, charities return to the same artists again and again.

"The number of requests for donations of your work jumps up geometrically after you give once," photographer Nicholas Nixon said. "You find yourself on everyone's list. They sometimes treat you as though they're entitled to your work and, once you start to say no, they are not particularly sympathetic. Sometimes, they sneer." Other artists have found the same to be true. "I get annoyed at the way you get asked again and again to give something," printmaker and sculptor Leonard Baskin noted, adding that "artists don't get a lot of feedback from the donation of works."

Artists handle this problem in different ways. Some donate a reproduction of their work or create a line of low-cost items. Sculptor Kent Ullberg, for instance, has a line of more affordably priced bronzes from which he may select a work for a charity auction, and Goodacre said that she does "a series of terra-cotta plaques every year around Christmas, and those I give away. They're inexpensive to produce, and I don't mind the loss of income. I certainly don't give away my big, expensive pieces."

At some charity auctions, artists are allowed to establish minimum bids. This would ensure that the art is not sold unless the bidding reaches a certain amount, ensuring that the sale price does not have a deleterious effect on the artist's market and reputation. The National Museum of Wildlife Art in Jackson Hole, Wyoming, holds an annual "Western Visions" show of two- and three-dimensional miniatures, and all of the works (usually 100) are put up for sale at a silent auction at the conclusion of the exhibition. The artists set a minimum price for their work and receive between 60 and 80 percent of the auction proceeds, with the remainder going to the museum for collection conservation. This style of charity auction prevents works from selling below market value and, if the pieces do not sell at all, from becoming a public embarrassment to the artist.

Also at some charity auctions, artists are permitted to offer works for sale, donating the money earned (or a certain portion of that money) to the charitable cause, which they may deduct in full on their tax returns. George Koch, president of Artists Equity, noted that "charity auctions should not pressure artists to offer their pieces but, instead, approach collectors rather than artists to donate works. Collectors can receive the full fair market value of the work as a charitable deduction on their taxes." Otherwise, he added, artists should try to gauge what their feelings will be if they see their work selling for relatively little money. "If the prospect of that is too painful, they probably should not donate their work."

The New York Question

One of the main articles of faith in the New York art world is that one has to live in Manhattan (at least part of the year) in order to be relevant and known. Something about the high concentration of artists, the large number of critics and art galleries presenting a smorgasbord of art styles and innovations is assumed to keep a creator stimulated and on his or her toes. Many artists find that, after they have reached a certain level of proficiency in their art or have exhausted the local galleries and collectors, their hometowns begin to look a little small to them. They seek bigger challenges and a more critical audience but are unsure to what lengths they would go to develop a market for their artwork. New York City presents itself as a question for these artists: Am I a real artist if my work isn't exhibited there? Should my work be more in line with what is being created and shown there?

Young Lee Kim decided to accept the challenge of New York. A prosperous artist in her native South Korea, the 33-year-old Kim left

Seoul in 1985 to establish her career in New York. Back in Seoul, the several galleries representing her semiabstract, black ink-on-paper paintings all afforded her one-person exhibitions that usually sold out, and she earned the equivalent of more than $20,000 a year from those sales, which goes a little further in South Korea than in New York City. "Things were going very well in Seoul," Kim said. "My work won high honors at various competitions, and I was making a lot of money selling my paintings, but I felt that South Korea was too small for me. I wanted more stimulation; I wanted more challenges. I wanted to be a player in a big playground."

Only those artists who believe in reincarnation, it might seem, would want to go through the experience of building an art career twice. Starting over as an unknown, going door-to-door to art dealers with packets of slides, trying to get people to remember your name and style of work is enough headaches for one lifetime. "It was a small market, with not that many dealers, in Korea," Kim stated. "It was easy to get to know everybody and for everybody to know me. Here, it is a big market and I don't know people. That's a little scary for me." There are not only unfamiliar faces but different dealer practices as well in the respective art worlds.

"In Seoul, dealers buy your works outright if they like them," Kim said. "Here, they buy provisionally"—that is, take works on consignment. She has had one exhibit at an established midtown gallery during her time in the United States, and many of the paintings were purchased by members of New York's Korean-American population. Kim also continues to send works back from time to time to her South Korean dealers, which she will do with even greater frequency after completing her degree (in printmaking) at Pratt. She has found that being in the New York art world, even though (currently) as a bit player, makes her work even more sought after in Seoul. "You have to struggle a lot more in New York than in Seoul," Kim noted, "but that's what I came for. I wanted the human contact; I wanted the challenges of doing my best here and succeeding."

Not all artists who believe their work to be at a professional level feel the need to conquer New York. The good news for artists is that the art world has become more decentralized since the early 1970s. Regional art centers and markets have developed that enable artists to live and work where they like, and the growth of art departments and art schools around the country have reduced the concentration of artists in just a few areas as well as increased the opportunities for the public to see and create art.

"I don't think I suffer from isolation up here," Scott Pryor, who has never lived in Manhattan and appears quite wedded to Northampton, Massachusetts, where he has lived and painted since 1970, said. "I have a number of friends who are artists and give me support, inspiration or maybe just camaraderie." One of those fellow artists is his wife, Nanette Vonnegut (one of the two painter daughters of novelist Kurt Vonnegut, Jr.). He added that "I don't lack for ideas about what to paint; in fact, I wish there were more hours in the day to paint everything I want to do." He also doesn't lack for patrons who purchase his oils and watercolors through the two galleries handling his work, Alpha Gallery on Boston's Newbury Street, which has represented Pryor's work since the 1970s, and the Maxwell Davidson Gallery in SoHo.

Once a month or so, Pryor does travel to Manhattan (about 175 miles away) to "drop off paintings at my gallery and look at what's being done in the other galleries; sometimes, I just drop off the paintings and head back home." He added that it is "important to follow what's going on. I read the magazines and think about what's going on in the art world, but it's also important to forget about all that, too, and concentrate on your own vision." Pryor is quite aware that the pace is faster in Manhattan, that ideas fly about, but has found that "there is a concentrated media network that lets you find out what's going on very easily. If it's important for you to know what are essentially changes in fashion, then it's important for you to be in New York. I prefer the way I live in Massachusetts, and I think I keep up with what's going on down there."

Artists Owning Their Own Galleries

Most artists, it is fair to say, want to get their work shown in an art gallery at some point in their artistic development. There is something about those white walls, having a dealer, not seeing one's art competing with a bowl of soup (when it is exhibited in a restaurant), and the knowledge that potential collectors may look at and buy it, that gives artists a sense of getting a fair hearing.

There are generally not enough art galleries in the country for all the artists who want to be represented in them and relatively few of those live up to the hopes and expectations of the artists who have found a place in them: the dealer doesn't advertise and promote exhibitions or the artist; the art is displayed randomly; the overall quality of the art in the gallery is uneven; commissions are too high, and the artist isn't paid promptly when a sale does take place. These are standard complaints, and one frequently finds that, when artists get together, they are more apt to discuss what their gallery or dealer isn't doing for them than what they are currently working on.

Some artists have taken the matter into their own hands, setting up their own galleries that feature their own artwork as well as that of others. As with everything else artists may do for their careers, there are benefits and drawbacks to this. On the plus side, owning a gallery solves the problem of where and how to exhibit one's art. Painter Barbara Halliday Montgomery's decision to open the short-lived West End Market Gallery in North Adams, Massachusetts, in 1988, for instance, "evolved from my needing a place to display my own work."

Art generally needs a certain artistic context in order for it to be viewed as art—that is what separates graffiti from graffiti art—and a gallery can help an artist feel more like a professional. "The gallery atmosphere has a certain formality," Richard A. Heyer, owner of the Beaver Pond Gallery in Williamstown, Massachusetts, said. "You walk in and really feel you are looking at serious art." A watercolorist of landscapes, Heyer added that, since starting up the gallery in 1978, he is "not just pursuing art without a goal. The gallery creates goals for you, such as finishing enough paintings and having them all in frames and looking presentable."

There are some notable examples of galleries owned and run by individual artists in major cities—Alfred Stieglitz's "291" gallery in New York City back in the 1910s featured his own photography in addition to photographs, paintings and sculpture of fellow modern artists, and a number of the loosely structured East Village galleries in Manhattan in the 1980s were established by avant-garde artists—but these types of galleries are most commonly associated with small towns and rural regions. Today's artist-owned galleries grew out of the idea of artist cooperatives, which are art spaces that a group of artists pay for and jointly run in order to show their own work and gain control over their careers. Frequently, galleries owned and run by an individual artist are located on the first floor of that artist's house, which is convenient and allows substantial business write-offs.

For watercolorist Lou Lehrman, owner of The Gallery at Mill River in Mill River, Massachusetts, an entire gallery "gives me a showcase for my painting, and people can see my work in depth. I am represented by other galleries—a couple in Scottsdale [Arizona], one in Sedona [Arizona], and another in West Hartford [Connecticut]—but they may only show two of my paintings. They may have another two paintings, but they're probably somewhere in the back, maybe in a bin. You have no control in other people's galleries but, in my own, I can show more of my pieces if I like. I also get to keep 100 percent of the sale, since there is no commission."

The Gallery at Mill River, the West End Market Gallery and the

Beaver Pond Gallery have included work by other area artists, although others may not or do not represent other artists consistently. It may be an inherent conflict for artists to discuss the work of competitors with the same enthusiasm or objectivity as when attempting to sell their own. Over the years that he ran his gallery, Alfred Stieglitz quarreled, and ultimately broke, with most of the photographers whose work he represented over matters of aesthetics. Artists who are considering consigning their work to a gallery owned by an artist, created largely to showcase that artist's work, should be confident that the gallery will represent their work and ideas fairly.

There are some drawbacks to artists owning and running their own galleries, among which are the cost and time involved. Nina Pratt, a business consultant to art galleries, stated that having one's own gallery is "not the easiest or the best way to show or sell your art. It's much more practical to just have shows out of your studio once or twice a year or even to use your studio as a gallery. You might see three or four people a day; you wipe your hands off and shake hands with the people who come in. That way, you don't have the huge overhead of a gallery and use up time that might otherwise be spent on your art in maintaining the gallery."

Operating a gallery, even in one's home, can become a major expense. Clemens Kalischer, a commercial and fine art photographer and owner of Image Gallery in Stockbridge, Massachusetts, which he started in 1965, doubts that "the gallery has ever broken even, not when you figure the overhead, the taxes, the heat, the electricity."

It cost approximately $59,000 for Barbara Halliday Montgomery to buy a family-owned meat market and another $20,000 to convert it into the West End Market Gallery, taking down and putting up walls, replacing flooring and adding lights, putting in parking spaces, landscaping the back and installing a second bathroom with handicap access. Meanwhile, electricity cost a monthly $200, the telephone another $100, printing and mailing amounting to $75, and wintertime heating (oil) averaging $200–$300 per month. The expenses quickly proved too much and, despite the money Montgomery earned as a singer (in her now ex-husband's folk band) and the fact that she "received some help from my family to open the gallery," the gallery closed.

Any business expense may be written off, whether the gallery is located in one's home or elsewhere, but if there has been no profit in three out of five years, the Internal Revenue Service will disallow the deductions, viewing the gallery as a hobby rather than as a serious commercial enterprise. Artists contemplating creating a gallery of their own work need to know what regular art dealers know—how to sell art and make money from it. In the smaller towns where galleries of this kind are more likely to be found, there does not tend to be an active market for art, certainly not with prices for individual works that can support an individual or gallery.

Most of the galleries in Berkshire County of western Massachusetts are owned by the artists whose work is featured therein. This region attracts thousands of tourists, especially from New York City, during the summer each year for the internationally renowned music, dance, and theater festivals—a large potential audience for art—but, still, few of these galleries are able to break even. (Were they able to do so, more commercial galleries and dealers would probably spring up.) "Everyone has said to me, 'You must do so well, with all the New Yorkers who come up here,'" Kalischer stated, "but you can't assume that everyone in New York is interested in art, nor that they are particularly interested in looking at contemporary art, especially contemporary art by Berkshire County artists." Even the more art-conscious New Yorkers are reluctant to buy anything because they "assume that in a small town like Stockbridge there can't possibly be anything of interest to them."

Many artists already have a full-time, pay-the-bills job and creating art itself requires a lot of time. There is very little time left to run a gallery, and the art is usually the first thing to go. "To do it right," Kalischer noted, "you have to do it more than just on a part-time basis but, if you have to live on it, you can't possibly do it full time." With all the drawbacks, artists who look to create a gallery for their own work (and artists who might join a gallery set up by an artist) recognize that there are other reasons for exhibiting than specifically selling art. Simply getting one's art before the public or being able to say that an artist's work is represented in the Such-and-Such Gallery has value, letting others know where it may be consistently seen. A decided benefit of artists owning galleries is the ability to meet potential collectors, and many artists note that the personal element directly affects sales. "My work sells better in my gallery than in the various commercial galleries representing me," Lou Lehrman said, "because I'm there and people want to meet me."

Pop Quiz

Who or what is an artist, and what makes an artist a professional? Neither question generates an easy answer but, perhaps, there are ways to approach them.

The United States Government has answers for both questions, however the answers contradict each other because different agencies are looking for specific kinds of information. The Census Bureau (whose data on artists is extrapolated by the National Endowment for the Arts), for instance, claims that there are over 100,000 visual artists in the country. The decennial census asks at what job an individual worked on April 1, or what career activity occupied the largest portion of that day, and, for statistical purposes, the answer to this determines one's employment area. Someone who painted most of that day is a painter unless the respondent indicates otherwise.

The Internal Revenue Service, on the other hand, does not consider someone a professional artist—able to deduct art-related expenses from gross income on tax forms—unless that person made a profit on the sale of his or her work in three out of five years. The government, therefore, may deem someone an artist on one hand but a rank amateur on the other hand.

The art market may or may not provide answers to these questions. Certainly, there are many people who exhibit their artwork in galleries and in other art spaces; a portion of these people sell their work regularly, while others sell occasionally or just enough to cover expenses or sell rarely if ever. Anyone can sell something once, if only to a parent. Somewhere on this continuum one may want to place the idea of being a professional, or even being an artist all all, if it is decided that collectors define what art is through their purchases.

In addition, if sales define an artist or his or her professional standing, where does one place Vincent van Gogh, who only sold one or two paintings during his lifetime but was lionized as a towering figure posthumously? Was van Gogh an amateur in life and a professional in death?

Perhaps, an artist is someone who attains an art degree (a Bachelor or Master of Fine Arts, for example) from an art school or even teaches art privately or at a school. Many artists also belong to professional associations, such as a watercolor society or an artists union, which exist to help members' careers in some fashion. However, the lack of a market for their work may undercut the claims artists may make for themselves, regardless of where they studied or teach and to what groups they belong. Most faculty at art schools would have no other money coming in if they gave up their teaching.

Within that 100,000-plus group that the NEA has defined, there is a wide spectrum of talents and marketability. Categorizing people in too fine a manner often results in numerous exceptions and contradictions. The twentieth-century view, first articulated by Marcel Duchamp, is that artists define themselves, with no other external forms of validation required. One might add to this that artists who behave professionally are professionals.

Part of being a professional is understanding, first, the variety of ways to exhibit and sell one's artwork, second, the value of joining an artist membership organization or society, third, what art schools look for in prospective faculty members, and, fourth, what the federal government requires for artists claiming art-related deductions. In fact, a number of profitless artists have successfully defended their deductions to the IRS on the basis of having made efforts to exhibit and sell their work, belonging to an artist organization, earning an art degree or otherwise taking art classes as well as teaching at an art school. Saving receipts and maintaining good records, these artists have been able to document the extent to which art is their vocation, and this process establishes them as professionals.

☙

CHAPTER 5

■

Success Stories

*T*HE MEANING OF SUCCESS IN THE ART world is as personal and wide ranging as the art itself. For some, success is finally seeing one's work included in an exhibition, or maybe having a one-person show; for others, the mark of achievement may be seeing one's face on the cover of *ARTnews* or learning that Sotheby's just auctioned off one's work for millions of dollars. Somewhere in-between is selling one's art with or without a dealer. There are lots of ways in which an artist can begin to make or increase sales, all of which require some exertion on the artist's part.

Using a Consultant

Joe DiGiorgio "slowly became a success. I became known after one of my paintings was in the 1975 Whitney Biennial. Before that, forget it. I was trying to sell my work off a pushcart in the Village [in New York City] in the 1960s. I've got lots of horror stories about trying to make some money from the paintings. How much do you really want to hear?" The only real luck DiGiorgio had during that time, which he now sees in hindsight, is that his SoHo loft rent was so very low. "It was cheaper to live and work in a loft back then," he noted. "I didn't have to work so hard just to support myself, so I only worked part time"— in advertising agencies and publishing houses—"and had time to develop my art. Young people can't find such bargains today. Now, it's all about real estate."

Like many artists, DiGiorgio has been represented by various art dealers over the years, but most of his sales have come through art consultants who have recommended his work to their corporate and private clients. "You have to get a consultant," he said. "I just go through *Art in America*'s annual guide, which lists various consultants around the country, and I send them slides of my work as well as some material on myself. The consultants keep the slides on file and periodically review them when their clients ask them for a certain kind of work. A number of consultants have shown my work to their clients who liked it and have become repeat buyers."

Many artists send slides to consultants but ask to have them sent back because slides are expensive to produce and they don't want to have to make a lot of them, DiGiorgio stated, "but that's wrong. If the consultant doesn't have the slides, how will he remember the artist? For them, it's out of sight, out of mind. A lot of artists also get discouraged because they send something out and don't get an immediate positive response; so then they don't send anything out. My feeling is that you have to keep pushing yourself. I know that it's embarrassing for artists to talk about their work. I used to cringe to do it, but now I do it without hesitation because I know that if I don't do it no one else will. I've sent out slides to consultants lots of time and not gotten positive responses but, instead of getting discouraged, I just send out more slides to those same people six or twelve months later, with a note that says, 'Here's what I'm doing now.' I think it has paid off."

Being Prolific

At Paier College in New Haven, Doug Brega, a commercial art student, took one painting class and it changed his life. Nothing else was quite as good as painting. So, after a year or so of working as an art director in a plastic container company, Brega quit to spend a year painting in Martha's Vineyard. For most of the time since, he has supported himself from the sale of his work.

"Being prolific is the secret," Brega said, noting that he produces approximately 40 dry-brush watercolors a year. "You have to realize that not every painting will sell, not every painting will come out wonderful, but the more you have the better off you are. That's why you have to paint every day or just paint enough pictures so that you always have something to sell."

His first one-person exhibition was at the Silvermine Artists Guild in New Canaan, Connecticut, in 1976, and he has also shown in New York City and elsewhere. Each showing has brought him buyers, many of whom have become repeat customers. "I've currently got a list of 25 prospective clients who have all told me that they want to see the next thing I do," he stated. "I've compiled the list over the past 12 or 13 years and, every year, I add one or two more."

Selling It Yourself

Peyton Higgison is really two artists living in the same body. He is, on the one hand, an acrylic painter of aerial imagery based more on his imagination than on anything he has ever seen in the sky (he has a pilot's license) or in photographs. On the other hand, he is also a silkscreen printmaker of hard-edge, abstract images that look nothing at all like the paintings.

"I separate myself," he said. "I have two studios in my house. Downstairs is the print studio where I do the prints for about a week. These are my bread-and-butter pieces, which have always sold well for me, so I stick to the formula. But, after a week, I'm sick of the printing chemicals and don't want to see another print for a year. So then, that part of my personality is over and done with and I can get to my paintings"—that studio is upstairs—"where I can explore and take chances."

Higgison claimed that he "would love to be part of a gallery" in order to be able to produce even more work. However, the Brunswick, Maine, artist is his own representative, traveling around the country between May and October doing outdoor art shows every weekend. For more than a dozen years, he has supported himself in this way.

"I didn't study art in order to leave school and paint houses, like a lot of my friends," he said. "I knew that I wanted to be a professional artist and live by selling my work. Outdoor art shows aren't taken seriously by the mainstream art world, but there's money for a good artist to make there. Some of the shows offer prize money for the best work, sometimes thousands of dollars, and I've won some of those." He has also won a number of loyal customers who come back to these shows year after year to buy his latest pieces. "I have a list of 600–700 people on my Rolodex," Higgison said, "and when I am going to be doing a show in, say, Buffalo, I get out my Buffalo file and send out cards to people there, telling them when I'll be there. I've thought about getting a computer to print out cards to people, but most people seem to prefer a personal note." In addition to information on where he'll be and when, the cards also include a picture of one of Higgison's latest paintings. Considering the fact that most of his patrons are print buyers, this could cause a bit of a problem. However, "whichever painting I put on the card never fails to sell," he noted, "and no one else has ever been too bothered."

Lots of Dealers

With abstract artist Deborah Remington, "one things feeds off another."
One exhibit leads to another, one dealer leads to more, a write-up somewhere leads to articles in various magazines—after a while, a career is
pieced together and the creation of art becomes a full-time activity. A
New Yorker, Remington started out, as many others have, working on
her art part time while teaching and waiting tables the rest of the time.
Her first big break came when one of her works was included in the
1965 Whitney Annual. "After that, dealers began to call me up,"
Remington said. "They traipsed through my studio, looking at my work,
and one of them asked me to have a show at his gallery. That show was
a sellout. Right after that, I got a call from a dealer in Paris who wanted
to do a show, and that, too, sold out. One thing feeds off another."

The secret to success, she noted, is having "a lot of dealers all over
the place. Having these dealers frees me up considerably so that I can
do more work. I think an artist should have as many dealers as he or
she can deal with directly. I have a very special relationship with my
dealers, and I have a better sense of what's going on in my life when
I'm in touch with them. They tell me what the various critics have been
saying or how the public is reacting to my work." Each of the dealers
may have several pieces as well as slides of more to show prospective
buyers. "There are hills and valleys in everyone's career," Remington
stated. "I may be active in Cleveland and Phoenix while things are slow
in Los Angeles and New York, so I might have to send more works
where the activity is. A lot of artists believe that their one New York
dealer will arrange shows for them all over the country, but New York
dealers can't be bothered like that. No one dealer can do it all."

Thinking Positively

Self-help and assertiveness training talk comes at you a mile a minute
when Len Garon gets into his can-do mode: "You have to share with
the world who you are and what you want to do;" "People will succeed
to the level of their self-image;" "I'm not a victim but someone who is
in control of my life;" "Success is a marathon, not a sprint." The success
and mind training course that this Paoli, Pennsylvania, painter took
back in 1970 (the main book for the course was *Think and Grow Rich*)
served him well then and it continues to set the agenda for his life today.
At present, he produces approximately 100 original works a year (half
watercolor, the others oils and pastels) plus various print editions (litho-
graphs as well as photoreproductions of his paintings), almost all of
which sell.

Back in 1970, however, he was working in personnel and later grants management in the Denver public hospital system, just a year removed from his Masters in Public Administration studies at the University of Colorado. Painting was a pastime but not yet an obsession. In order to make the transition from student to administrator, he spent $3,500 for new clothes and a car. Overcoming that debt helped change his life. "I worked real hard that year on my painting and started to sell them," Garon said. "I made $3,700, and it was all because I had a goal, and that goal was to make $3,500. But the next year, I only sold about $700 because I didn't have a goal. I didn't need to make the money as much, and I sold my work more casually, not putting myself in front of the public as much. After that, I took a long hard look at what I was doing and realized that I needed to set goals and meet them."

Among the goals he currently sets is to finish five paintings a week. "It's easy to start five paintings, but not so simple to finish them," he noted. Between 1971 and 1976, when he left office work for good to become a full-time artist, Garon worked steadily on his painting and on marketing his work. Sidewalk art shows, knocking on gallery doors, putting on exhibits from his studio (in his home) and letting friends and co-workers know that he was creating pictures were some of his methods.

The art print field, however, was his main entry into profitability. "You have to work at getting your name and artwork out to the public, to put it in front of people," he said. "I recognized the power of the print field to get one's name out." It wasn't automatic. Garon sent out pictures of his work to over 100 print publishers and only three responded favorably. Some time elapsed—he needed to learn through trial and error the lithographic print process and then create an image that publishers would risk paying to print—but, eventually, sales from publishers' catalogs took off. At present, half of his income is derived from the sale of prints in one medium or another.

He aggressively pursues that market through renting booths at the Art Expos of New York City and Los Angeles as well as Art Buyers Caravan (a for-the-trade show hosted by *Decor* magazine). Over the years, Garon has put together a network of 900 galleries, interior designers, frame shops and others that buy his prints with some level of frequency. He also acts as an agent to distribute the prints of other artists. "I say that there is creation time and marketing time," he stated, "and each is equally important. Ignore one and the other inevitably suffers."

Garon credits the success and mind-training course with showing him how to set and achieve goals. "Back then, I knew what I didn't want," he said. "I didn't want a job that has a lot of stress and causes ulcers, and I think I was on the way to an ulcer at the time. There is stress in the art field, don't get me wrong, the living between checks and shows, but I'm in control. I'm not just a cog in the wheel, answering to some bureaucrat who can tell me what to do and ruin my whole day for me. I'm not a starving artist. I'm not a victim."

Selling Art Through the Mail

The first introduction most people may have to Edmund Sullivan is through his catalog. The 24-page (8½-by-8½-inch) booklet, which looks like the sort that L. L. Bean or a department store might send out, is full of photographs of framed paintings by the artist. And, just as in the department store catalogs, there is a little something for everyone— landscapes, seascapes, still lifes, prints, even plates with his images on them—at a variety of price ranges, payable by credit card and through a toll-free number, with a money-back guarantee and an order form. "There was with me a gradual coming to awareness that art galleries are just stores that have to use marketplace tools to sell their wares," Sullivan said. "I said to myself, 'I have those tools. Why can't I use them to sell my own work?'"

In 1973, Sullivan was a mirror salesman, earning $1,000 a week but not enjoying what he was doing. A longtime urge to paint took over, and he quit his job to live on his savings. His knowledge of how to market salable items also eventually took over. "I didn't have a system of distribution or contacts," he stated. "I had no plan for promotion. It was a gradual evolution in my thinking, but I began to see that mail order was the way to go." Sullivan did some homework in evaluating printing techniques and prices, rented mailing lists from list brokers, hired a writer to do the copy for the catalog and began doing test marketing. So much for distribution.

Next came subject matter. Sullivan's main interest is the landscape or seascape, but lots of artists do that. A specialty was needed, and Sullivan found a winner—pictures of the Old Sod in Ireland. Once again, it was more a matter of a gradual evolution in Sullivan's thinking than an immediate decision. "I kind of fell into the Irish thing," he said. "About the time I quit my job, my family went over to Ireland, and they invited me to go with them, but I didn't want to. I was (and still am) a patriotic American and wasn't really interested in the Old World stuff, but when I saw the pictures they took on their vacation, I was bowled over."

Sullivan began making paintings from photographs and postcards of Ireland, finding that a vast audience of Irish-Americans existed which longed for the nostalgic scenes he depicted. He made contact with some potential buyers through an Irish-American newspaper, later setting up a gallery at an Irish-American convention and hanging paintings up in an Irish Tourist Board office. "When you grow up with an Irish mother and father, you wear your Irishness all the time, and people really wanted this sort of picture in their homes," he stated. Ninety percent of his catalog sales are of Irish scenes.

In fact, Sullivan's catalog notes when his next trip to Ireland will be (he has traveled there annually since 1976) for people who want him to paint a particular scene at a location of their designation. There is a $30 application fee, and a 33 percent deposit of the total price is payable roughly two months before he leaves for Ireland. "You have to have a plan," he said. "The world takes care of itself, and that means you have to take care of yourself. Be tenacious. I learned in the marines that dogged perseverance always overcomes the resistance it receives."

Know Your Audience (And Have Your Audience Know You)

"All politics is local," the old politician said and, perhaps, all realist art is, too. Certainly, creating images of places that his potential collectors know has been a key (and successful) strategy of watercolorist William Mangum of Greensboro, North Carolina. More than most, he has identified a market and paints for it—buyers between Virginia and Florida, where he is represented by 180 galleries. It is even more local than Virginia to Florida, because approximately 100 of those galleries are in North Carolina, 20 in Greensboro itself. One of those Greensboro galleries is his own, the Carey-Mangum Gallery that only carries the artist's work. The gallery's largest competitor in the sale of William Mangum works is "about half a mile away," Mangum said, "but to exclude other dealers is slitting your own wrists. There is enough for everyone to make money from."

Such a magnanimous attitude is based on experience. More than half of the artist's sales come through other dealers and, he noted, "customers are often very loyal to particular dealers. They have worked with their local dealer before. They know that person and they don't know me. It's as simple as that." Personal knowledge also informs the decision of what to purchase in art, he believes. "Why do people buy art?" Mangum said. "It's because they have a relationship with it, that it tugs on their heartstrings. With landscapes and architecture that they know, the art stimulates memories of the world that they see every day. There's more romance in familiar subject matter than with a painting that's a splash of colors composed on the canvas."

Call it a twist on what every creative writing teacher tells his or her students: write about what you know. Mangum paints pictures of what his audience knows. But it is even more involved than that, as the artist strongly believes in making personal connections with would-be collectors. "It's who you know that puts you in the driver's seat, and I try to know people," he stated. Considering the fact that between 80 and 90 percent of all sales of Mangum's work takes place in North Carolina, the strategy is clearly paying off. As a way of knowing people, Mangum became a member of the local chapter of Rotary International as well as an elder in his church, board member of Urban Ministry and Young Life (two Christian civic groups in Greensboro) and joined a couple of watercolor societies (National Watercolor Society, North Carolina Watercolor Society). "The more you are involved with your community," he noted, "the more you plant the seed."

Some of those seeds have sprouted into commissions from local foundations and institutions to create original works. Greensboro's local newspaper, the *News and Record*, for instance, commissioned him to portray the city in celebration of the publication's 150th anniversary in 1990. In 1991, the Foundation of Greater Greensboro selected Mangum to make a painting of the statue of Revolutionary War general Nathanael Greene (after whom the city had been named), which had been restored following an act of vandalism against the statue's pedestal. The artist then solicited the local Jaycees to put up half the money— $5,000—for a limited-edition print of the image ("It's better when some group endorses you, because you don't look as though you're just out for yourself," he said), which was published in time for the rededication of the statue. He repaid the Jaycees, in effect, with a donation of $5,000 to the Greensboro Police Dependents' Foundation based on the sale of those prints. More favorable publicity, more mileage from one picture: Mangum knows how to make things happen.

Another local Greensboro group, Vanford Communications, asked him to create a work in recognition of the 100th anniversary of the University of North Carolina at Greensboro, where Mangum received his Masters of Fine Arts degree in 1977. Not content to rest there, the artist was also commissioned to make a print edition of this painting, which has contributed to increasing his visibility in the community. Prints of the University of North Carolina picture, "Centennial Roots," were marketed to the school's alumni ("You kind of have a captive audience there"), and the image also appeared on the cover of the next edition of Southern Bell's telephone directory, of which 800,000 were distributed ("I just called up Southern Bell and asked someone there, 'What are you going to put on the cover of the next telephone book?'").

Eighty percent of his sales come from reproductions of his originals, sold in a variety of formats—poster-sized prints, postcards and some sizes in between. The prints range in price from $5 to $115 apiece. "I think every artist who wants to support himself has to choose," he said. "You can either make some very expensive paintings and hope that a few sell, or make your work affordable and get a lot of people to buy them." Certainly, collectors like Mangum's work, but buyers also like him. "I had a terrible time getting through the MFA degree," he stated, "but I remember the dean of the art department, Joan Gregory, said to me, 'I know a lot of people don't agree with the kind of art you do, but I also know you'll always succeed because of your personality.' I am people oriented; I'm not shy or reclusive. I like to get involved.

"I've always thought it important to show myself in a very professional manner, to give a good account of myself, to never let on that times were challenging for me at home. If I seemed poor or desperate, some people might buy a painting from me out of sympathy, but they would never become long-term collectors, and they're the kind of people you need to survive as an artist."

Mangum's strength as a "people person" may not be much help as he aims to sell the watercolors and prints beyond North Carolina and the Southeast. He thinks about taking part in an ArtExpo show. He thinks about finding a print publisher who could distribute his work throughout the country, but his one experience with a Salt Lake City, Utah, publisher left him with royalties still unpaid and a sour taste in his mouth. He thinks about having his work represented by dealers elsewhere in the country, but "dealers generally want an exclusive arrangement, and I've never bought into that." "The challenge of going national," he said, "is that people generally buy local artists first. Will people in different areas of the country buy me if they don't know me?"

Breaking Out of the Mold

It is usually actors who are typecast, but there is a certain kind of typecasting for visual artists as well. They are often identified with a certain image—Jasper Johns and his American flag paintings, for instance, or Jackson Pollock's drip paintings—that achieves good prices and widespread acceptance but that also limits them as they seek to expand their vision and ideas.

Linda Roberts, who had been known primarily as a ski and snow watercolor artist, decided in the late 1980s to start painting landscapes of other seasons and other (nonmountainous) locations as well in order to expand her reach as a painter. This took some planning—"In my shows, I have gradually introduced a small percentage of summer and beach scenes among the other works that my collectors are more used to," she noted—and some reeducation: "I'm still trying to fine-tune this. Green grass and blue water, even sand, are colors I didn't have a lot of experience with, and I don't feel I've conquered the problems yet. There's a lot more I need I need to learn, but I'm making good strides and I'm glad I took the risk." A number of resorts in Aspen and Vail, Colorado, have commissioned her to create ski scenes that are used as posters. Most of Linda Roberts's clientele live in the northern half of the country because that's where the snow is. "People often say to me, 'You must live in Colorado, right?' because of all the snow scenes I've painted," she said. No one believes that I live right here in Baltimore."

Having found success with snow and ski scenes and better known from (self-published) limited edition photographic reproductions of her work than the originals, Roberts decided that it was time for a change. It was then that she opened her own art gallery in nearby Clarksville, traveled to Europe for the first time and got divorced (not necessarily in that order). She began pursuing galleries—there are three at present, in Aspen, Colorado, Annapolis, Maryland, and Manchester Center, Vermont—to exhibit her originals and introduced new imagery into her work, such as beach scenes and other spring and summer settings. "Before, I had thought, 'Well, I can paint the winter, that's something,' and worked on a wholesale level, just getting it out," she said. "I had built walls around myself in a number of areas at the time, and I began to realize that I could do more than just this one thing."

It was the marketing people for the Jerry Ford annual golf tournament in Vail, Colorado, who helped provide some of the push, commissioning a limited-edition print series to promote the annual event. They had known (and, presumably, admired) her snow scenes and "assumed that if I can paint winter, I can paint summer," she stated. Many of the same ingredients of her winter imagery are used in the two golfing works she painted—the low-lying foreground, with hills beyond and mountain peaks in the back—but a new emphasis on color, a greater figurative range and more overall painterliness was required and achieved.

She noted that not all of her collectors "are interested in seeing change. My mother came to one of my shows and said, 'Who did this?' My very own mother! I had to take her over and put her nose in my signature." However, there had been other people, such as those living in Maryland and nearby Washington, D.C., "who had appreciated my style and technique but weren't interested in snow. They only think of snow in terms of traffic jams and car accidents." Some of them have become buyers, and the change in subject matter has also enabled Roberts to win collectors in the Southwest and Southeast.

Roberts also contracted in early 1990 with Voyageur Art of Minneapolis, Minnesota, to publish and distribute her limited-edition prints, which has freed her from needing to spend so much of her time making prints and marketing them. She has used that time to paint more, enabling her to develop her skills with spring and summer scenes and also have more original works to show in galleries.

Going Door-to-Door

Geoffrey Stiles walks up and down the streets of the better neighborhoods of Baltimore for a living. He's neither a policeman nor a thief. The artist goes door-to-door to some of the more architecturally interesting houses asking whether or not the owners would like a pen-and-ink drawing made of where they live. "People with nice houses like to talk about them, even if they're not willing to commission me," he said. "It's very flattering to them that I come to their door, and many of these people generally like to talk about art. It's not at all like insurance, which scares people off."

Stiles knows all about the reaction to insurance agents, having at one time sold life insurance. He had also sold vinyl replacement windows, made technical illustrations of military hardware for advertisements (he was laid off from Ford Aerospace because of the shrinking military budget), worked as an arts coordinator in Philadelphia and spent a certain amount of time just looking for work. Going door-to-door for one purpose or another is not entirely a new experience for him.

Many of his house rendering clients reduce the pictures he creates to put on their stationery or cards, and some place the pictures on their walls as pieces of art. They sell for between $350 (for a five-by-seven-inch postcard size) and $650 (for a nine-by-twelve-inch picture for a home) and, in his first full year of doing this kind of work, Stiles has eked out a living for his wife and child on four or five commissions a month. Each rendering takes him approximately two or three days, bunched up when the demand is great, spread out when customers are fewer. Christmas has proven to be a busy season, with trade slowing down for a time shortly thereafter, but his market is largely wealthy people for whom seasonal vicissitudes in spending are not so severe. "Retired people generally won't pay as much as those who are younger, with a family," he stated, noting that one of his customers was 95 and wanted to have him draw the house she had lived in more than 50 years earlier. "I like to find people who are younger and, maybe, renovating their house and want some artistic documentation of what they own."

To balance out his workload, and ease some of the need for door-to-door selling, Stiles has begun advertising in various national magazines—a pricey way to get work, costing $600 for a two-month ad in *Historic Preservation* magazine, for instance—and has received some responses. Customers would send him photographs of their houses that he, in his studio, would render in a pen-and-ink drawing. Even when the house is in Baltimore, Stiles still takes photographs and works from them in his studio.

"There's no question in my mind that sketching on the site is far superior to working from a photograph," he said, "but I clearly can't travel everywhere. It takes too much time and money and isn't cost effective. The studio is also a controlled environment. Baltimore is a humid environment. During the summer, if you work outside, the paper gets damp from your perspiration and you can't keep working at your best. The camera distorts things, but I couldn't live without it."

Where the ability to do architectural renderings came from Stiles cannot say. He studied drawing and painting in college, but never tackled this kind of assignment. His sister, Susan Stiles Dowell, is a writer on architecture and author of *Great Houses of Maryland*, so perhaps pictures of houses runs in the blood. Until the magazine ads produce more customers, Stiles will continue to solicit business door-to-door, which currently has the discouraging ratio of one commission for every 10 homeowners approached. "It's very humiliating to go door-to-door," he stated, "but there's a barrier to break through and, when you can do that, it can be really good."

Overcoming Obstacles

Artists need places to show their creations, time to work, a studio to work in and, obviously, talent. But, most importantly, artists need self-confidence and patience. Without the trust that one's vision will be recognized eventually, an artist may give up early or try to adopt a style that appears elsewhere in an effort to be "marketable." That confidence in oneself and in one's art may entail enduring some hard days and long nights. One gallery may go bankrupt, another may decide to get rid of the artist, and the color of one's skin may not open too many doors either. Sam Gilliam's success has been based on a determined self-confidence in the face of adversity.

"The system of segregation that existed while I grew up helped make a lot of black people, including myself, more self-reliant than they might have been," he said. "It taught you to rely on information beyond the book, on a sense of yourself beyond how white society sees you. I don't believe you should enslave a people in order to develop that sense, but I learned a lot of confidence in what I did despite what others might think, because a black man is used to having others think poorly of him."

For ten years, from 1958 to 1967, Gilliam (who was born in 1933) worked as an art teacher in the public schools of Lexington, Kentucky (elementary and junior high) and Washington, D.C. (high school), all the while learning his craft. The last five of those years were spent in the nation's capital where, after work, he associated with painters later known as the Washington Color School, including Morris Louis, Kenneth Noland, Howard Mehring, Thomas Downing and Paul Reed. He had come to Washington as a portrait painter but began to paint in an abstract style—a not very popular form of art there at the time, which only added to the burdens of an African-American man (in a low-paying job, with a wife and three children to support) in a white art world.

His breakthrough year came in 1967, with a fellowship from the National Endowment for the Arts, a one-man exhibition at the Jefferson Place Gallery (in D.C.) that sold out and a show at the Phillips Collection, also in Washington. The next year added New York City gallery representation and the purchase of a house as well as the ability to give up full-time, public school art teaching for part-time painting instruction at the University of Maryland. "My feeling of success was dominated by being able to get a house, with each kid having his own room, and the fact that a single art show could do that," Gilliam stated.

Kenneth Noland told Gilliam that "you have a better gimmick than the others—your face," that is, being unique for being African-American. That "gimmick" has been double-edged, as was his rise to acclaim as a "second-generation" Washington Color School painter. "Being compared to Noland and [Morris] Louis and even to [Jackson] Pollock establishes you as a follower, which is hard, but it also means that something is expected of you. And what that is, is to become a leader. Getting that kind of recognition helped give me the confidence to be an artist on my own terms and, by doing that, I became a leader for a lot of other black artists. Noland was right, but what is even more interesting is that black artists who are abstract artists created the interest for black artists who are nonabstract."

The road to success was not so easy. The crash came in 1970, as the Jefferson Place Gallery folded under financial stress—Gilliam lost "a lot of money" as he hadn't "gotten around to collecting receipts for a number of shows"—and Gilliam's New York gallery, the Byron Gallery, "tossed me out" when the artist decided to forego the stretcher for canvases that were now to be draped or folded into floral shapes. Other galleries showed little enthusiasm for representing his work. "In 1970, and even in the 1990s, it's hard to get a quality gallery to take on a black artist," he said, still feeling with bitterness that certain galleries in which his style of work would "feel right at home, such as the [Andre] Emmerich or [Leo] Castelli galleries"—in New York City—"weren't at all interested."

The years between 1970 and 1972, when the Barbara Fendrick Gallery in Washington, D.C., took him on, were hard, as he had to go back to earning a living through teaching and arranging private sales through his studio. "Friends helped, and I started doing the visiting artist thing," Gilliam noted. "The significant thing is to make it back from a loss." From his hardships, he learned never again to become dependent solely on a gallery for a living. Gilliam has done commissions of three-dimensional, multimedia works for corporations, government buildings and institutions of higher learning since 1979 as well as create print editions that sell when the paintings don't. Success no longer means just a house with enough bedrooms for his children but also two assistants (he claims to need a third as well as a larger studio) and the creation of collages, drapes, prints and painted sculptural pieces—usually, 20 larger-scale works a year that sell in the range of $20,000 to $40,000—to meet the demand. "I was always confident," he noted. "I just wasn't always this calm."

The Lives of Women Artists

All artists share the same search for ideas and for their own ways to express them, and most face similar tests of their resolve along the way. Some, however, may have additional obstacles to overcome. For many women, their artwork may not be taken as seriously—or viewed as somehow alien—in a still male-dominated culture, and their artistic pursuits may have to take a backseat to family obligations, such as child-rearing. Women may need to bring more dedication to their art-making than many of their male counterparts.

Attaining equal recognition has never been easy for women. Edgar Degas, never one to compliment quickly, showed only a grudging appreciation of Mary Cassatt ("I will not admit that a woman will draw so well"), and it took a long time for others in the art world to be more forthcoming. Cassatt and Berthe Morisot both influenced the work of their more celebrated compatriots in the impressionist school, but the two women also made themselves useful to the group by arranging sales of their male colleagues' paintings to wealthy collectors.

"I did a lot of wifely things in the 1940s," Louisiana painter Ida Kohlmeyer said, "accompanying my husband to Fort Bragg, where he was stationed during the war, and having two daughters." By 1950, however, she was also ready to devote some energy to making art, earning a Master of Fine Arts at Newcomb College of Tulane University where she later taught. "Having children required me to better organize my life, and I realized that there was no time to waste. I had grown up a lot during the war. I put aside the dilettantism that had been part of my life before the war and began to really dedicate myself to art—as well as my children." In 1963, she won a Ford fellowship for her art and briefly considered moving to New York City in order to further her career there, "but I had a family, and it might have broken up my family, so I stayed."

Finding the balance between raising children and pursuing one's art is no simple matter, and it is often complicated by the need to hold a job and have a supportive spouse. Still, the desire to make art remains, even if it must be deferred for a period of time. Both Louise Nevelson and Louise Bourgeois, two of the most important women sculptors of the postwar era, took time off from their work to raise children—an important full-time job in itself—but they came back. "You have children for 15 years, not for 80 years," said Louise Bourgeois. "It's just one episode in your life. There's a lot more to life than that."

Another hurdle women may face is having spouses who are also artists and, in fact, it is often the case that artists have married other artists. The benefits of having an artist-spouse are self-evident, as art is an approved activity and each partner may receive encouragement and in-house criticism. Unfortunately, such pairings may also occasionally lead to competitiveness and jealousy or, most commonly, someone having to take a backseat. Historically, it has just as often been true that the husband's art has taken precedence with the wife subordinating her work or career or both. This has tended to be a common phenomenon in the art world where, except for the rare example of Georgia O'Keeffe and Alfred Stieglitz and a few other pairings, husband and wife artists seldom are accorded equal attention. New attention has been cast on the careers of Marguerite Zorach (painter wife of William Zorach, the American cubist sculptor) and Suzy Frelinghuysen (painter wife of George L. K. Morris, a painter and founder of the American Abstract Artists group) as well as on a number of other artists who happened to marry male artists. However, recognition does tend to come late—often posthumously.

Bernarda Bryson Shahn, for instance, lived with success and greatness for most of her life. Unfortunately for her painting career, that greatness belonged to her husband, painter and graphic artist Ben Shahn, whose success overshadowed everything his wife could accomplish. Bryson Shahn has created paintings, drawings, prints and illustrations throughout her 60-plus-year career. She is an artist who shared a home, family, and left-wing political ideas with her husband but never his style or subject matter. Nonetheless, Ben Shahn's renown has always colored the art world's perception of her and her work. "People tell me all the time—I heard it again from a friend of the family just the other day—how they see the influence of Ben Shahn in my work," Bryson Shahn said. "I think they just look for it and find it regardless of what it is in front of them. You couldn't possibly find any real resemblance to Ben's work in mine."

Born in Athens, Ohio, in 1903, Bernarda Bryson came to New York City in 1933 as a journalist for the *Ohio State Journal* in order to interview Diego Rivera who was painting an ill-fated mural in Rockefeller Center. A year later, Bryson moved to Manhattan and was soon employed on the artist's project of the Roosevelt-sponsored Works Progress Administration where she met Ben Shahn. They married the following year. From 1936, when their first child was born, until 1972, three years after Ben Shahn's death, Bryson Shahn didn't paint. "The marriage contract was just like that back then," she said. "It was never the intention of my husband to stop from me from painting—in fact, he always encouraged me and others to express ourselves, and he never felt that there was only one way, his way, to paint—but one has obligations as a wife. I never intended to hold off on my career, but I just found myself in that circumstance."

Bryson Shahn never ceased creating, but she pursued other markets, such as creating illustrations for books (*Pride and Prejudice, Wuthering Heights*) and magazines (*Fortune, Harper's, Scientific American*) and other media, such as pencil sketches and printmaking. "With drawings, you can put your pencil down and go back to it in a way that you can't with painting," she stated. "When the kids were growing up, when Ben was entertaining, there was always something to do, and I never had large blocks of free time." In 1972, Bryson Shahn brought herself to go into the studio of Ben Shahn, where she found a canvas he had stretched but never got around to painting. She painted it and, through considerable trial and error, worked herself back into the fine arts career that had been interrupted 36 years before.

The effort to be taken seriously has been decades long for Bryson Shahn. Art dealers were always interested in representing her work in their galleries but rarely, she felt, because of a true liking for her paintings. "A dealer might want to take me on because he really wanted to represent Ben Shahn and thought he could get Ben by helping me," she stated. "It's been a rule with me not to be in the same gallery as my husband, and that has definitely hurt my career." That rule has even led her to call herself Bernarda Bryson professionally, but her current gallery pressed her to use her married name and she finally agreed to do so after her husband's death.

"I've often thought about what my career would have been like had I not married Ben Shahn," she said. "I'm sure that I wouldn't have had all the international contacts nor would I have gotten the Olympian view of the world that came with marriage to Ben, but I would have had galleries in New York and elsewhere to show my work. I might have been taken seriously sooner. Not that I'm complaining; you can call it a struggle but, for me, my life has been a hell of a lot of fun."

In 1983, she had her first one-person exhibition and, in 1989, the National Women's Caucus for Art presented her with an award for outstanding achievement. That award might have just as easily been for perseverance and not becoming embittered, the lot of many women artists whose marriages to more famous men have overshadowed and, in some cases, eliminated their careers. Lee Krasner and Elaine de Kooning, the painter wives of Jackson Pollock and Willem de Kooning, respectively, certainly spent decades attempting to assert their own artistic vision. Sally Avery, widow of Milton Avery, claimed that she never let the attention paid to her husband's painting (and the concomitant lack of interest in her own) "bother me too much. I wasn't going after the same notoriety as my husband. I just went at my own pace and tried to ignore all the people who said 'Oh, pity the poor wife who can't get anyone to look at her work.'"

Some artist-wives, such as Helen Sloan (John Sloan) and Emma Bellows (George Bellows) to name a few, completely gave up on their art. Jo Hopper, wife of painter Edward Hopper, never fully gave up but was unhappy for years at the art world's lack of interest in her painting. Gail Levin, a former curator at the Whitney Museum of American Art in New York City, noted that the museum "was given a number of her paintings along with the Edward Hopper bequest [in 1968], but most of her work was either given away or thrown out. Jo Hopper was not as good a painter as Edward Hopper, who was one of the greatest American artists ever, but she was as good as many a minor male painter who is currently in the Whitney's collection. Edward Hopper's fame was just too much for her career."

Moving (from a Nonart Career) to an Art Career

Pursuing one's art interests on the side is clearly more the norm than the exception. As noted in chapter seven, Tony Smith was an architect before devoting himself fully to sculpture well into his middle age. The French painter Henri Rousseau was frequently called "le douanier" by his artist friends for his job as customs official that he was loath to give up.

Herbert Ferber, a painter and sculptor born in 1906, did not give up his dentistry practice until the late 1970s. He did not become interested in art until age 20, while a science major in college. "I knew that painting and sculpture couldn't support me, so I became a dentist," he said. "I quit being a dentist when I realized that I could make money from art." Those intervening years were quite busy for him—he maintained a private practice, taught at Columbia University's dental school and researched and published numerous articles in a variety of dentistry journals, all the while making art and keeping his hopes alive that, someday, he might not have to do anything else. When it finally came true, "it was like a holiday."

Another well-known dentist-turned-sculptor, Seymour Lipton seemed almost embarrassed about his previous career. "The fact that I was a dentist has nothing to do with my artwork. Dentistry was just an oddity I did for a number of years in order to make a buck. No one talks about Wallace Stevens because of his work as an investment banker in the insurance industry. The important thing is the poetry he wrote."

To a degree, Lipton was right. His work makes no reference to his past "day job." Rather, it reflects thematic influences of the surrealists (birth and death, primordial shapes, celestial imagery), just as Ferber's sculpture suggested the gestural qualities of abstract expressionist painting made three-dimensional and captured in welded steel. No one would think to look for images of tooth decay in either artist's work. However, desiring to create artwork and the need to earn a living are well-known concerns to almost every artist.

The Art World's Slowpokes

Sure, everyone likes Jan Vermeer *now*, 300-plus years after the seventeenth-century Dutch artist's death, but most art dealers want little to do with artists who can only produce two or three paintings a year—Vermeer created fewer than 40 in his lifetime.

"There are lots of difficulties in building a career when you don't have a large inventory," New York dealer Louis K. Meisel said. "You want to have one-person shows every two or three years, but the artist may not have enough completed works to exhibit. You want to show the artist's work at galleries in other cities, in order to attract out-of-town buyers, but you can't do it because there is just nothing to spare. You also have to sell each painting for more money than other artists might receive just because the artist has so few other works to sell."

Meisel, who has represented the work of photo-realist painters (most averaging four works a year) since the early 1970s, developed a number of creative approaches to surmount these difficulties, but many other dealers just don't want the bother and will forego otherwise promising artists. "Admittedly, there are times when you get frustrated, waiting and waiting for the works to dribble in, for the shows to take place," said New York dealer Nancy Hoffman, who represents a number of nonprolific artists. "It's much harder to keep an artist in the public eye if there are five years between shows. Shows give context to the work."

Finding an accommodating art dealer is no small challenge for artists with low productivity. "I've had dealer after dealer tell me that they like the images I do but not the low volume," William Beckman, who produces an average of two paintings a year, said. "Dealers just can't appreciate the length of time it takes me to get that image right, and they say they can't show me and pay the overhead." Beckman never was much faster. He may apply as many as 100 layers of paint, which he then scrapes and sandpapers ("I have an obsession with a certain surface"). In 1969, he worked all year long on a single six-foot-tall painting of his (now ex-) wife, which he sold two years later for $10,000, keeping only $5,000 after the commission was paid. "I really began to question whether I could do this," he noted. "Now, I had a wife and child to support." Ohio State University offered him a teaching position in 1971. "I flew home [Brooklyn, New York] to talk to my wife about it and, as soon as I got through the door, she told me there was a buyer for the painting I was then working on, so I tore up the contract and stuck with it."

Even the most understanding dealers may show exasperation from time to time at artists who do not produce many paintings. Barbara Dixon Drewa, a trompe l'oeil painter in Houston, Texas, stated that "I've had dealers suggest to me that I get an assistant to do the finishing touches, to speed everything up. Others have suggested that I spend less time with my family and just paint. I'm working 30–40 hours per week in the studio on my painting as it is." Her one-person shows at the Fischbach Gallery in New York City take place when she is able to complete enough works to fill the space. A single oil-on-wood painting takes between 10 and 12 weeks to create, and each is sent up to her dealer as soon as the paint is dry. Usually, they are sold quickly but with the proviso that the gallery may borrow the works back for exhibitions—that is a common solution to the slow-producing artist problem, filling up the gallery walls for exhibitions even though half or more of the works may not be for sale.

At times, the walls just cannot be filled. Beckman noted that he has had shows with only two paintings, displaying each spotlighted painting in a darkened room, which adds a certain visual excitement to the event while making a virtue of necessity.

There are certain options for dealers of slow-producing artists and others for the artists themselves. In order to help artists work full time on their art, some dealers offer advances against future sales or suggest foundations to which artists may apply for grants and fellowships. Similarly, some dealers also arrange commissions for their artists as well as recommend them for teaching positions. Some artists also become more productive when a specific exhibition date is scheduled. Artists are usually appreciative if their dealers are understanding and supportive of their slow processes, not carping at them or dropping them from the gallery when they don't produce a certain number of pictures. "Artists aren't factories," Robert Fishko, director of Forum Gallery in New York, said. "You can't put on a second shift. You just have to accept the artist with whatever level of productivity he or she has."

Expanding the regional or national exposure for artists with relatively few works to show sometimes entails a dealer placing advertisements in art magazines and other publications. Louis Meisel noted that he has been able to put together exhibitions of his photo-realist artists for loans to galleries in other cities by including "two of this artist, two of that artist, two of another and two of someone else, because there just aren't eight works by one artist to lend out." In general, artists who may go long periods between one-person exhibits are more likely to be included in group shows.

All other things being equal, realist painters, especially those who concentrate on fine details, are more likely to have a small output than artists in other media and styles. "When I was an abstract expressionist, I produced lots and lots of work. It's the nature of the beast," said painter and sculptor Audrey Flack. "When I started doing the photo-realism, that's when everything slowed down. I'd say to myself, 'Here I am working all this time on this finger and, during this time, someone else has already done 20 paintings.'" She noted that the slower pace of productivity increased the problem of earning a living as well as "raises the stakes" when the completed work is finally exhibited to the public. "You show your work and people don't get it, or some critic condemns it, you may wonder, 'Have I wasted the last few years of my life?' If I do just three paintings in two years, and only one sells, I think, 'How am I supposed to live off that?'"

The labor-intensive approach of painstaking realism requires career expectations as patient as the artistic technique itself. Realist artists cannot expect that their paintings will sell for much more than another painter's work simply because it took them longer to create them. Photo-realist painter Don Eddy, who said that he "lived from painting to the painting" in the early 1970s and produces only four or five works a year, noted that he always spends "less than my income, and I've created a reserve that now could carry me through three or four years if there were a fallow period. That takes the pressure off."

Another way of taking at least some more of the pressure off is by creating works in different sizes and media that do not take as much time as the larger pieces. Audrey Flack and Janet Fish, for instance, both paint in watercolors (Flack: "because you can finish them in a day, and it's a way to get out of the studio and into nature"; Fish: "because I can do three or four a day, and it has helped me open up my larger paintings").

Studies for larger, more time-consuming works also flesh out an exhibition as well as provide more affordable pieces. William Beckman also helps "fill the gallery's walls with drawings," both in pencil and charcoal, that sell for between $3,000 and $11,000, far less than the large (six-by-five-foot: $160,000) and small (two-by-three-foot: $45,000) paintings. Candace Jans, a Boston artist, exhibits and sells the studies (gouaches and alkyds) for her larger oil paintings, of which she may only produce two a year. While the studies sell for far less ($2,500 for a five-by-eight-inch or $5,000–$6,000 for a 12-by-18-inch) than the oils ($25,000–$30,000), their more plentiful supply increases the likelihood of something selling right away. The studies are also less taxing for her: "They are straightforward exercises," she said. "It's what I see in front of me. I don't have all the compositional problems of the larger paintings. The studies are a palette cleanser."

Varying the size also increases the artistic output of Scott Pryor, a painter who spends an average of two months on his four-by-six-foot paintings but just a few days or weeks on his smaller (five-by-eight-inch or one-by-two-foot) paintings. "After I finish one of the larger paintings, I think, 'Gee, I don't want to do that much more again for a long time,'" he said. "And even though I get more money for the larger paintings, proportionately I make more from the smaller works because I can do so many more of them." He added that he creates the larger paintings "on a lot of faith, because the larger works may be harder to sell since they cost more."

At times, the obsessive concern with detail that makes a large painting so difficult to finish can invade the smaller works as well. Douglas Safranek, a Brooklyn, New York, artist who takes five months to create one three-by-two-foot painting in egg tempera, began to paint smaller works (from three-by-three-inch to eight-by-12-inch) "because I could do them more quickly. But now I find that making these miniatures is even more difficult because everything has to be exactly right—perfect. They became more and more challenging and a hell of a lot of work. I wonder how long my eyes will hold out."

The Big Break

When a big break comes in an artist's career, will that person realize it, or know how to take advantage of it? Artists who are just starting out look to the future with boundless hopes, most to be dashed by the reality of getting a paying job, and trying to find the time to create art on the side for a public that rarely shows any interest. The "career break" is the act of being discovered, a storied example of which occurred when starting-up art dealer Leo Castelli happened to walk into Jasper John's studio during a visit to Robert Rauschenberg. Castelli was intrigued by what he saw, and his gallery made both Johns and Rauschenberg rich and famous. The career break might be the first real sale of a work ("Here we go") or being awarded a prize as well as having some art dealer decide to represent one's work. Some breaks turn out to be temporary confidence boosters, becoming just one more line on a résumé (other works don't sell, the prize doesn't lead to sales, the dealer does very little to promote or sell one's artwork), while others elevate the artist to a new level of visibility and collectibility.

Dean Mitchell. Such an event, for watercolor artist Dean Mitchell, was the 1990 Hubbard Art Award for Excellence, for which Mitchell was one of five finalists. He didn't win the $250,000 grand prize—another painter, Howard Terpning, did—but the exposure from placing in the contest and the fact that the Hubbard Museum founders, R. D. and Joan Dale Hubbard, purchased his entry (entitled *Rowena*) for $25,000 raised his stature enormously.

The Hubbard Art Award, which was discontinued after 1991, was a significant event because of "the caliber of the artists invited, the prize money involved and the fact that it was promoted so extensively," Mitchell said. "After the Hubbard, politicians contacted me, wanting to be seen with me. I had gallery owners and museum curators asking to show my work. And, of course, having the Hubbards pay $25,000 for my painting meant that I could raise my prices in the marketplace." Prior to the contest, $10,000 was the highest price anyone had paid for Mitchell's work. A year afterward, a portrait of the artist's uncle who was dying of cancer, entitled *Release Me*, sold to a private collector for $40,000. Another painting, *Psalms 4:1*, a portrait of the artist's wife kneeling and praying, sold for $30,000. That picture, which he had painted in 1989, was originally priced at $2,500 and could not find a buyer at the time. "I knew, right after the Hubbard, that this was the time to test the market, so I raised the price to $30,000," Mitchell said. "If I couldn't get that sort of money then, I never would."

Perhaps most extraordinary is that the artist, who lives in Overland Park, Kansas, not only recognized that the Hubbard was a break in his career but knew how to capitalize on it. He had been entering, and winning, art competitions since the late 1970s, viewing each achievement as a stepping stone. Every new award resulted in a press release to local and regional media; awards also led to membership in the National Watercolor Society at age 23 and the American Watercolor Society at 28. Competitions were entered on the basis of how showing well there might advance his opportunities in the future.

"You can send to shows everywhere. You can win awards up the wazoo," Mitchell said, "but I wanted shows that were hooked up to major museums"—that is, the shows take place at museums—"because museums lend a certain prestige to the show and to the artists in them. And, also, museums buy works from these shows." Again, every museum purchase led to a new press release and brochures trumpeting a growing body of collections. Mitchell also studied the jurors for the shows he entered, selecting those who were connected to major museums ("they might someday buy my work for their institutions") or were members of the National Academy of Design ("I want to keep my name and work before them, because I may become a member that way").

Entering show after show has been important for Mitchell, as "the public forgets your name very quickly, and people want to know what's new." Leaving the show circuit for more lasting recognition, he added, requires "a retrospective or a book" about one's art. The renown from the Hubbard Art Award helped him here, as an ever higher level of exhibitions since 1990 had to a retrospective at the Marianna Kistler Beach Museum of Art at the University of Kansas in 1995.

An additional credit that Mitchell gives the Hubbard is "breaking the ice for museums buying a black artist's images of black people," he said. "Museums will buy the work of primitive black artists or stylized images, like those of Romare Bearden and Jacob Lawrence, but not the realist images of an academically trained artist." He noted that the art world still has a long way to go in breaking the color barrier. His earliest and still largest area of sales were of white figures, generally women, although slowly his paintings of black women have begun to sell. Mitchell's audience has been principally white buyers. "It's hard to get the black community interested in buying art," he said, "and, when they buy, it's usually Picasso or Matisse, because they think it has to be blue-chip investment art." He added that "it's easier to sell the female figure, white or black. The male figure is much tougher, and the black male figure is almost impossible."

Wendy Ewald. Artists value fellowships and awards highly not only for the money received but for the endorsement of their artwork that is implied. The award not only assures the artist that his or her work is understood and appreciated by someone but informs the rest of the art world (collectors, critics, curators, dealers, other funders) that here is a talent to be noticed. Of course, the more prestigious the award, the more notice the artist will attract.

Perhaps the most significant award in the United States is the MacArthur Foundation fellowship, which pays between $37,500 and $60,000 per year for five years and has been called the "genius" grant. There is no application process for these awards, as unidentified nominators for the foundation select finalists in a range of arts and humanities areas. Wendy Ewald, a photographer in Rhinebeck, New York, who works with children, learned that she had been chosen for a MacArthur Foundation award in 1992 through a telephone call while in Washington, D.C., where she was serving as a panelist in the visual arts program of the National Endowment for the Arts.

Ewald had no idea that she was under consideration or that many other people had ever seen her work. Although a book of her work, called *Portraits and Dreams*, had been published by a small press, she had no gallery representation, selling only to people who called her at her studio, and earning money through teaching at Bard College and Duke University. "Some people had seen my book, and others had heard of me but weren't willing to commit to showing or buying my work," Ewald said. "After the MacArthur, suddenly a lot of curators and dealers were interested in my work."

Almost immediately, her résumé ballooned. Within the next two years, her photographs were featured in one-person shows at the George Eastman House in Rochester, New York, the Ansel Adams Center in San Francisco and the Southeast Museum of Photography in

Daytona, Florida, as well as at a number of university and commercial galleries. Noting that "I've always wanted to work in Europe," Ewald said that she began to receive requests to exhibit in Portugal and Holland, hold a workshop in Spain, "and there's something I'm supposed to do in Germany—I forget what." European magazines have also commissioned her work.

The James Danziger Gallery in New York City became her exclusive representative ("the market for my work was so small that I never even tried to get a gallery before"), and the prices for her pictures jumped from $200 to between $500 and $1,000. A major New York publisher, W. W. Norton Company, brought out a new book on her work, entitled *I Dreamed I Had a Girl in My Pocket*, which is physically larger and has better quality reproductions than the one produced by Writers and Readers Press.

If receiving the prestigious MacArthur gave Ewald credibility within the art world, it also fortified her own self-confidence. "The money and recognition made me much more relaxed and able to just concentrate on my work and take more chances," she said. "It made me more willing to trust my ideas." She has continued to teach at both Bard and Duke, recognizing that "the MacArthur gives me more negotiating power for more money and tenure, if job permanence is what I want now." Prior to 1992, such an idea would have been unthinkable for her.

The immediacy of her move from obscurity to acclaim was not easily absorbed. "I have the problem of saying yes to everyone," she said, "and everyone was asking me to let them exhibit my work. I found myself inundated, apologizing right and left for not doing everything I said I would." MacArthur grants are frequently given to creators of complex, difficult work, as Ewald's is. Her photography could not be produced as fast as the demand. The speed of the turnaround in her career outstripped Ewald's ability to adjust to new circumstances. "I'm a very cautious person, basically. I assumed that people are interested at the moment and would cool down later. I didn't take everyone seriously, and that may have been a mistake."

Ewald assumed, for instance, that correspondence from a publisher at Harcourt Brace and Company, "wanting to see what I was working on," was a form letter sent to all MacArthur grant recipients. By the time she began to seriously contemplate publishing a new book and attempted to contact that publisher two years later, that person had been let go by Harcourt Brace in a corporate restructuring move. No one at Harcourt Brace was as interested now. However, the fired publisher had moved on to W. W. Norton and produced the book there.

Dennis Evans. "Slow and steady wins the race," Aesop moralized, and many art careers follow a progression of smaller to larger exhibitions, from group to one-person shows and from a few reluctant buyers to a Rolodex of eager collectors. A few careers receive a great big push early on, which may take the artist years to comprehend and appreciate. Four years out of graduate school at the University of Washington, Seattle, multimedia artist Dennis Evans was selected to be in the 1979 Biennial exhibition at the Whitney Museum of American Art, arguably the most prestigious showing of contemporary art in the United States. Evans was only the second artist from the state of Washington to be included in the Whitney Biennial, which brought him a great deal of local and regional attention.

"The prices didn't change for my work, but I began to sell a lot more of them," he said. "Collectors don't have their own eye and need the approval of recognized authorities." Dealers on both coasts expressed interest in representing his work, and Evans was invited to create installations at both the Portland Art Museum and the Portland Center for the Visual Arts in Oregon, the Whatcom Museum in Billingham, Washington, and the Los Angeles Institute of Contemporary Art in California.

"There is no question that the Whitney Biennial makes a real affirmation in an artist's career," said Patterson Sims, a former Whitney curator and now a curator at New York's Museum of Modern Art. "The real change in an artist's life is when he or she is given an important fellowship or starts to sell works, but the Biennial is a step in that direction. I can remember one show, the 1975 Biennial, where almost none of the artists in the show were affiliated with a gallery; after the show was over, they all were." "The Biennial is a confidence-boosting experience, as much for the artist as for the collector," he said. "People discover you. Eventually, commercial galleries want to represent you and sell your work and send you checks. Sounds great."

The problem was, this opportunity occurred too early in Evans's career; he wasn't ready for it and, as a result, did not know how to take advantage of it. Perhaps, this was a case of "fear of success" or an unwillingness to take seriously the business of being an artist, but recognition that comes too soon or for the wrong reason may lock an artist into one area of activity, limiting the ability to grow and evolve. "I wasn't mature yet as an artist," he noted. "I was still learning about art and what I wanted to do. I thought about moving to New York. [New York City art dealer] Ronald Feldman sold a few pieces for me, but that's as far as it went. I wasn't sure what I wanted and didn't pursue the gallery connection aggressively. It would have been better if I had been in the 1989 Biennial—by then, I had a better idea."

The strength of the renown of the Whitney Biennial afforded Evans a steady stream of regional collectors, and teaching art at the college level provided him with a steady paycheck while he and his art matured. At present, four West Coast galleries represent his work, and he has been able to give up teaching for full-time art-making. "If I took on a new gallery," he said, "I'd have to drop one." Evans knows that he "lost some opportunities" after the Biennial, "because I never followed up. I could have pursued something with Ronald Feldman. If it were all happening now, I would be more persistent and aggressive. If some dealer said he were interested in my work now, I'd call him and show him work—make him say no. If someone called me up and said he'd like to represent my work, I'd fly out there to look at the space, meet the dealer and ask a lot of questions."

Should an Artist Be Told What to Do?

A common area of frustration for artists is when collectors or dealers want to alter some aspect of the artist's work, for instance, to get the same image but in different colors. Sculptors may be told, "Why not do smaller things that people can and will buy more easily?" Who makes these decisions—the artists or their dealers?

Art world opinion divides evenly on this question, and for obvious reasons. Artists believe that they have the final word, while dealers claim that collectors run the show. In large measure, both sides are right: no one can (or should) tell an artist what to do or how to do it, and collectors are free not to buy whatever they choose. However, having staked out these positions, both artists and collectors look for basic areas of common interest. Artists who are creating art to satisfy their own internal needs should determine whether or not they also wish to satisfy a market, which to artists' advisor Sue Viders translates into making "ego art or consumer art. You have to ask yourself, 'Who are you creating the art for, and why are you creating the art in the first place?' If it is to sell, then you have to accommodate the market."

It is not always the case that an art dealer will bluntly tell an artist to make smaller works because that's what collectors want. Frequently, a dealer will mention which pieces are selling and, if those happen to be all smaller works, the artist is apt to catch the subtle hint to work smaller. Arthur B. Davies, the noted American painter, is reputed to have advised his students in 1915 not to paint pictures that were longer than their arms as they probably would be carrying their works around with them from gallery to gallery in search of someone to represent them. Station wagons, vans and other types of modern transportation, however, may have solved part of that problem.

Collectors may not be the only reason that a dealer suggests the artist create smaller pieces. "We can't show paintings that are bigger than six-by-nine-feet," Penelope Schmidt, co-owner of New York City's Schmidt-Bingham Gallery, stated. "Larger than that, the painting won't fit through our front door or in the elevator. With sculpture, too, there is a storage problem, especially for very large works." Trying to tailor one's art to a particular market or the physical constraints of an individual gallery owner doesn't necessarily make for good art, however. The scale of the art may be very important to the art or the artist, and finding the market for this work can be difficult. Artists should, therefore, look carefully for the right dealer, art consultant or corporate buyer who can place large-scale public artwork in the proper venue. Among the sources of this information are *ARTnews' International Directory of Corporate Art Collections* ($109.95, which can be ordered from *ARTnews*, 48 West 38 Street, New York, NY 10018, 212/398-1690) or the Association of Professional Art Advisors (P.O. Box 2485, New York, NY 10063, 212/645-7320). *Art in America*'s annual summer guide also lists galleries and corporate consultants that might be interested in large-scale work.

The Other Side of Success—A Word About Frustration

In the life of every artist, from the newest kid on the block to the most revered, there is far more rejection than acceptance and success. Juried competitions may not want one's work, private or governmental arts funding agencies may not provide a grant to help create it, commercial art dealers may not be interested in displaying or representing it, critics or reviewers may ignore or pan it and collectors may pass it by with only a glance (if that). Every artist must learn not to take rejection personally.

Feeling hurt or disappointed by the reaction of others is natural. Artists have to remain focused, however, both on their art and their career, and remember that the enjoyment of creating artwork—rather than proving something to someone else—is the reason they started in the first place. There may also be a degree to which the opinions and reactions of others may allow artists to look at their work from a different vantage point; perhaps, some changes are worth considering.

Beyond this, opinions are not static and judgments vary from one person to the next. Art competitions usually have different jurors from one show to the next, so there is always the likelihood that the subjective opinions of someone who rejected certain artists one year will not hold sway the next. Art dealers may decide against showing the work of a particular artist, not as a result of something wrong with the artwork but, because they already have too many artists in their stable; the artist's work doesn't fit into the specific style (realist or abstract, for instance), media (photographs, watercolors, prints, drawings, mixed media are often difficult to place and, with works on paper, don't bring as much money) or theme (landscape, portraiture, regional artists, for example) of the gallery; the artist is not of the stature of the other artists in the gallery; or, the artist does not have a sufficiently established market.

Artists are less likely to feel personally wounded when rejected by collectors and dealers (who represent the commercial side of the art world) than that of art show jurors, art critics and museum curators (who theoretically inhabit a realm of pure aesthetics). Artists must keep in mind that these individuals aren't the final word on one's art—there is no final word—and that vindication often takes time. Alfred Barr, who for many years was the guiding intellectual force at the Museum of Modern Art in New York City, once stated that he felt vindicated if one contemporary work of art out of every ten that he acquired on the museum's behalf turned out to be validated by history as a good choice. The jurors for the better competitive art shows and fairs change every year—it is understood that preferences are subjective and, whereas a certain juror may not care for a certain artist's work, the next year's juror may think very differently.

Art critics may seem to be more of an obstacle, as their tenure is generally longer. Few issues get artists as incensed as the subject of critics, and many artists have tended to build up the assumed power of critics to mythic proportions: critics determine the market for art; art gallery-goers decide what to look at based on what was favorably reviewed; a negative review can ruin an artist's career; currying favor with a critic, perhaps even giving him or her an artwork, will get you on the critic's good side.

In reality, some critics do wield some power, while others do not. Theater critics, especially those in larger cities, are thought to have the most power—that is, the ability to make or break a show. The reason for this is not because their ideas about what constitutes good theater or good acting necessarily influence anyone reading them; rather, the cost of putting on a production may be so great that, if the backers fear that not enough theatergoers will fill the seats, they will close down a show early in order to cut their potential losses. Movie critics, on the other hand, have very little sway with the reading public. Consider the fact that certain actors—among them, Bruce Willis and Sylvester Stallone—have never received favorable reviews, yet so many of their action films rake in hundreds of millions of dollars. Probably, no critics have less influence than pop and rock music critics; radio and MTV airplay has far more to do with recording artists achieving popularity and brisk sales.

Art critics may have a bit more influence on their readers than film or pop music critics but not nearly as much as those reviewing theater. Beyond this, there are no documented instances of a critic irreparably damaging an artist's market or career. One recalls that many French art critics condemned the work of the impressionists but impressionism clearly triumphed and the words of its detractors have been long forgotten.

An art critic's role, as far as the interested public is concerned, is to indicate what is happening where, which is more in the line of straight journalism than opinion making. For this reason, artists should make sure that they notify the newspaper or magazine well in advance about any upcoming exhibitions and provide high-quality photographs of their work—black-and-white or color, depending upon the needs of the publication—for illustration. Getting one's name in the paper and, better yet, a picture of one's work, is what readers look for, because they are not nearly as likely to remember what the critic said as the fact that there is a current or upcoming exhibition they might like to take a look at.

This view contradicts what artists too often believe—that a critic's words are examined at length and revered by readers as gospel—and it also denies what critics themselves like to believe. Anyone who labors over words wants to believe that others will spend an equal amount of time thinking about those words. Deconstructivist critics have gone further, announcing that art itself is simply "text," which needs to be deciphered by a critic in order to be rendered intelligible by the public. It doesn't bode well for the artist, for instance, when critic Donald Kuspit writes that "it is inevitable that one acknowledge, however reluctantly—for both critic and artist—that 'the critic is artist,' in the fullest sense that the eroding idea of 'artist' retains. All the weight of meaning in the formula of their relationship is now on the critic rather than the artist." It serves the ego and the self-interest of certain critics to believe this, but only other critics of this bent and some impressionable (or insecure) artists will concur.

Counteracting the views of nonartists, a number of artists themselves have written art reviews, usually during the early stages of their careers. This exercise provides, perhaps, the fine artist's perspective on art and, in the process, makes the artist/critic known to the editors of publications that may someday publish articles about them. Sculptor Donald Judd and painters Peter Halley, Peter Plaegens and Fairfield

Porter all have written reviews of artists' exhibitions. Whether or not their criticism is superior, inferior or no different than that of nonartist reviewers is open to debate. They certainly did not write about their own shows and, as soon as they have disparaged some other artist's work, they opened themselves up to the same sort of complaints all other critics hear.

Artists do expose themselves to public scrutiny and comment when they exhibit their work, and it certainly seems unfair to put themselves in that position only to have some critic render a negative judgment. However, critics also expose themselves publicly when they discuss and offer their opinions on an artist's work. Readers are perfectly able to determine whether or not a critic has exercised sound reasoning and shown sufficient knowledge or understanding. Critics don't simply say, "I like it" or "I don't like it," and it is the explanations for their comments on which they are judged.

It is true that critics (and the public in general) may not understand what the artist is attempting to say in his or her artwork. Once a work of art is exhibited publicly, it is open to the ideas and interpretations of anyone who sees it; in effect, it no longer belongs to the artist in the sense that the artist is the final source of meaning but, rather, it becomes the property of the world. However they may want to, artists cannot control how their work is perceived. Critics are the most visible target of an artist's sense of, and frustration with, losing control. Artists certainly do not lose any of their power, because that power exists within the work itself, and someone else's opinions do not really affect what the artwork is.

It is best for artists to understand that, in all but the rarest instances, negative criticism isn't personal. Critics may write unfavorably about exhibits or artists because they prefer a different style or type of art— no one newspaper or magazine reviewer can be so knowledgeable and objective about all the art, past and present, he or she is required to write about that the critic can comfortably judge it equally. As Lawrence Alloway, the critic who coined the term "pop art" has described, most art writers are only interested in artists of their own generation as "[t]he critic's entrance into the art world also becomes a cutoff point."

Foundations, corporations and governmental agencies that provide grants or commission art each have their own idiosyncratic way of deciding who gets what. It is best to keep in mind that more people, including artists and critics, have been historically unhappy with the selections so-called experts and judges have made than pleased with them. The "Salon des Refusés" in 1863, for instance, best known for introducing the world to Édouard Manet's painting Le déjeuner sur *l'herbe*, was created by decree of the French government after the official salon (the Royal Academy of Painting and Sculpture) rejected a record 4,000-plus paintings. The Nazi regime in Germany, on the other hand, wanted to determine public judgment on contemporary art, creating a hostile "Degenerate Art" exhibit of European modernist painting for people to scoff at while lauding other official art exhibitions, now-forgotten pictures of hardworking Aryan laborers and patriots.

Errors in judgment, of course, are not limited to Europeans. The federal government of the United States thought so little of the artwork created under the Federal Artists Project of the Works Progress Administration that it baled thousands of canvases (by such artists as Adolph Gottlieb, Jackson Pollock and Mark Rothko), storing them in a mildewed state at a warehouse in the Flushing section of Queens, New York, and later selling them at an auction for four cents a pound to a junkman in 1944—the junkman and the antique dealers who bought canvases from him at $3 or $4 apiece all did much better than the government.

᙮

CHAPTER 6

Kindred Spirits

*B*Y THE NATURE OF THEIR PROFESSION, artists tend to be loners who use solitude as a means of collecting their thoughts and finding the right visual means to express them. However, working in isolation for too long can prove personally wearisome and even become a detriment to one's art, as art is a form of communication with others and not solely a conversation with oneself. For this reason, artists over the centuries have frequently banded together in some way, meeting in particular cafés or studios to create or talk about their art or just commiserate together.

Increasingly, the tendency of artists groups is less to define a specific style of art than to provide encouragement, instruction, information, camaraderie, career assistance, or opportunities for exhibition and sale of their work. Throughout the country, there are hundreds of artist clubs, local, regional and national societies for painters and sculptors, artist-run art spaces and cooperative galleries as well as membership organizations that offer services to artists. They each have somewhat different reasons for being, and artists may select the groups that best meet their particular needs.

Support Groups for Artists

Artists have a variety of very tangible needs—among them, art materials, time to work, a studio in which to work and a place to exhibit their work—and some less tangible ones, too. Inspiration (or one can just say ideas) and confidence in their own creativity are no less essential but are more difficult to discuss in a general way because these come from within. Where Jackson Pollock got the idea to wave a stick full of paint at a canvas on the floor, and how he allowed himself to exhibit these drip paintings are among the great questions of twentieth-century art.

The desire to create a supportive environment for creators has become more widespread since the early 1990s, as hundreds of artist support groups around the country have sprouted. In addition, a growing number of psychotherapists have begun to specialize in arts-related issues, leading groups or working with individuals. Although it cannot be guaranteed that one emerges a Jackson Pollock, artists may feel more understood, part of a community and more confident in the pursuit of their art.

Perhaps the most ubiquitous of these groups are the Artist's Way groups, which have taken their name and inspiration from Julia Cameron's 1992 *The Artist's Way*, a book offering a 12-step program for discovering one's creative self. A second book by Cameron, published in 1996 and called *The Vein of Gold*, has also inspired a growing number of Vein of Gold groups, primarily composed of people who have been in Artist's Way groups. Artist's Way groups, according to Cameron, are "peer-run circles—'creative clusters'—where people would serve each other as believing mirrors, uniting with the common aim of creative unblocking."

Although called the Artist's Way, there is no requirement for group members to be visual artists, composers or performers, writers or involved in some other recognized art activity. One may be creative in every field, and "group members often include bankers, salesmen, teachers, housewives, lawyers, someone who runs a café," Cameron said. "The support you get is more diverse. It's better than a group of just painters, who may all agree that you can't show this-or-that kind of work. Someone in the group who isn't a painter and doesn't share the tribal assumptions of artists, may say, 'Well, why can't you show it or show it somewhere else?' and that gets people to thinking about what they can do instead of what they can't."

Artist's Way groups are not franchised, run by teachers accredited by Julia Cameron or any institution, but are formed by people who have read and been moved by the book. Each group's makeup will be different, but they all follow the same basic tenets laid out in the book: There are "Morning Pages," in which one fills three pages with stream-of-consciousness writing in longhand (in order to overcome one's natural "censor" or "critic"); group members look for and assess their personal strengths and passions (to discover the type of creative work they individually seek to accomplish); and there is a "reframing" of past failures into current strengths (in order to learn from one's mistakes and "minimize one's aversion to risk").

While many Artist's Way groups are "peer-run," some are led by therapists and others who may charge a fee for running the sessions. Who leads the group, how it is led and the fact of paying someone to lead may change in subtle or unsubtle ways the nature of the experience for group members. Mark Bryan, who cofounded the Artist's Way workshops with Cameron, noted that "groups that are led rather than convened are acceptable as long as they adhere to the principles outlined in the book. However, one should ask of everyone who teaches the Artist's Way groups, 'Have you been through the process and gained something from it?' and 'Are you currently involved in some creative endeavor?' The Artist's Way is supposed to be about a group dynamic that is nonhierarchical."

Bryan and others stress that there is a significant difference between Artist's Way and psychotherapy groups as the focus of the Artist's Way is on solutions rather than an airing of problems. "In psychotherapy groups, you are verbally processing thoughts and feelings," said Terrell Smith, a massage therapist in Boulder, Colorado, who has run Artist's Way groups since 1993. "In Artist's Way groups, we celebrate creativity together." Carol Floyd, a bookseller in Akron, Ohio, who has run Artist's Way groups intermittently since 1995, noted that there is less advice offered in an Artist's Way group than in therapeutic groups. "No one says, 'You ought to leave your husband,' or something like that," she said. "People offer each other options, saying something like, 'I know how you feel. My husband used to do that, and here's what I did.'" Some of the same issues may come up at an Artist's Way group as at a therapeutic group, Mark Bryan added. "An Artist's Way group won't solve a history of child abuse, but it may give one a voice in order to express it. The focus is how do you turn a complaint into a creative work."

As groups are not under the control of an organization, there is no one place to find an existing Artist's Way group. Some people who form groups take out advertisements in alternative newspapers or put up a notice at a bookstore where *The Artist's Way* is sold. One may write for information about how to form an Artist's Way group to Cameron's office (Power & Light, P.O. Box 1349, Taos, NM 87571, 505/751-2156 or 505/758-5424) or to Cameron in care of the publisher of her two books (Tarcher Publishing, G. P. Putnam Sons, 200 Madison Avenue, New York, NY 10016, 212/951-8577, *http://www.putnam.com*—click on Artist's Way). There is an Artist's Way bulletin board on America Online, which may be found through the keyword "Exchange," then click on

"Home/Health/Careers" and then "Support Groups, scrolling down for Artist's Way (much of the information consists of Julia Cameron's schedule of workshops). One may also make a Web site search, using as keywords "Artist's Way" or "Arts" or "Cameron." Some Artist's Way groups on the Internet discuss individuals' problems and solutions, following the program as much as possible.

Before writing her book, Julia Cameron attended meetings of Arts Anonymous, a group founded in 1984 that similarly focuses on overcoming mental blocks and other reasons that artists' lives are out of balance. Arts Anonymous (P.O. Box 175, Ansonia Station, New York, NY 10023, 212/873-7075, *http://www2.cybernex.net/~jaymark/arts*), modeled specifically after Alcoholics Anonymous and other 12-step programs, is designed to help artists who are "addicted to avoiding their art" for one reason or another, according to Jill F. (the last names of 12-step program members are always initialized), the organization's executive director. "Basically, the person's relationship with art is not as they would wish. They may avoid their art—we refer to the 'anorexia of avoidance,' in which people martyr themselves to their art—while some people do art night and day, neglecting their jobs and families. Some people who come to our meetings simply have no community in the art world, and others want to be involved in a spiritual program."

There are between 80 and 100 meetings of Arts Anonymous in existence at any one time and may be found in most major cities in the United States. Just as with the Artist's Way, Arts Anonymous offers members a "safe" place to discuss their desire to create art, free from critiques and other judgments and with no promises of fame or fortune as artists. Members are "encouraged to create art on a daily basis—that's our road to sobriety," said Abigail B., the founder of Arts Anonymous, who describes herself as a painter/sculptor/writer. "I have talents in many areas. We all have a basket of gifts."

Many Arts Anonymous members also have a basket of problems, as the majority of them previously have been through other 12-step programs, Abigail B. noted. Jill F., for instance, had attended Alcoholics Anonymous and Al-Anon meetings before joining this program, and others are veterans of programs to combat overeating, drug abuse and more. "They have other problems," Abigail B. said, "and they come to Arts Anonymous because they have found that 12-step programs work."

Having a specific leader or following Julia Cameron's book or the catechism of Arts Anonymous is useful for many peer groups, which "often fall apart in a short period of time when they have no guidelines for dealing with conflict between members," said Dale Schwartz, director of the New England Art Therapy Institute, where artists are treated individually and in guided support groups.

Support groups differ from membership organizations, societies and associations in that the people involved in these groups are not specifically uniting to put on a juried show, lobby lawmakers for certain issues, gain credentials in the field or develop services for other artists. An artist's support group does not judge members' work but provides encouragement and emotional sustenance. "The primary reason that people come to us is because they are so isolated as artists," said Ivan Barnett, a Santa Fe, New Mexico, sculptor who, with two other people (a psychotherapist and a financial advisor), runs the support group Artist's Solutions (2202 Camino Rancho Siringo, Santa Fe, NM 87505, 505/471-1014). "Someone may not have a burning problem or a question; they just want to be in a place where there's another artist. And, when you're in an artists' mecca like Santa Fe, that's really saying something about why we're needed." He noted that while some people talk about mental blocks at Artist's Solutions meetings, as they do at gatherings of Artist's Way and Arts Anonymous, "that's not all we talk about. Some people want ideas on how to get their artwork into a gallery—very nuts-and-bolts stuff. Other people want to network and just make friends."

Barnett called Artist's Way groups "too therapeutic in its approach," but noted that the reason Artist's Solutions has a psychotherapist co-director is because "some people's problems are of a psychological nature." Distinguishing between specifically creative problems (such as a mental block) and issues not peculiar to artists (a personality disorder, for instance) is not a simple matter. Perhaps, a mental block is the result of deep-seated trauma or the inability to overcome a reproving parent, and overcoming the block may be only the first step in resolving another problem. Treating the symptom is not the way to gain mental health, which may occur when personal problems are treated as artistic ones. One's background and how one generally deals with problems are what leads an individual to either a support group or to a therapist in the first place, and it may be just the treatment of a problem that differs from one to another. Artist support groups, such as Artist's Way, are about "creating the nurturing environment that makes it possible to be creative," Cameron said, but they won't cure personal trauma. In fact, Carol Floyd noted, someone in an Artist's Way group who describes a significant psychological problem "will be directed to get professional help outside the group."

A number of therapists around the United States work with artists of all disciplines and media, either in support groups or as individual clients, and one may find them through the associations to which they belong, such as the American Psychological Association (750 First Street, N.E., Washington, D.C. 20002-4242, 202/336-5500, 800/964-2000 for tie-line to state psychological associations) and the American Art Therapy Association, 1202 Allanson Road, Mundelein, IL 60060, 847/949-6064, *http://www.arttherapy.org* for state chapter groups). A third organization whose members offer relevant help is the Performing Arts Medicine Association (c/o Dr. Ralph Manchester, 250 Crittenden Boulevard, Box 617, Rochester, NY 14642, 716/275-2679). The association's resource directory includes mental-health professionals who work with visual as well as performing artists. All of these associations provide lists of appropriate therapists in one's area.

Art therapy and therapy for artists are not synonymous. Art therapy uses art-making activities as a way to help people describe their feelings who may not be able to express them in words, and it has been used frequently used for trauma victims and children. However, it is the understanding of both how images reflect an artist's feelings and the artistic process in general that leads artists of all media and disciplines to art therapists for counseling and support. The major drawback to art therapy as opposed to other mental health practitioners is that most art therapists are not covered by insurance.

"Most art therapists have artist patients," said Beth Gonzalez-Delinko, an art therapist and president of the New York Art Therapy Association. "Some artists can't do purely verbal therapy and are more comfortable with their images than with words. Through examining their work—the use of space, the subject matter, color—you can discover the artists' personality." She added that, in general, artists come to therapy for the same reasons that most other people seek out a therapist—relationships and family issues.

Dale Schwartz noted that it is not important whether the people taking part in her creativity groups or in one-on-one sessions are professional or amateur artists, as "art-making becomes a metaphor for increasing consciousness of our own patterns. The art activities we do allow participants to go deep within themselves for renewal and regeneration in their own expression." As in Artist's Way, creativity has a larger meaning than the completion of a work of art, and the approach is forward-looking rather than focusing on one's history or childhood. There are instances, however, when Schwartz works with artists on specifically art-related concerns, such as an art project that has become overwhelming to the individual "or how to regain their artistic inspiration."

Many other mental health practitioners who are not specifically art therapists also may examine artwork as part of their work with artists.

"The biggest problem with artists is that they are nonverbal and, consequently, you don't see many of them as patients," said Hyman Weitzen, a psychiatrist in Miami, Florida, who has treated a number of artists over the years, frequently using their artwork in place of talking therapy. One of Jackson Pollock's psychiatrists, Joseph L. Henderson, also made artwork a substantial element of his sessions, writing later that "Since he was extremely unverbal, we had great trouble in finding a common language and I doubted I could do much to help him. Communication was, however, made possible by his bringing in a series of drawings illustrating the experiences he had been through. They seemed to demonstrate phases of his sickness."

Richard Rice, a psychiatrist in Northampton, Massachusetts, who also has a Masters of Fine Arts degree in sculpture, noted that he encourages his patients to draw (or write a poem or a song) because "these images come from their feelings, which is what you're really trying to get at. I don't have to interpret the images too much but just let the patient talk about the images and see where it goes." The particular image itself may only be important in itself as a starting point for a discussion. "The patient and I are trying to tell a story, and the images are markers or signifiers in that story."

Many in the mental health field follow a psychological definition of art. According to Jay Harris, a New York psychiatrist, "art is a resolution of conflicts, and in a work of art we see both the conflict and the way in which it is resolved. When I look at my artist patients' work, I see how they resolve conflicts in their art and, by extension, in their lives."

Artists frequently worry that, through a therapists' tinkering with their personalities, their art will be significantly and irrevocably altered. Rice pointed out that "some artists are afraid that, if they resolve some conflicts, they won't have anything left to do their artwork with. I've generally found that getting some help for your problems has never hurt anyone and is usually helpful." Still, there is the famous example of German Expressionist Oskar Kokoschka, who for a time painted pictures of flowers while a patient of Sigmund Freud. Jay Harris also noted that the colors of one of his patient's paintings began to reflect his office decor, which is beige. Looking around his office, he said, "I think it looks nice."

Social Encounters

There are many professional and emotional reasons why people in the arts want to find one another, but sometimes the interest is purely social. Evening hours at art museums or the Baltimore Museum of Art's once-a-month "Single Sundays" add more opportunities than may be found solely at art gallery openings and seem safer than bars or gymnasiums. There is also a nationwide dating service—Art Lovers Exchange (ALX, Box 265 HA, Bensalem, PA 19020, 800/342-5250)—that arranges get-togethers for twos or groups at art galleries, museums and elsewhere.

Ann Keesee, president and founder of Art Lovers Exchange, noted that "I have been an art lover all my life. I should have been an interior designer but, to please my father, I became an accountant," which was her profession for 32 years. Most of her members are between 32 and 48, including many divorced or widowed women looking for a second husband. "It's hard to find older men, whether they like it or not," she said.

While she hasn't helped herself to any of the available men in her club, Art Lovers Exchange has indirectly provided her with a steady date in the form of an attorney whom "I went to because of my problems in trying to run this club." Keesee said that unattached club members have had success, including a 58-year-old widow who met a 63-year-old retiree. "That was our first marriage, though I have heard about a number of other alliances." The newlyweds' common interest was Spanish art, and they "honeymooned in Madrid so they could go to the Prado" museum, she added.

Art Lovers Exchange has been in existence since the early 1980s. Few other dating services stay in operation for that many years (Classical Music Lovers Exchange is the only other exception in the arts), and a growing number of people in the arts and elsewhere are meeting each other online, such as on an artist's home page or on an organization's Web site chat room.

Meeting strangers, regardless of the context and circumstance, implies a certain degree of risk. Susan De Monco, a painter in Swamscott, Massachusetts, who had "wanted to meet another artist," described a "scary experience" with someone she briefly dated through the now-defunct Art Lovers Network. "No one ever tells the whole truth that you meet in dating services, but that's par for the course," she said. "But this man started telling one lie after another. He hadn't gone to Boston University as he said. He told me he worked undercover for the CIA, and that the CIA had given him an assumed name. The story just got more and more bizarre and, when I confronted him on his lies, he threatened to set the CIA on me. I called Art Lovers Network to tell them what had happened to me, but I never heard from anyone there again."

Patricia Moore, president of the International Society of Introductory

Services, noted that there is "no absolute way of knowing that someone you meet through a service is undesirable," but added that a reputable dating service should have some screening process that limits the likelihood of predatory people becoming members. Online meetings have fewer safeguards, and one must exercise the same caution as with any other total stranger.

Art Clubs and Societies

Many artists also look for others with whom they can create art. "Most of our members join for the 'paint-outs,' when people get together once a week and paint," Maxine White of the Delta Watercolor Society of Stockton, California, said, adding that 10 members on the average are on hand for the weekly paint-out sessions. The approximately 75 members of the society get together for the five annual business meetings, which usually include painting demonstrations by outside professional artists, as well as for the three annual member exhibitions that take place at a local bank.

At the New Rochelle (New York) Art Association, the Iowa Watercolor Society and the Shenandoah Valley Watercolor Society, the emphasis is less on creating together than on talking about one's work with other artists. "People are pretty isolated out here," Jo Myers-Walker, a past president of the Iowa Watercolor Society, said, "and we exist so that people don't feel they're completely alone. When I was president, I was contacted by members who called up to say 'I've done a really good painting today.' They just needed someone they could talk to about it."

Both the Iowa Watercolor Society and the New Rochelle Art Association provide newsletters to their members in order to keep them abreast of news in the field, such as which member is having an exhibit where and providing tips on techniques. Once a month, the New Rochelle group holds meetings that give its 150 members a chance to talk about their own work as well as watch a demonstration by a professional artist. The group's four member shows and large annual juried competition provide additional opportunities for members to discuss what they and others are currently doing. For its part, the Iowa Watercolor Society schedules a weeklong workshop during its annual juried exhibit for members to learn from a professional artist.

The monthly meetings of the Shenandoah Valley Watercolor Society are intended to provide support and technical advice to artists in the group, according to Mary Ann Baugher, a past officer of the group. Members often bring in their paintings for group critiques; those who have recently attended a workshop will discuss what they learned; and, on occasion, an art professor will be invited to speak to members. Baugher noted that she also belongs to the Virginia Watercolor Society. "They have an annual juried show, which is very good, but there really is no opportunity to meet fellow members," she said. "Meeting other members and talking about their work is what a lot of us need and want."

Most clubs and societies hold at least one exhibition per year, perhaps featuring the work of members or juried competitively, and this is another compelling reason for someone to join. Singly, an artist may not find a venue in which to exhibit his or her work but, in a group that sponsors its own shows, there is a chance for personal recognition and the prestige that may be attached to the particular society. Eligibility and membership costs for artist clubs and societies vary widely. Some allow all comers, while others require jurying in or a different kind of admissions process. The Shenandoah Valley and Delta watercolor societies, for instance, permit anyone to join, requiring only the annual dues of $25 and $18, respectively. Membership in the Suffield, Connecticut-based Academic Artists Association, on the other hand, requires acceptance into two of the group's juried exhibitions within a four-year period as well as the $15 annual fee.

There are three levels of membership to the Florida Watercolor Society, starting at associate membership, "which can be anyone who is a Florida resident and wants to pay $20 to be a member," James Koevenig, a past president of the organization, said. A participating member, who is allowed to vote for officers, policies and venues for the society's annual juried exhibition, must have had one painting in a juried show. A signature member, one allowed to use the society's initials (FWS) after his or her name, must have been accepted into three juried exhibits.

The use of the signature letters after one's name is more likely to carry weight for those artists who are members of recognized national, as opposed to regional or local, societies. The National Sculpture Society, for example, is a well-recognized association of artists from all over the United States who work in a variety of styles and materials, while the Cowboy Artists of America and the National Academy of Western Art— both of which offer signature letters to members—are more regional in focus and specific in content.

Both the American Watercolor Society and National Watercolor Society divide their members into two levels. The National Watercolor Society has both associates and signature members—the first group may join without jurying, paying $30 a year and receiving the society's newsletter, the second ($40 a year) requiring acceptance into the society's annual exhibition and then an additional jurying of three more paintings—while the American Watercolor Society has sustaining associates and active members. At the highest levels, members are permitted to include "AWS" or "NWS" after their names for professional purposes.

The National Academy of Design also has two levels of membership, both of which include signature privileges: the first is an associate member (ANA), who is proposed by a current associate and approved in an election by at least 60 percent of the entire associate membership; the second is an academician (NA), who is chosen from the associates and elected by 60 percent of the academicians. Unlike the national watercolor societies, no jurying of individual works of art or acceptance into past or current annual exhibitions is part of the entry process.

Members of the major regional and national groups claim that signature initials confer stature upon an artist and may help advance one's career. "The National Watercolor Society is a very prestigious organization, and the jurying in is so strict that to be able to put NWS after one's name is really a feather in one's cap," Meg Huntington Cajero, a past president of the society, said. "The letters NWS matter to dealers who would be more inclined to represent an artist with them, knowing that the artist has been seen as having attained a very high level of skill and accomplishment, and dealers would point out the NWS to potential collectors." Ed Gallagher, director of the National Academy of Design, also stated that "it is worthwhile for an artist to let others know how he is esteemed by others."

The degree to which signature letters appended to one's name aids an artist's career is not fully clear. James Koevenig noted that a juror for a watercolor competition is often selected on the basis of that person being a member of either the American Watercolor Society or the National Watercolor Society, but many art dealers have little reason for believing signature letters help a sale. "We've shown artists, some of whom put the letters AWS after their names, and we've shown other artists who didn't put those letters in (or may not even have been members of an organization or society, and it never seems to have made a bit of difference," Jo Chapman, owner of the Chapman Gallery in Santa Fe, New Mexico, said. "Someone may look at the signature letters and ask, 'What does that mean?' and then I explain it to him, but with most collectors, if they like something, they like something."

Lawrence diCarlo, director of the Fischbach Gallery in New York City, stated that signature letters don't mean anything to his collectors or to himself, and Frank Bernarducci, director of Tatistcheff and Company, another New York art gallery that represents artists who work in watercolor, claimed that all the signature letters may do for artists is "help keep their egos under control, perhaps." Painter Will Barnet, who is a national academician as well as a member of the American Academy of Arts and Letters and the Century Club but does not use any of these signature letters after his name, said that the letters "have more of a human value than they are a benefit to one's career. It means something to me personally that other artists have accepted my work, but it doesn't matter to people who buy my work."

The larger regional and national societies do attract more people to their annual juried exhibitions, and they contain a higher percentage of professional artists—including those who live off the sale of their artwork as well as full-time art instructors—than smaller and more local groups and clubs. The larger societies offer little to no social interaction among members, however, unless one happens to meet at the annual shows. Artists seeking more support and camaraderie would be better off looking closer to home.

The only problem in this is that one may more easily find out about the larger regional and national groups than the smaller, more local ones. *American Artist*'s annual spring watercolor issue contains a listing of the major watercolor societies in the United States and Canada. The International Sculpture Center (1050 Potomac Street, N.W., Washington, D.C. 20007, 202/965-6066), a service organization for sculptors as well as craftspeople, performance artists, and video artists, has an 11,000-member mailing list that includes local and regional sculpture societies in the United States and around the world—the Center will provide information on applicable societies for free. There are no specific sources about societies devoted to oil painting, printmaking or other art media.

Local, state and federal arts agencies can provide information on art clubs and societies in one's area. (For names, addresses and telephone numbers of these agencies, contact Americans for the Arts, 927 15th Street, N.W., Washington, D.C. 20005, 202/371-2830, or the National Assembly of State Arts Agencies, 1010 Vermont Avenue, N.W., Washington, D.C. 20005, 202/347-6352.) However, arts funding agencies are most likely to have information on groups that have previously applied for funding rather than general lists of all the clubs and societies in their domain. It is worthwhile noting that, although some of these organizations have post office box addresses, most are located at the home of the current president, and that job is usually rotated annually. One may have to make a few telephone calls before ascertaining the group's current headquarters.

Since most of these clubs and societies do eventually hold member or juried exhibitions, the venues for these shows—banks, arts centers and galleries, museums—will be able to provide contact people for the organizations. One may find out where these shows take place from editors of local newspapers that list such events. Of course, one would not wish to join any group blindly; those who are interested in being part of an artist club or society should visit the organization during a meeting or view a show that it has organized to determine whether or not one feels comfortable with the kind of work being done and the people in the group.

Miniature Art Societies

Most art clubs and societies have rather loose rules for membership. Academic Artists Association of Springfield, Massachusetts, for instance, clearly looks for traditional realists, while other groups may specify the medium, such as sculpture or watercolor painting. Their aim is to bring in as many people as possible rather than be exclusive—with the exception of selecting people who meet a certain level of artistic quality. Some groups, however, have very strict guidelines, such as the miniature art societies.

There are several societies of miniature artists in the United States—in Florida, Georgia, New Mexico and the District of Columbia—and these groups establish the rules of what a miniature is. They define miniature art, specifying the image size of a two-dimensional work to be no greater than twenty-five square inches and the largest dimension of a sculpture eight inches. They also all have a "one-sixth" rule: The image—say, a man's head—must be one-sixth the actual size of the object; larger than that disqualifies the image as a miniature. There is also an "outside-the-frame" rule for two-dimensional works—the size of the total work, including the mat and frame—that varies from one society to the next. The Washington, D.C., group only permits the entire work to be six-by-eight inches, while Florida increases that to eight-by-ten inches. In the somewhat fussy field of miniatures, the rules all have their ardent supporters and critics.

The purpose of these societies is not only to bring like artists together and provide an opportunity for exhibiting a particular type of artwork but to improve the reputation of the miniature, which has traditionally been viewed as an attractive novelty. After the development of photography in 1839, when the camera began to produce the portraits that had been the miniature artist's major activity for over a thousand years, the field of miniatures became thought of as an eccentric novelty.

As a result, the market for miniatures has been relatively small.

Many collectors tend to see miniatures as fun and decorative but not necessarily as serious art for which they should pay serious art money. Margaret Wisdom, who is secretary of the Miniature Art Society of America, noted that most art galleries also show no interest in exhibiting these works. Among the reasons for this is the fact that they would have to raise prices—currently averaging between $35 and $100 per object—considerably to cover their own commissions, and that would turn off potential customers. Affordability tends to be a major consideration, because no collector buys just one painting to hang on the wall—a wall of any size would swallow up a tiny picture. Buyers frequently purchase five or ten or more, grouping them together to fill up the space that a larger picture would cover. Affordability also tends to work against artists in the miniature field, as hardly any are able to make a living from selling only miniatures.

Most self-supporting artists who create miniatures, in fact, earn their livelihood from larger, more expensive artworks that may not sell as quickly but bring in far more money. "It's a challenge," said Connie Ward Woolard of Silver Springs, Maryland. "It's a whole different approach than what I otherwise do, which is very large. It appealed to me to try something very, very tiny." Her miniature acrylic on watercolor paper scenes of barns, Victorian houses, small-town street scenes and landscapes range in size from one-and-a-half-by-one-and-a-half-inches to four-by-six inches, while a mural she orchestrated on Courthouse Square in Rockville, Maryland, measured 90 feet long and 10 feet high. To Woolard, miniatures represent "a break from other, paying projects."

Art gallery owners have also expressed reluctance to handle miniatures because of the difficulty in providing adequate security for tiny objects. "Miniatures are also very easy to steal, and that also concerns dealers," Wisdom said. "You can put one into your pocket and walk right out the door. A dealer can solve that problem by wiring the work to the wall or putting the work under glass, but that is an additional problem that most normal-sized artwork doesn't face."

The larger art world has also not tended to take miniatures seriously because of the low prices and the fact that many miniature paintings are sold with little brass easels for display on coffee tables—more frequently sold by interior decorators than through art galleries. There are some art galleries around the country that handle miniatures, although most collectors tend to follow the arts and crafts shows that either specialize in or include miniatures as a special category. The miniature art societies themselves have helped foster sales for members by sponsoring annual exhibitions, and many artists join these groups—

frequently more than one society—simply in order to have a place to show these works to the public. Richard Haynes, who belongs to the miniature art societies of Florida and Georgia, noted that "you get to put three works in a show if you're a member, as opposed to only one piece if you're a nonmember." Residency in a particular state is clearly not a factor in membership.

Prices tend to be higher at the shows than at most galleries, sometimes reaching several thousand dollars per work, because the best work by the nation's top miniaturists is there. There is no directory of galleries representing miniatures or of arts and crafts shows featuring these works. The best way to find out where these galleries or shows are is by reading the newsletters of the various societies:

Miniature Art Society of Florida
Jeanne Boyers, P.O. Box 867, Dunedin, FL 34698

Miniature Art Society of Georgia
P.O. Box 75, Marietta, GA 30061-0075

New Mexico Miniature Arts Society
Betty Morgan, P.O. Box 2928, Roswell, NM 88201
(505) 624-2755

Miniature Art Society of America
1595 North Peaceful Lane, Clearwater, FL 34616

Miniature Painters, Sculptors, Gravers Society of Washington, D.C.
Margaret Wisdom, 5612 Massachusetts Ave., Bethesda, MD 20816
(301) 229-2463

The most common forms of miniatures in the crafts field tend to be utilitarian objects—although, of course, they are too small to be actually used—such as ceramic vases, jewelry, painted cigarette and jewelry boxes and wooden furniture. This utilitarian focus has meant that these objects are sought after for dollhouses and, in fact, the main market for miniature crafts has been at dollhouse shows, which take place at various venues around the country. (Among the best sources of information for upcoming dollhouse shows are the monthly publications *Art Calendar* and *Sunshine Artists*.)

An added benefit of belonging to one of the miniaturist societies is having a group of fellow artists with whom to compare notes on such matters as which materials are best for painstakingly small work and how to handle some of the physical discomforts of miniature work. For instance, some artists use jewelers' caps, which contain a magnifying lens and a lamp, to enable them to see what they are doing; as it is an unwritten rule of miniature societies that the object must look as highly detailed under a microscope as to the naked eye, the ability to work with great precision is essential. Obviously, a miniature painter must forget about broad brush strokes and have a delicate hand with a firm wrist. The traditional techniques of working small in paint are hatching (using fine lines to indicate shading), pointillism (dots) and stippling (dots, in a more generic sense), and this requires rather small brushes with tiny, fine points. Jane Mihalik, a painter in Basye, Virginia, needs an ongoing supply of new brushes with few bristles, while Louis Stern of Washington, D.C., prefers "small watercolor or acrylic brushes," even though he paints in oils, "because you can't get that much of a point in an oil brush."

Artists who create miniatures in other media must simply be careful or inventive. Bob Best of Great Falls, Virginia, whose miniature collages are three-by-five inches, has a "drawerful of tiny scissors" and otherwise makes use of tweezers to hold the image he is cutting out or pasting down. Margaret Wisdom, who fashions miniature animal motif sculptures in ceramics and wood, has used dental tools or whittled twigs in order to fashion her own tools for carving and shaping.

Working small may be more physically taxing than working large. Get-togethers of miniaturists frequently lead to conversations about work-related ailments and methods to relieve them. "Working this small gives me headaches," said Richard Haynes of Fairfield, New Jersey, whose oil and watercolor paintings average three-by-three-and-a-half inches in size. "After a long day of painting—and I put in some very long days—I can't focus on the TV in the evening. I listen to it and watch the colors. By morning, everything is back in focus again, thank God." Jane Mihalik agreed, noting that "it's very tough on the back. You have to be very still, sort of scrunched over. After a little while of this, I need a heating pad, or my husband will have to give me a back massage."

Nature and Wildlife Art

There are many different genres in the art world, all with their own societies, rules and venues. As with the miniature art societies, acceptance into juried exhibitions enables one to apply for membership, and membership confers a broader recognition among would-be collectors. To apply for associate membership into the American

Academy of Equine Art, for instance, "you must have been accepted into three shows," said Werner Rentsch, president of the group. "For full membership, you must be a full-time practicing artist who paints horses, not just a landscape painter who includes a horse now and then." Other organizations, such as the Cowboy Artists of America and the Society of Animal Artists, make no requirements of having been in previous shows but make their decisions on the basis of the strength of the applicant's submitted slides as well as, in the case of the Cowboy Artists, history of earnings from selling western art in the realistic style of Frederic Remington and Charles Marion Russell.

Acceptance into one of these societies does not make an artist's career, but they reflect the place that one has earned in the eyes of his or her peers, which may bolster an artist's standing with the buying public. These groups also have newsletters, meetings and other ways of keeping members abreast of opportunities and events in their fields. Magazines, such as *The Equine Image*, *Southwest Art*, *U.S. Art* and *Wildlife Art*, are also devoted to these genres and frequently include the main galleries in the United States where these types of work are sold to the public, while R.R. Bowker's *The Official Museum Directory* lists the institutions that specialize in showing these works.

Among the main societies of specialty artists in the United States are:

American Academy of Equine Art
P.O. Box 1315, Middleburg, VA 22117
(540) 687-6701; e-mail: *WadeAAEA@AOL.com*
http://www.horseworld.com/IMH/AAEA/Home.html

American Society of Marine Artists
1461 Cathy's Lane, North Wales, PA 19454
(215) 283-0888

Audubon Artists
32 Union Square East, Room 1214, New York, NY 10003
(212) 260-5706

Cowboy Artists of America
P.O. Box 396, Blue Springs, MO 64013
(816) 224-2244

Guild of National and Scientific Illustrators
P.O. Box 652, Ben Franklin Station, Washington, D.C. 20044
(301) 762-0189

National Sculptors Guild
2683 North Taft Avenue, Loveland, CO 80538
(907) 667-2015

Society of Animal Artists
47 Fifth Avenue, New York, NY 10003
(212) 741-2880

Western Academy of Women Artists
1550 North Stapley Drive, Mesa, AZ 85203
(602) 834-1201

Wildlife Artist Association
5042 Casitas Pass Road, Ventura, CA 93001
(805) 649-3914

Women Artists of the West
15455 Glenoaks Boulevard, Sylmar, CA 91342
(818) 362-4941
or
31061 Via Limón, San Juan Capistrano, CA 92975
(714) 496-2628

For artists of specialty genres, the most practical way of earning recognition in the field is winning an art competition—among them, the Prix de West award for cowboy artists, and Arts for the Parks or the federal duck stamp awards for nature and wildlife artists.

Every year since 1934, the United States Fish and Wildlife Service of the federal Department of Interior holds its annual duck stamp competition, selecting one painted image of a duck that will be used on a stamp, which every waterfowl hunter in the country must purchase and affix to his or her hunting permit. In 1996, 477 artists submitted their work for this annual event. The award for the artist whose work is selected by the judges of this contest isn't monetary, but recent winners tend to earn upwards of half a million dollars from the sale of prints of the artwork to wildlife art collectors as well as receive name recognition that lasts for years and years. Winners will have ready buyers for their original paintings and prints for their other wildlife images and, at a higher price range, they will receive commissions and the opportunity to license their images for use on calendars, clocks, clothing, coasters, note cards, puzzles, outdoor thermometers, and anything else.

"Before I won the contest," said Wilhelm Goebel of Somerset, New Jersey, who submitted paintings to the duck stamp competition for 17 years before winning in 1995, "I made a good living as a wildlife artist, maybe averaging $40,000 or $50,000 a year. But after I won, that was a different story. People call to commission me to paint something, like International Ducks Unlimited. Customers keep coming back wanting more. I'm now virtually out of originals—I've got nothing left. Usually, I paint between 20 or 30 works a year, and some of them are slower to sell than others, but now there's nothing in stock."

Managing this influx of money itself becomes a second career, so much so that Phil Scholer of Cassen, Minnesota, who won in 1983 and grossed "considerably more than $1 million" from the print sales of that duck stamp image, took time off from his painting in order to "make critical choices concerning my investments. That's very time consuming on the front end." Both he and Dan Smith of Bozeman, Montana, who won in 1988 and also earned in excess of $1 million, assembled their own investment teams, consisting of an accountant, lawyer and financial planner.

Managing one's time also becomes a major activity as duck stamp winners are courted by print publishers, art fair organizers, charities and entrepreneurs, "all of whom want to make money from your work," Scholer said. "You have to pick and choose carefully among all these people who are coming to you for one reason or another. There is a Queen-for-the-Day aspect to this contest—really Queen-for-the-Year— because of all the exposure you receive. You can run victory laps every day of the year."

After establishing his investment portfolio and participating in a variety of events, Scholer reduced his annual output of paintings from 20 to 12 or so, raising his prices and turning some of them into limited-edition prints. Dan Smith, on the other hand, used his duck stamp notoriety to "help me make the transition from duck stamp artist to limited-edition print artist." Between 1983 and 1990, Smith had earned the majority of his income from winning commissions and competitions for duck, pheasant and turkey stamps on the state level (Alaska, Arizona, Arkansas, Georgia, Minnesota, New Jersey, New Mexico, South Carolina, Texas, Utah, and West Virginia, among others) and internationally (Australia, United Kingdom). The award amounts varied widely, from $10,000 to $100,000, and he created three or four stamps per year.

After winning the federal duck stamp competition and his own year of running "victory laps," Smith became a more prolific painter, creating pieces that could be sold as originals and made into prints, and entering the more general category of wildlife artist. "I've always painted with an eye for how it will look as a print," he said. "But, whereas I probably earned 80 percent of my income from prints and licensing and 20 percent from selling originals before winning the federal duck stamp, now the ratio is more like 60 percent prints and 40 percent originals. Winning gave me the opportunity to be a more complete artist."

Winning the contest also has had a magical effect on the careers of three brothers, all wildlife artists, in Minnesota—Jim Hautman, who won in 1989 and 1994, Joe Hautman, the 1991 winner, and Bob Hautman, who won in 1996. Both Bob and Jim had earned the same amount of money as Goebel prior to winning and, like Goebel, had submitted entries for years. Joe had also sent in duck paintings for four years before winning but, unlike his brothers, he was a hobbyist and not a full-time practicing artist and the duck picture was his entire artistic output for the year. "It was good that the contest had a deadline, because that forced me to have something to show for the year," he said. Joe was a physicist, working as a postdoctoral researcher on theoretical condensed matter in the chemistry department of the University of Pennsylvania, when he received word that he had won the contest. Within a year and a half, having earned $500,000 from prints of the duck stamp image, he had left the academy for good for the life of a full-time artist.

"In some ways, it has been a great transition," he said. "In physics, there are only about six people in the world who appreciate what you are doing, and only a handful of people can understand it. Not even my family could figure out what I was doing. Now I go to shows where everyone understands what I do, and I can have informed, two-way conversations." Where the transition had been more difficult was his incomplete knowledge of painting as well as a lack of older works to sell and convert into prints. Not having a cache of other paintings is troublesome as federal duck stamp winners rarely have time to produce many more in the following year. They are invited to appear and speak at various stamp and wildlife art fairs around the country throughout the year, and the business of finding and negotiating with a print publisher is also time consuming.

"Painting was always a hobby, but one I didn't have much time for," Joe said. "After I won the duck stamp contest, I started learning how to paint, because I still had a lot of technique to figure out." Whatever technique he lacked, however, did not deter several individual and corporate collectors as well as the state wildlife agencies of New Jersey and Texas from commissioning him (the state agencies sought stamp images).

All of the states have their own game and nongame (eagle, for instance) stamps, for which there are either commissions or competitions open to anyone around the country. Bob Hautman won the Minnesota duck stamp contest in 1987, and his brother Jim won it in 1989—Jim also won duck stamp contests in Delaware and Nevada in 1988. "Winning the state contests gave me some recognition and helped sell my work," Jim said. "I could start to afford better art supplies, but winning mostly let me see that I could make a living at this."

All three brothers contracted with Wild Wings, a wildlife print publisher in Lake City, Minnesota, to produce limited-edition prints of their duck stamp and other wildlife images. As Jim was the first big winner in the family, he had the earliest contact with Wild Wings and advised both of his brothers to sign with the publisher as well as make other career moves. Wild Wings, which has marketed most of the federal duck stamp prints over the past 12 years, sends out direct mail catalogs to five million individuals and art galleries in the United States and Canada, selling prints (between $95 and $250), some original paintings (between $1,000 and $50,000) and wildlife bronze statues (between $3,000 and $40,000). Sara Koller, art merchandising manager at Wild Wings, stated that the size of a federal duck stamp limited-edition print is 12,000–13,000 copies, down from 25,000 a few years ago.

There are differing reasons given for the decline in the size of these editions. Koller noted that "interest is down. It used to be that duck stamp winners earned a million dollars from these prints, but now it's really more like half a million." However, Terry Bell, special events coordinator at the United States Fish and Wildlife Service who runs the actual duck stamp competition, said that publishers have started to rein in the number of prints they put in circulation: "You can't print thousands and thousands of these prints and still call them limited editions. People start to realize all that's limited is the number of people who will buy them."

The Hautman brothers also contracted with MHS Marketing Consultants in Minneapolis to license their images. Marty Segelbaum, president of the company, noted that he is principally licensing "their combined work as the Hautman Brother Collection rather than as individual images. I'm not an image house, although I may license out just one image for a calendar. I'm trying for long-term relations." Among those licenses are one for throw blankets, clocks and even turning a duck stamp image into three-dimensional sculpture. With licensing deals that include guarantees and royalties, Segelbaum projected earnings for the three brothers in the six figures.

Learning how to paint wildlife in this exacting manner takes times and study, which is perhaps a reason that many artists submit work to the federal duck stamp and other contests for years before finding any success. Terry Bell noted that "many of the winners have a background in commercial art, and it shows. They know how to make something clean and informative." In order to better his chances of winning, Goebel began attending the judging of the contest, which is open to the public and takes place in an auditorium at the Department of Interior. There are five different judges each year, who are selected for their knowledge in one or more categories, such as art, biology, environmental awareness, ornithology and even taxidermy. The judges are not permitted to confer with one another, "but, if you watch closely, you see what they're zeroing in on, what they tend to select, and then you study what they select. You see they want warmth and detail; they want a tight rendering and an uncluttered design. They also go for strong lighting—you can call these Hollywood ducks for the way they are spotlighted, standing out and looking alert. The judges change from year to year, but they all seem to pick the same types of work. A number of artists and I tried to analyze if there is a formula, and we couldn't, but there are ways to capture a judge's eye."

Winning the federal duck stamp contest turns little-known wildlife artists into well-known artists and well-known artists into much better-known ones. For instance, Jim Hautman was commissioned to create the national duck stamp for the Australian government. Goebel called the Fish and Wildlife Service's duck stamp a "winner-take-all" competition, as his second-place finish in 1990 did nothing to help him sell more work or receive commissions. He had won trout stamp contests in the states of Delaware, Illinois and New Jersey, "which may have been more of a psychological boost than financially rewarding. It led to some exposure, but not all that much." After attending the jurying for a number of years, he added, "I started coming in higher, finishing in the top 20 for a number of years. In 1995, I finally put all the pieces together."

The federal duck stamp is the only art competition run by the United States government. The ten-year-old Arts for the Parks competition is run by a private, nonprofit organization, National Park Academy of the Arts, in cooperation with the National Park Foundation, itself a foundation created by Congress in 1967 in order to raise private funds for the National Parks System. Between 2,000 and 3,000 artists annually submit slides of paintings that "capture the essence of the landscape, wildlife and history of the more than 300 units of our National Parks System."

Similar to the duck stamp competition, Arts for the Parks winners receive considerable publicity and opportunities to sell their work both as originals and in limited edition prints. Unlike the federal duck stamp competition, Arts for the Parks presents a cash prize—$50,000 to the winner—and keeps the painting, which it publishes as a print and sells, using the proceeds to pay for the prize money and the costs of running the contest. Remaining money is contributed to the National Park Foundation. While the duck stamp is a winner-take-all event (those who come in second do not benefit), Arts for the Parks publishes the images of eight of the top works on a stamp and makes smaller awards to as many as 20 other artists (including $3,000 regional awards and $6,000 purchase awards). In addition, the top works each year are exhibited together at five or six museums or national park sites around the country.

Fifty thousand dollars, the largest art competition cash prize in the country, doesn't permanently change one's economic status in the same manner as winning the duck stamp competition does. Rather, it helps pay bills and upgrade one's lifestyle. Paying bills was a primary consideration for Tom Antonishak, the 1993 winner, and 1995 winner Howard Hanson "bought a few things for around the house and got Barb [his wife] a new car." Winning may also offer a psychological boost, announcing to the public that this artist has entered the top tier of artists in this field. "Winning the grand prize gave me more confidence and pride in my work," Antonishak said. "It helps you take yourself more seriously. I had a few publishers looking at my work before I won the competition. They all said, 'Very nice, we'll keep you in mind.' After the contest, they all wanted to take a second look. In the art world, people always need someone else to recognize your work first."

Painting nature or wildlife for a stamp is a highly specialized skill, requiring considerable tolerance for problems other artists rarely if ever face. "Tight realism is what we're looking for," said Terry Bell, yet much of the detailing will be lost as the image itself small, seven-inches-high by ten-inches-long—is reduced to the size of a postage stamp. Sara Koller also noted that "the market is just not as interested in any other style than a closely rendered realism. People want to see all the feathers." There is also a high premium placed on accuracy, rather than artistic license or invention, in this field, requiring artists to conduct considerable research on their subjects for both a market and jurors who are well informed. "If you make a mistake anywhere, people will point it out to you at shows," Antonishak said. "It may be the wrong habitat, wrong plumage, wrong season of the year."

The market for nature and wildlife art, by all accounts, appears to be growing, comprising not only the traditional buyers (hunters and sportsmen) but environmentalists, hikers, urban dwellers with homes in the country and others who simply enjoy the outdoors. This expanding market has broadened the field of wildlife art from predominantly depictions of game animals to others that are protected by law (such as wolves and bears), creatures that are usually not hunted at all (song birds, for instance) and images that feature the landscape as much as the animals.

The market for nature and wildlife art is largely for reproductions. Spor'en Art in Sullivan, Illinois, produced Goebel's federal duck stamp print in three different limited editions, a 17,000-copy edition for $175, a 2,000-copy "medallion" version that contains a reproduction of the duck stamp contest medallion won for $350 and an "executive" edition (of 225 copies) of the duck image with the medallion as well as a hand-painted sketch by the artist in the margin for $950. When all the sales are made, Goebel expects to gross $500,000. Spor'en Art had won the right to commission and publish the duck stamp images for the states of Alaska, New Jersey, North Dakota and Virginia, and Goebel was offered those painting assignments as a "signing bonus." "I'm not a stamp artist," Goebel said, "and I don't revolve my year around ducks, but this has been a duck stamp year."

A drawback of the emphasis on reproductions is that the photo-lithographic process generally flattens images, and a number of painterly concerns are also lost. "You spend a lot of time trying to get the color just right in the painting, but you never get the same color when it is printed," Jim Hautman said, adding that he has also learned not to add texture to the painting, "since it just gets lost in the printing process anyway." In many cases, the point of the painting becomes creating an image that will reproduce well.

The focus on what will sell in quantity as a print sometimes works against artists who have otherwise achieved notoriety by winning one of these competitions. "There are some images that are very good as works of art but don't fall into the consumer category," said Lisa Laliberte-Belak, director of art publishing at Hadley House, a print publisher in Bloomington, Minnesota. "A problem may be the subject matter, for instance, a form of wildlife that is uncommon or odd, or maybe the color palette is tough to sell." She added that decorators and gallery owners are frequently asked about which colors and subjects are currently popular.

One of the artists who has proven a challenge for Hadley House is Nancy Howe, the 1991 winner of the federal duck stamp competition, for whom color and subject matter have been important issues. Laliberte-Belak noted that, after studying an entire year's output of Howe's paintings, she finds only one or two images that are potential print candidates. Hadley House has created limited-edition prints of Howe's images of kittens, swans and chickens in a henhouse, but the artist's painting of a calf sleeping in a barn wasn't usable since "people don't collect paintings of calves," and a painting of a partridge was also ruled out as "it was an odd type of partridge, and the painting was also done as a portrait, without much background." For her part, Howe said that suitability for "prints are not the measure of the quality of my painting. It isn't an art consideration."

The size of a print edition in nature and wildlife art may often be quite large, sometimes as high as 20,000, and publishers send out mail-order catalogs to several million individuals and art galleries in the United States and Canada. Without an available print edition, an artist may be largely invisible to his or her market. Rita Skoczen, the 1988 winner of the Arts for the Parks grand prize, was told by Voyager Art, the publisher for the Arts for the Parks competition, "that my picture was too serious, not decorative. They didn't want to publish it because it would never sell and they wouldn't recoup their costs." Her image featured the Vietnam Veterans Memorial in Washington, D.C. "Winning the grand prize didn't help me professionally, because I didn't get any visibility," she said, "and people didn't hear of me. The only people who saw it were those who went to the places where the painting was exhibited."

Wilhelm Goebel noted that, since winning the federal duck stamp contest and gaining financial security, he can be less dependent upon painting images suitable for prints. "I can give more time to paintings of wildlife that are artistic but maybe not so commercially viable. I've done one of a red-tailed hawk with a half-eaten rabbit in its mouth— who would want a limited-edition print of that? I'm sure it will be salable to one collector in the world, but I won't have to sell a thousand copies of it."

Co-op Galleries

Before their work enters major museum collections and is featured on the covers of important art magazines, valued in the six- and seven-figure range, artists need places to show their art. Getting a start in the art world, which involves finding an exhibition site where sales may result, is no easy task. Art galleries and dealers, who barely have time to attend to the artists they already represent, are swamped with requests by other artists to handle their work. Juried art fairs and competitions usually turn down more artists than they accept. Town arts centers, alternative art spaces, even banks and restaurants that allow artists to hang their work on the walls are also often backlogged with requests.

The battle required simply to enter the art world has led many people to band together and join cooperative art galleries, which are run (and paid for) by their artist members. Co-ops solve the where-can-I-show-my-work problem for artists, although they are less likely to lead to substantial sales. The cost of joining a co-op and paying monthly dues may prove a drain on some artists' bank accounts, and a stigma is occasionally attached to co-op artists for apparently not being good enough to get a "real" art dealer to represent them. For some artists, however, co-ops are places where careers may begin, although advancement frequently means that the artist moves on to a commercial gallery.

The A.I.R. (Artist-in-Residence) Gallery in New York City, which was founded in 1972 as a feminist cooperative, has launched a number of noted and successful artists. For some, the co-op was a clear starting point in their success, attracting the attention of collectors and commercial art dealers, while others found success coming despite their association with A.I.R. Nancy Spero, one of A.I.R.'s founding members who left the co-op in 1983, stated that her work "didn't really sell much there, but it was seen by a lot of people, including dealers who later asked me to show at their galleries." Among the benefits for her of being in a co-op were "learning how the art world worked and understanding how to pursue my own interests, not being pushed around" as well as creating art without having to keep an eye on the market. "The work I did at A.I.R. was crucial to my artistic development," said Spero, who is currently represented by New York's Josh Baer Gallery. "I wasn't worrying about sales. I was supporting myself in other ways. Being able to create and exhibit noncommercial art, and get feedback from people on it, gave me a lot of confidence when I finally went to a commercial gallery."

That freedom is not without cost, as A.I.R. requires a one time $500 acceptance fee from new members as well as monthly payments of $90 to cover the costs of heat, light, power, rent and incidentals. At other co-ops, there may also be a commission—smaller, certainly, than those charged at commercial galleries—for all pieces sold, with that money used to pay salaries or other expenses. One cannot be assured of recouping that money through sales of artwork, as co-ops are not the main stops for serious collectors and newspaper or magazine reviews of exhibits at these spaces are rare.

For Dotty Attie and Barbara Zucker, who were members of A.I.R. from 1972 to 1987 and 1972 to 1974, respectively, the opportunity to have their art exhibited, especially in the context of a politically oriented artistic cooperative was vital to their careers. "A.I.R. gave me the opportunity to show my work," Zucker, a sculptor, stated. "Once you've shown, that's a rite of passage. You have a different view of yourself once you've had a one-person exhibition, and what I also learned was how to show my work." As with Spero, dealers came to Zucker, either having seen her work at shows at the co-op or through hearing about her from those who had been to her exhibitions. Dealers also told Attie that they admired her work at the co-op ("I always remembered those dealers and had a warm feeling for their galleries," she said), which proved encouraging when she decided to move to a commercial gallery. "Through years of being at A.I.R., I was able to build up a reputation," she noted.

Attie began inviting dealers to her studio in September of 1987. By December, the New York City gallery P.P.O.W. asked her to join, giving her a one-person exhibition the following September that completely sold out in one month. "At A.I.R., I wasn't able to support myself by selling my work," she said. "After the first show at P.P.O.W., I was able to, and I've been able to ever since." The ability to reach a larger, more serious audience of collectors is a major reason these women left A.I.R. and others leave their co-ops; it is the difference between starting out and making a career move. Attie stated that no museums showed her work during her almost 16 years at A.I.R. but, within a short period of time after moving to a commercial gallery, the Brooklyn Museum and the Museum of Modern Art in New York City both exhibited her pieces.

Elaine Reichek, a past A.I.R. member who currently exhibits at the Michael Klein gallery in New York, said that it is "hard to sell collectors work from a co-op. They look to dealers to guide them in what to buy." While attributing her growth as an artist to the freedom of exhibition without the pressure to sell artwork at A.I.R., her move from co-op to commercial gallery had less to do with the prestige she earned at A.I.R. than with her efforts to make contacts with people during those years. She was introduced to dealer Michael Klein, for instance, through friends of friends rather than at an A.I.R. exhibition. "Everyone at A.I.R. functioned as her own marketer," Reichek stated. "A.I.R. did give me a place to show my work, but it certainly didn't advance my career."

There are scores of cooperative, artist-run galleries around the country, and they each are as individual as their current roster of member artists. All of them exist because artists need somewhere to exhibit their art, although only some of them are viewed by their members as places to start careers. That is because becoming a self-supporting artist isn't a primary goal for many members. "Back when we started, in 1966, there was hardly anywhere in Reno to show your work," Marge Means, president of the Nevada-based Artists Co-Operative Gallery, said. "Now, there are a lot of galleries where you can show your work in Reno, but a lot of people just like being part of a co-op."

At both Artworks Gallery in Hartford, Connecticut, and the Artists' Cooperative Gallery in Omaha, Nebraska, members are more likely to leave the co-ops because they have moved elsewhere or stopped doing their art than as a result of stepping up to a commercial gallery. "We have a number of activities that people want to be part of," Judith Green, director of Artworks Gallery, noted. "We bring in guest lecturers; we hold juried exhibitions. A lot of the members like to spend time with the other members."

Co-op galleries certainly do entail maintaining a personal, as well as financial, commitment to a group, and they permit a greater diversity in styles and subject matter than is found at many (if not most) commercial art galleries. Cooperatives, however, may not be for everyone. The commitment of time and energy can be enormous. "You have to be on committees; you have to sit at the gallery," Dotty Attie said. "You have to do all the work, and you just get burned out after a while."

Co-op membership also changes over time, and older members may feel less affinity with some of the newer ones, resulting in a withdrawal of that initial commitment. Ultimately, co-ops are statements about the art world, a claim by certain artists that they have been shut out of the process, due to the kind of artwork they create, the exigencies of commercial art dealers, the race and gender of the artists or some other cause. In this regard, they are as much political as aesthetic groups, and political ideas change with new faces and the passage of time. There may be a certain time limit after which career-minded artists will move on from a co-op.

Although there have been instances over the past 200 years of artists cooperatively taking control over the display of their work—all of the French impressionists' exhibits of the 1870s and 1880s, or the Ashcan school's shows in the United States in the first decade of the twentieth century, for example, were organized without benefit of commercial dealers—the co-op-as-alternative-art-venue took hold widely in the pluralistic 1970s. Many co-ops and alternative art spaces came into existence at this time and some, such as A.I.R., drew critics, dealers and collectors.

The 1980s signaled a retreat from alternatives, with both new and established commercial art galleries as well as a number of major and smaller museums reclaiming the enthusiasm for discovering new artists. That decade's association of artistic novelty and excitement with monetary worth meant a turning away from the noncommercial emphasis of co-ops. Whether the art world shifts back to an interest in alternative spaces and co-ops during the 1990s and beyond is yet to be seen.

Another potential drawback of co-ops as starting points in an artist's career is an unstated stigma attached to these kinds of galleries, perhaps because of their association with political rather than purely aesthetic concerns. With A.I.R., "a lot of people complained that an all-women's co-op ghettoized women artists," Nancy Spero said. "I think belonging to A.I.R. may have set me back," artist Mary Beth Edelson stated. "Co-op artists are generally stigmatized in the art world and, through my association with A.I.R., commercial galleries assumed that I had made a commitment to exhibit my work in a certain way." After leaving A.I.R. in 1982, where she had been a member for almost 10 years, Edelson claimed that she needed "to reinvent myself" in terms of how the art world perceived her, becoming involved with the artists and galleries gaining popularity in Manhattan's East Village during the early and mid-1980s. Art dealers began to give her work a second look at this time.

Winning an audience, a dealer and recognition in the art world is a battle, however one goes about it. Co-op galleries are but one line of attack for artists, some of whom will draw the attention of collectors and dealers, while others gain the experience of exhibiting their work and running a gallery, free from the pressures of earning a living in this way. "Many commercial gallery owners have a very fixed idea of what they want to show," said Sarah Savidge, director of A.I.R. Gallery. "You may not fit into that fixed idea, and many artists have found co-ops to be an answer to that problem."

Geoffrey Homan, president of the board of directors of the one-time Association of Artist-Run Galleries, noted that there is often a "conspiracy of silence" among the critical establishment about co-ops, a result of economics. "Dealers are fearful of losing market share, and art publications, which rely on advertising from dealers, don't want to offend the dealers by reviewing an artist-run space." However, he stated, the benefits of belonging to a co-op outweigh the disadvantages, since there are no expectations about the sale of one's work and "you can control your own destiny as an artist. At a lot of commercial galleries, the plan is to have all of an artist's work sold before the show even opens. If the work doesn't sell very well, or doesn't sell at all, the dealer may just kick you out of the gallery. Now, that's got to interfere with the creative process. You avoid all that at artist-run galleries."

Artist-Run Spaces

Artist-run spaces differ from co-ops in that they are not devoted exclusively to the presentation of artwork by the people operating the space. They are generally nonprofit arts centers, and their orientation is toward artists as opposed to the general public. That tends to mean, first, that the kind of artwork that will be displayed is of an experimental (less commercial or more avant-garde) nature and, second, that the organization is run as a community rather than as a strict hierarchy.

Zone Art Center in Springfield, Massachusetts, for instance, is run by a 15-member committee of artists who are not allowed to exhibit their own work but who raise money for programs by artists who aren't members. Zone has an additional 450 members who pay between $7.50 and $25 a year. A different kind of artist-run group is the Fort Point Arts Community in Boston, which has 300 artist members each paying $40 a year. Similar to the Zone Art Center, Fort Point is also run largely by volunteers who find, renovate, and negotiate leases for buildings in which artists may obtain studio space at discounted rents. Open studio days and periodic exhibitions of the work of artists in these studios also offer the opportunity for valuable exposure.

Many artists spaces (sometimes called alternative spaces) don't often have long lives, as they are largely dependent on public funding and usually display the work of artists who have not yet built up large public followings. Others, most notably The Clocktower, Franklin Furnace and P.S. One in New York City, have developed into long-standing institutions that act as spawning grounds for new artists. All of these spaces represent an opportunity for artists to gain experience in exhibiting their work, perhaps even receiving a critical notice in a newspaper or art periodical, without the pressure to sell. Many of these spaces also offer slide registries, where artists may leave slides of their work for potential collectors to browse through, and are often the sites of meetings for artists.

One of the best sources of information for artists spaces is the National Association of Artists' Organizations (918 F Street, N.W., Washington, D.C. 20004, 202/347-6350), whose detailed membership directory, *Organizing Artists*, costs $25.00. State and local arts agencies, to which the majority of artists spaces apply for funding, would also be of help.

Membership Organizations

A final type of group that artists may join are membership service organizations, which are largely volunteer, nonprofit bodies that assist artists in career and work-related areas. The Chicago Artists' Coalition, for instance, provides a monthly newsletter of news and information for members (who pay $30 a year), discounts at art supply stores in the Chicago area, a no-interest emergency loan fund, monthly seminars on such subjects as taxes and record-keeping, a slide registry of member's artwork, a resource center of books for developing one's career, and group rate insurance for one's health and artwork. The NOVA in Cleveland, Ohio, Boston Visual Artists Union in Massachusetts and National Artists Equity Association in Washington, D.C., also provide similar kinds of assistance to their artist members.

Opportunities are sometimes available for members to meet, such as at the Artist Dialogue Series that NOVA developed a few years ago, in which practical concerns (for instance, consignment agreements between artists and their dealers) or technical matters (such as advances in print media) are discussed. The International Sculpture Center also holds periodic conferences and symposia on subjects that range from the aesthetic and philosophical to business and technical issues.

Other, more specialized service groups provide help to particular segments of the artist population across the country, such as the Asian-American Arts Alliance (in New York City), Chicano Humanities and Arts Council in Denver, Colorado, ATLATL (aiding Native American artists) in Phoenix, Arizona, National Conference of Artists (aiding African-American artists) in Washington, D.C., Association of Hispanic Arts in New York City, and Women's Art Registry of Minnesota in Minneapolis. Separate organizations exist for artists working in various media, such as crafts, film and video, performance art and sculpture. (Again, for more information on arts service and artist membership groups, contact the National Association of Artists Organizations at the address above.)

In addition to the specific services to the field, an important element that these groups provide is advocacy. Power in our society exists in numbers, and organizations that can draw upon a sizable constituency may help to overturn laws that adversely affect artists or apply pressure on legislators and agencies to create new regulations and statutes that protect or assist them. In addition, studies that are conducted about artists—who they are and what they need—generally rely on artist organizations, as these groups are the fastest and easiest resource for this kind of information. Many local, state and regional arts councils also look for artist members for their boards, which allow artists to have an important say in establishing policies concerning such areas as funding, arts festivals, and public art. Historically, artist clubs and societies have become permanent fixtures in the art realm. For instance, the black artist Edward M. Bannister (1828–1901), while suffering slurs such as what was printed in a New York newspaper—"while the Negro may harbor an appreciation of art, he is unable to produce it"—founded the Art Club in Providence, Rhode Island, which later became the Rhode Island School of Design. The French Royal Academy of Painting and Sculpture was organized by the seventeenth-century painter Charles LeBrun in 1648 in order to elevate the status of the independent artist and ensure that they would be selected for royal commissions in France. It was, in turn, because of the conservative policies of this academy that artists from the Impressionists on chose to band together in their own groups for the purpose of exhibiting their more modern styles of painting.

Similarly, in the United States, artists broke away from the conservative American Academy of Fine Arts (which had also been founded by artists, in 1802) to form the National Academy of Design in 1826. That group, in turn, was seen as overly restrictive by other artists, such as Robert Henri and the American Impressionists, who created their own respective organizations to display new work in independent exhibits. Henri's group was called The Eight; the Impressionists were referred to as The Ten. Yet another short-lived group of National Academy dissidents, the Association of American Painters and Sculptors was formed in 1911 to hold regular shows of contemporary art. That association's greatest achievement was the 1913 Armory Show, which traveled to Boston, Chicago, and New York City and brought the work of Brancusi, Cézanne, Duchamp, Matisse, Picasso, and other advanced European artists before the American public for the first time and forever changed the (somewhat stodgy) tenor of American art.

Banding together in groups may give artists far greater visibility than they may ever achieve individually. All clubs, societies, co-op galleries, artist-run spaces and service organizations to which artists may belong take away a certain amount of the solitude that creators cultivate for their art-making, but the return on this investment of time may be far greater than anything lost.

Arts Wire

Most organizations that artists may join bring them together face-to-face for various purposes. Some groups, however, connect artists electronically through their personal computers (via a modem and existing telephone lines). The most broad based of these, Arts Wire, provides timely news, job opportunities, information and areas of discussion to subscribing artists and arts organizations (performing and visual) for a $60 annual fee (for individuals, $100 for organizations) in addition to the monthly maintenance charge from one's Internet service provider, such as America Online or other company.

Material on Arts Wire is largely posted by the subscribers themselves, and among the interest groups that contribute information are the American Music Center, the Association of Hispanic Arts, the Association of Independent Video and Filmmakers, the Center for Safety in the Arts, the American Craft Council, the National Alliance of Artists' Communities, National Campaign for Freedom of Expression, National Institute of Art and Disabilities, and Visual AIDS. A painter in search of private and governmental sources of funding, for example, would look in the "Money" conference ("conference" is the Internet term for targeted subject matter), while those seeking information on current legislation affecting the arts might examine the conferences on "Advocacy" or "Artists." A ceramicist who wishes to obtain information on upcoming arts and crafts shows (dates, location, deadlines for submitting applications, booth fees) would tap into the CraftNet database that the American Crafts Council had submitted. A printmaker interested in finding out about the toxic ingredients in certain products that he or she is using, or how to safely dispose of them, would examine some of the data sheets that the Center for Safety in the Arts has placed onto the system. There are more than 50 public conferences, covering a wide range of topics, as well as a number of private ones in which subscribers may develop a one-on-one relationship with other individual or organizational members.

Those already on-line may sample Arts Wire's home page (*http://www.artswire.org*), which includes a newsletter, *Artswire Current* (updated every Tuesday), that lists news and events in the arts, job listings and opportunities. To set up an Arts Wire subscription, one may download a registration form from that home page, which may be filled out and sent to New York Foundation for the Arts (155 Avenue of the Americas, New York, NY 10013-1507), or e-mail a request for information to *Artswire@Artswire.com* or telephone 212/366-6900, ext. 247 or 510/758-1878. The registration packet includes a user rights and responsibilities agreement, cost sheet and an accounts name sheet (on which an artist may assign his or her own computer password). After the packet is returned, Arts Wire provides a user guide that enables the artist to get online.

❧

CHAPTER 7

Sources of Artistic Inspiration

*W*HY PEOPLE CREATE ART IS A SUBJECT
for philosophers and psychologists, but the sources of an artist's
inspiration tend to be somewhat less theoretical. Sometimes, the
inspiration can be just about anything. "A real object can prompt an
idea for a painting or a sculpture," Joan Miró said. "It might be the shock
of a very small real object that starts me off. . . . This line on the table,
this black spot here, or that little mark there. . . ."* Frequently, color
itself serves as a starting point for artists. Vincent van Gogh wrote to
his brother, Theo, from Arles in early November, 1888, ". . . we saw a
red vineyard, all red like red wine. In the distance, it turned to yellow,
and then a green sky with the sun, the earth after the rain violet,
sparkling yellow here and there where it caught the reflection of the
setting sun."

Among the most common sources of inspiration are specific themes
that resonate strongly within the artist (the landscape or a powerful
feeling about modern life, for instance), viewing the work of other
artists (past and present), growing up in a family where art is created,
new art-making techniques occasioned by changes in technology and
simply enjoying the process of making art.

Art and Social Change

Art is by nature subversive. It intends the viewer to look—and look
closely, for a period of time—at life or the world in a new and different

*Quoted in *Matisse, Picasso, Miró: As I Knew Them* by Rosamond Bernier. Knopf, 1991.

way, undermining the complacency of the everyday. As such, art aims to enhance the world around us by changing the way we look at it. Increasing our appreciation of the world is not the only way that art may prove subversive. Some artists want to change the world by provoking viewers to a sense of outrage and, perhaps, action. Whether that has ever happened, or ever could happen, is questionable considering the rarefied group of people who look at contemporary art. A prime motivator of certain artists to create environmental art, graffiti art, performance art and public murals is the fact that they take art out of the confines of the galleries and museums to the "real people."

Historically, many artists have sought to use their creations as a tool for social or political change. To a degree, these artists have had no other choice, as alternative methods largely involve giving up their art for direct action. Francisco de Goya's series of aquatints, *The Disasters of War*, as well as his paintings *The Colossus* and *The Third of May, 1808*, were an indictment of the barbarity that war visits on common people; the same may be said of Pablo Picasso's *Guernica*. Yet, in both artists' work there is also a suggestion that the common people should fight back in order to oust the oppressor, that the dead must be avenged. This kind of ambiguity is inherent in the idea of political art, in which the politics say change yet the art itself calls for contemplation; this uncertainty is reflected in *Guernica*, where an antifascist, procommunist fist raised in salute was originally drawn in and later painted out. Social and political concerns providing the inspiration for the creation of art is different than the desire to use art to treat the ills of society.

This distinction becomes even more evident with the passage of time. The inspiration that led Goya to paint his great works is lessened for contemporary viewers who are unlikely to take up arms against Napoleonic invaders. Similarly, with *Guernica*, the Franco regime is long gone in Spain. Works of art that have been inspired by political or social concerns rarely pass the test of time, as the quality of the art seldom matches the intensity of the moment in which they were created. Precious little of the "antinuke" art of the early 1980s has held its ground, for instance, as it was created for the moment but stayed behind with that moment.

Art That Changes Society. While discussing a painting by Eugene Delacroix, the poet and occasional art critic Charles Baudelaire rhapsodized, "Now I must change my life." This is a sentiment every artist would wish to hear, knowing that their efforts have resulted in some shift in the world (or, at least, in some viewers). Artists in the early twentieth century still believed in this possibility, issuing manifestos (a distinctly European, as opposed to American, tendency) and creating art that indicated how the world could be remade or reimagined. Very few artists maintain that kind of modernist optimism today. "I'm not so naive as to think that looking at my artwork will make people completely change their lives and thinking," said Leon Golub, a painter who is best known for images of racist incidents and other scenes of societal brutality. "That's an impossible expectation. My paintings may have a strong effect on people who are already convinced, but it may also have a strong effect on other people who may be shocked and feel nervous the next time they discriminate against, or speak derogatorily about, black people, for instance." Noting that "the function of art is to report on society," Golub claimed that his aim is to "reflect, criticize and enter into a dialogue" through his paintings with a wider audience.

Among the major influences on Golub's work are German Expressionist Max Beckmann and Mexican muralist José Clemente Orozco. Beckmann's paintings and graphic work used a distorted realist style to document the anguish, violence and uncertainty of life in Germany between the two world wars. Unlike Diego Rivera and David Alfaro Siqueiros, two other well-known Mexican muralists and avowed Marxists who were his contemporaries in revolutionary Mexico, Orozco was never an advocate for a particular political movement. (In fact, Rivera and Siqueiros were bitter enemies, the former being a Trotskyite and the latter a Stalinist.) Orozco's art chronicled the misery of Mexican street life and, after the revolution, developed into a more narrative, didactic, monumental style in which the poor, oppressed masses were depicted overthrowing their rulers.

Golub's own art has highlighted topical issues throughout his career, beginning with the Vietnam War. "I look at what I do as reality-testing," he explained, "finding out what the world is like, and how what is happening in the world affects individual psyches and national destinies."Social issues go in and out of favor in the art world on a cyclical basis and, for many years, Golub's work was overlooked when abstraction or nontraditional media assumed the spotlight. Political and social issues, absent from the visual arts since the social realism of the 1930s, returned to the fore in the 1980s, due in part to the increasing reacceptance of representational imagery. Angst-filled neo-expressionist painting and pop art–inspired critiques of mass-media portrayals of women and minorities came to be displayed side-by-side with the more formalist art that had previously displaced the socially concerned art of the past.

The mass media certainly had as much influence on the work of the American social realists in the 1930s as on today's artists. Social realist art was heavily indebted to the style of newspaper cartoons and comics—especially the caricatured figures and shrunken space—as well as the graphic styles of advertising posters of the time. William Gropper, for instance, worked as a graphic illustrator for the *New Masses*, and his paintings of bread lines and tycoons were quite similar to his illustrations. Ben Shahn, who first focused on celebrated legal trials—Dreyfus, Sacco and Vanzetti, Tom Mooney—and later evolved to depict more generalized images of working-class life, created poster illustrations for brief periods for both the Congress of Industrial Organizations and the United States Office of War Information.

Gropper, Shahn and Abraham Harriton are among the social realist influences on Sue Coe, whose career is divided between illustrations for leftist magazines and large-scale paintings. In all of her artwork, she evokes a nightmarish environment of anarchy, violence and injustice, using the elements of distortion and caricature. "We live in a nightmare world, the great panorama of the nightmare of capitalism," Coe stated. "Anyone who doesn't see or understand that isn't actually awake." Describing her work as "visual journalism," Coe noted that she was "not politically formed in any way" when she began her career as an illustrator at age 15: "I just read and worked with the text and learned about the world that way," she said. "I kept getting jobs about social issues and only worked for left-wing periodicals. On occasion, a right-wing periodical would ask me to do something for them, and I would turn them down." She added that "I'm not a passive pencil who goes along with whatever the text says. I feel that I'm interactive with the text, investigating what can't be recorded by a camera."

American social realist art largely disappeared from art gallery and museum walls after World War II, viewed with embarrassment in the anticommunist fervor of the early Cold War years and overwhelmed by the onslaught of the apparent apolitical abstract expressionism. Coe is one of a small minority who believes that the subordination of social realist art and the elevation of abstraction was effected as part of a right-wing campaign. Unlike Leon Golub, Coe believes that her art can assist significantly in altering society by "reinforcing reality"—that reality being a host of injustices. Most art, to her mind, is politically right wing because, by not attacking the existing social structure, it rather serves as a buttress. "Art that doesn't deal with the realities of life as people live it is right wing," she said, "but right-wing art, right-wing ideology, creates its own resistance and, ultimately, its own demise."

Barbara Kruger, who uses photographs and text to create artworks that comment on how groups in society are oppressed, is another who believes that art can, "if not offer solutions to major problems, at least ask questions and raise issues that others, such as politicians, may be afraid to ask." She looks to raise these issues not only through exhibits at art galleries and museums—"the art world is a subculture of the larger world I'm involved with"—but by creating magazine covers (*Esquire, Ms., Newsweek* and the *New York Times Magazine,* among others), pro-choice posters and other politically charged imagery on T-shirts and shopping bags. Furthermore, she has also developed billboard projects in the United States and Europe that present her thinking to a wide audience. Her San Francisco billboard project, for example, is based on the theme of violence in the family. "Pictures and words have the power to make us who we are, and I want to address that power and see how it defines a culture in my work," Kruger said. "The more people who begin to think about these issues, perhaps by seeing my work, the better."

Art That Changes Art. The fame of Picasso's *Guernica* is perhaps out of proportion to its importance relative to his entire artistic output. Certainly, it was not nearly as much of a breakthrough work as his painting *Les Demoiselles d'Avignon.* Neither was it as novel as his collages or welded assemblage sculpture nor as influential to other twentieth-century artists as his analytical and synthetic cubism. The picture was created more than a decade after Picasso had ceased being an innovator. According to some critics, *Guernica* is not even a particularly good painting. Critic Clement Greenberg pointed out that "this huge painting reminds one of a battle scene from a pediment that has been flattened under a defective steam roller. It is as if it had been conceived within an illusion of space deeper than that in which it was actually executed." Still, *Guernica* is probably Picasso's best-known and best-loved work precisely because it spoke to a larger segment of the population than the contemporary art audience about a subject for which the public had strong feelings. The work traveled extensively, first to Paris (where it was hung in the Spanish Pavilion at the 1937 International Exhibition), then to Norway, London and New York. Millions of people saw it and could understand this work of modern art.

Most artists today don't set their sights on the general public but on the groups of artists, collectors, critics, dealers, museum officials and art exhibit-goers that constitute what is called the "art world." Certainly, that world has grown considerably in size over the past few decades. The change that politically and socially conscious artists now strive for is within the art world itself; possibly, change in that realm will eventually lead to new thinking in the larger society, or, perhaps, political concerns within the art world mirror those in the larger society, such as in academia and book publishing.

"I'm speaking to other artists in my work," said Faith Ringgold, a painter and creator of "story quilts" that offer visual narratives of growing up as an African-American in the United States. "I want them to know that you can change the course of art, to make a place for women and people of color, that art isn't just about the lives and work of white men, that art isn't just about the lives of other people but about your own life. The reason why I wanted to become an artist was to express the way I felt living in America." The artist Jacob Lawrence, who is well known for his paintings of African-American history in America, was "a guiding force in my art," said Ringgold, whose use of story quilts is intended to reflect a folk tradition. She departs from Lawrence in telling a more personal narrative.

In addition to the example of her own work, Ringgold has also offered guidance to other women and artists of color by founding an organization called Coast to Coast, which creates exhibitions of artists who have been excluded from the mainstream art world. These exhibits travel around the country, allowing many people to look at previously unseen artwork. "I'm trying to find ways to open up doors so that others can participate in the so-called American dream," she stated.

Hans Haacke is another artist who views the art world as a battlefield, weaving together corporate advertising images and his own commentary to draw attention to the issue of who owns art and why they collect. One of Haacke's installations, concerning the provenance of Édouard Manet's *Bunch of Asparagus*, documented how that painting was originally owned by artists and appreciative collectors before coming into the hands of German industrialists and later being rejected by a museum in Cologne. His aim was to "present the social and economic position of the persons who have owned the painting over the years and the prices paid for it. . . ." Other Haacke installations at museums have examined who sits on the trustee boards of those museums and the less benign activities of their companies over the years.

"The art world is not as isolated as we usually think it is," Haacke said. "It does not lead an ivory-tower existence, but is part of a general field of perception. Since the 1960s, art has become almost fashionable. You see that general readership publications now devote more and more pages to arts subjects. You see that corporations have moved in to collect art and support arts activities; these corporations, in turn, try to attract people they want to have work for them by showing how much cultural activity there is. Certainly, the art world is my immediate audience, because art galleries and museums are the locations where I show these things, but, in an indirect way, the artwork affects the public mentality of the larger community. All public articulations, which is what artists produce, have an impact on the general fabric of ideas, opinions, values, perceptions and goals that make up the Zeitgeist."

Technology as a Springboard for Art

Advances in technology may seem to be far removed from the creation of art. The methods used by ancient Roman painters and artists today to make colors, mix them and use them to form images seem to have more in common than ancient and modern ways of living, traveling or entertaining. Nonetheless, artists—especially in the nineteenth and twentieth centuries—have been quite sensitive to these technological advances, frequently making use of them in their art. The printing press, for instance, was developed in the fifteenth century for the purpose of increasing the circulation of Bibles and other books, yet also became a major vehicle for disseminating art prints to the multitudes. The introduction and use of copper for printing plates led artists to switch from the burdensome woodcut technique to engravings and etchings, which allowed for greater detail and more visual information in a single image.

While artists are rarely the inventors of the technology that transforms art (or society), they do put such technology to use in creating art. And sometimes, artists make technological breakthroughs, becoming inventors themselves. Fifteenth-century Flemish artist Jan van Eyck, for example, is generally credited as the creator of oil-based paint, which replaced fresco and egg tempera as the medium of choice for painters. In 1794, Aloys Senefelder, a Bavarian artist, developed the printmaking process known as lithography, which freed artists to create far more expressive images in printmaking. Watercolors were also principally formulated by artists, first for illuminated manuscripts, later as toned preliminary studies for oil paintings and, finally, in the eighteenth and nineteenth centuries (in England, France, and the United States), as works of art in themselves.

Photography (invented in 1836 by Frenchman Louis Daguerre, a painter of stage backdrops) was another advance in technology that has had an enormous impact on how artists work and the images they make. The invention of the camera freed artists from the need to record the world in exact detail, allowing them to offer more personal and abstract visions. Photographers largely took over the artist's traditional work of creating highly realistic scenes of faraway places or historical events by producing large editions of relatively inexpensive pictures to meet the particular segment of the art market that wanted these images. Mathew Brady, George Barnard, Alexander Gardner and Timothy O'Sullivan in the United States, and Felice Beato, Roger Fenton and James Robertson in England, were among the pioneering photographers who documented wars for their countrymen. The French brothers Louis Auguste and Auguste Rosalie Bisson, the Englishman Francis Frith and the American Carleton E. Watkins were leading photographers of sites of wonder around the world, such as the pyramids of Egypt and the Yosemite Mountains in California. Others took balloon rides to record cityscapes from above.

Photography freed artists to paint in the advanced expressive styles now associated with modernism. The camera itself allowed artists to record moments that they would later paint in their studios, and the often random and unplanned images in photographs—the person in the background whose head is looking the "wrong" way, the cropping of the image which reflects a world not as self-contained as that of a classical painting—became a part of picture-making. Starting with the Impressionists, images became more a "slice of life" than a grand view of life itself, with the subject frequently off-center or focusing on something outside the viewer's field of vision. The overhead cityscape photographs, with their strong sense of architectural line and geometry, had a significant influence on a wide range of artists, from French Impressionist painters Gustave Caillebotte and Camille Pissarro to Russian abstract artists El Lissitzky and Kasimir Malevich, as well as on later fine art photographers, such as Alvin Langdon Coburn, André Kertész and László Moholy-Nagy.

Sculpture is another area where advances in technology have played a major role in influencing the work of artists. Perhaps most noteworthy is the way in which many sculptors have adopted steel for the same reason that architects have—its strength, even in thin sheets, and suitability for creating very tall structures. Artists have frequently used steel architecturally to comment on city life.

New technology, in the form of larger printing presses that were able to capture a broad spectrum of colors and designs, revived fine art lithography in the 1960s, and, today, the computer is increasingly becoming an important tool. Art created on the computer dates back to the late 1950s and the genre started to gain some attention by the end of the 1960s. Now, a growing number of commercial artists produce work on computers and submit floppy disks or digitized images to publishers and advertising agencies rather than paintings, which must be photographically reproduced. More and more fine artists are moving in this direction.

Some artists, such as Keith Haring, Philip Pearlstein and Andy Warhol, have experimented with computer "digital paint boxes," largely translating their painted imagery into computer-generated designs that are only distinguishable to the degree that paint looks different from computer dots. Others have turned to the computer to manipulate images from other sources—such as a photograph—that are scanned or digitized into the computer's memory.

Nancy Burson, for instance, has used scanning to fuse two or more disparate images, such as landscapes by Cezanne and van Gogh, into a composite work. She has also taken photographs of various people and altered them on the computer to show how they would look at an older age. (On occasion, the Federal Bureau of Investigations has asked her to project how a child would look when aged a few years, as part of its hunt for missing children.) "I started out as a painter. That's what I went to study in college," Burson said. "I thought of myself as a conceptual artist and got into photography, later video, because I was really interested in seeing someone get old."

As with many other artists, the idea of what to do preceded the sense of how to do it. Burson knew nothing about computers, but was directed in her artistic efforts to Experiments in Art and Technology, an organization cofounded in 1967 by artist Robert Rauschenberg and Bell Laboratories laser physicist Billy Kluver. From there, she collaborated with computer scientists at the Massachusetts Institute of Technology "who helped me utilize the tools that were available and that were being developed to make the images I wanted." If the idea came before the technology, the technology also gave rise to new ideas, which Burson has pursued over the years.

One of the best-known computer artists, David Em, also started out as a painting student at the Pennsylvania Academy of Fine Arts in Philadelphia. His early work was heavily realistic but gradually became more expressionistic and abstract, with thick, textured layers of paint. The concern with texture brought him to try his hand at sculpture, and Em grew increasingly interested in the issue of how to light his works. Eventually, the question of how to light his art became more interesting to him than the sculpture itself, and he became absorbed in videotaping artworks, later creating what he called "abstract videos. It was the abstract videos that really got me interested in looking at the electronic image. The problem with video, however, is that you quickly reach a limit to what you can do with it. What I found I wanted was to control the color of every dot on the screen."

By 1975, Em found computer software at the Xerox Research Park in San Francisco that finally allowed him to control color this way. A year later, he moved to Los Angeles where he began to experiment on the larger computers at the Jet Propulsion Laboratory (JPL) of the California Institute of Technology in Pasadena. Between 1977 and 1987, Em was artist-in-residence at JPL, creating landscape images (frequently of other planets or stars) and more abstract designs in bright colors. Unlike Nancy Burson or Philip Pearlstein, Em does not work from other sources, such as photographs or his own paintings, but composes from scratch completely on a powerful computer, a process that he finds exciting. "The computer is a mirror of the thinking process," he said. "Computers work so quickly, and your ideas can jump very fast from one to the next to the next to the next with it." His only qualm about working on a computer is that it is such an artificial environment: "You are always inside laboratories; it's like living on a spaceship. After a while, I felt that I had to take some time off to see the outside world again; to really use my eyes."

Being well known in the computer art field does not necessarily make one well known, generally. It was 130 years after the invention of the camera before a gallery of photography (New York City's Witkin Gallery) was able to support itself—a number of previous efforts had tried and failed—and there are currently no art galleries exclusively representing the work of artists who create on the computer. Em's creations are sold through an agent to the small group of collectors who have shown an interest in this field of endeavor. Holography and xerography (or photocopying) currently suffer the same fate, as yet to be fully distinguished from mere novelty by any postmodern eclecticism. Perhaps it is ambivalence on the part of the public toward the computerization that is coming to dominate contemporary society, or an age-old belief that art must be handmade and not worked out on a computer keyboard, that limits the acceptability of art based on new technology—at least for now.

A Sense of Place

Artists, like regional dialects, tend to be associated with certain places. In time, these locations are thought of in terms of the artists who painted there, as with Monet and Giverny, van Gogh and Arles, Gauguin and Tahiti, Georgia O'Keeffe and New Mexico, Richard Diebenkorn and Ocean Park, California. The School of Paris refers to a group of artists who lived or worked in the French capital in the late nineteenth and early twentieth centuries, frequently depicting aspects of Parisian life in their artwork. We know the nineteenth-century Barbizon school of French landscape painters, for instance, precisely for where Corot, Courbet, Millet and a few others met to talk art as well as to paint side by side. Similarly, the New York School of abstract expressionists indicates the location of their activity. The American Abstract Artists group of the 1930s, on the other hand, consisted of a wide range of artists who maintained the same dedication to non-objective painting but did not paint as a group or in the same locations. Almost every movement or school of art over the past 200 years has identified itself with, and met in, specific locations or organizations.

The nineteenth century's love affair with the landscape made artists (individually or in groups) possessive of the terrain on which they could tell their story. This sense of artistic territory spread throughout the world hand in hand with the concepts of impressionist painting. Thus, American Impressionists concentrated their attentions on Cos Cob and Old Lyme, Connecticut; British Impressionists seized on Bosham and Amberley; those in Denmark painted in Skagen, while the Belgian luminists (Belgium's version of impressionism) went to Astene, and the Australians found Box Hill and Eaglemont.

In certain instances, artists don't live or work in the place their art is associated with, but the imagery used in their art continues to refer to a certain specific locale. Many of Marc Chagall's paintings, for instance, recall the Russian town of Vitebsk, where he was born, more often than Paris and the south of France, where he spent most of his professional life. Similarly, Thomas Hart Benton's Midwest regionalism was formulated and practiced during his three decades in Manhattan.

While some artists understandably want a locale that isn't heavily associated in the public mind with some other group of artists, this is not the sole motivation that drives them to find their own place to memorialize. The artists of the Barbizon identified the French nation with the land and its common people, and many of their paintings feature peasants at work in the fields. The French Impressionists, on the other hand, sought out those places where middle-class Parisians might vacation or go for a nature hike or leisurely stroll through town.

The exotic quality of Tahitian life, so different from the tame world of Paris, prompted Gauguin to paint an idealistic world of strangely colored water, land and exotic natives. However, it was the same Paris, with its hectic modern pace of life and jumble of competing signs and advertisements that led Georges Braque and Pablo Picasso to develop their own alternative visual system—cubist paintings and collages. Theirs was an art based on the idea of the city itself rather than on any particular neighborhood. Romare Bearden's art, on the other hand, frequently reflected the Harlem section of New York City, using the collage technique to capture the jazz rhythms associated with the community as well as the mix of modern-day life and older, African-American traditions.

The land (the agglomeration of hills, trees, pastures and whatever else), of course, is different than a painted landscape, which has a cultural meaning. From the beginnings of the American republic up until the domination of the art world by abstract expressionism in the 1950s, a central cultural concern in the United States was "What is American art?" or "What is *American* about American art?" One sees efforts to define both American art and America in the allegorical paintings and sculpture of the neoclassicists in the early nineteenth century, in the landscapes of the Hudson River school, the naturalist paintings of the Ashcan school at the beginning of the twentieth century, the regionalist art of Thomas Hart Benton and Grant Wood and the Depression-era photography of Walker Evans, Dorothea Lange and others in the 1930s. In almost all of these efforts, America was identified in terms of the land and the small towns (and the people who lived on or in them), a Jeffersonian vision of the republic, quite in contrast to the art of twentieth-century Europe, which primarily associated culture and nationhood with the major cities. When the New York School of abstract expressionism began not only to dominate art stylistically but seemingly surpass all previous European work, a major shift took place in thinking: American culture became identified with a long historical line of Western art and the cities that produced it.

Cities tend to be memorialized more than most places in art simply because they are traditionally where artists congregate. Living and working alongside so many other artists, with so much art to see, is frequently a spur to creating. However, the search for teaching positions in schools has led many artists to live in far-flung locations, and many others choose to make their homes where the terrain itself is a source of inspiration.

By 1954, when young artists from all over the world were flocking to Manhattan, going to the galleries, clubs, and bars that the New York School of abstract expressionists frequented and hoping that some of the magic of the place and moment might rub off on them, Carroll Cloar decided that he had had enough of New York City and decided to return to his roots in Memphis, Tennessee. "I didn't know that people back here would ever buy my work," he recalled. "I had a gallery in New York, but I hadn't sold anything there yet. I thought about teaching, although there weren't too many places to do that, either." Cloar's work was then at a crossroads, as he was influenced by a number of different sources, but "I began to think of how I conceived of things as a child. I thought my father was as big as a tree, for instance, and I was anxious to get back to Memphis to paint those memories. I bought a used car and figured that I'd just stay in Memphis long enough to finish those paintings I had thought about and then head back to New York. I just never left."

Cloar was surprised that there were art collectors back in Memphis, and that they were willing to buy his work. Born in Earle, Arkansas, Cloar attended art school in Memphis. He is a regional artist with a mostly regional market. His realistic pictures reflect the area of his childhood and one that his buyers would know, with cotton fields, farms, back roads and small towns. The air of reminiscence in his work, combined with an artistic indebtedness to Bonnard and Vuillard, strikes a fond chord with fellow Southerners.

"I go back and forth in time in my painting," he said. "A lot of the paintings are inspired by my childhood, and I either use old photographs or my wife and I roam around a lot to find things to photograph. Then, I create in the studio from the photographs." His work continues to be represented in New York City, where prices fetched for his paintings are considerably higher than in Memphis, but the bulk of his work hangs on the walls of collectors within a 50-mile radius of his studio. "If I had been an abstract artist, it probably wouldn't have mattered where I lived," he said, "but my subject matter is here." Besides maintaining close ties with his roots, Cloar had also been also in frequent contact with his fellow Memphians and their connection to him kept them loyal buyers. While he refused to do work on commission, Cloar often heard suggestions about what he might paint next. "Most of the time, their suggestions are lousy, but sometimes they will turn up something interesting."

Artist-Children of Artists

There are many sources of inspiration that compel someone to become an artist, but a rather common reason is that one parent or another is an artist. Three generations of Wyeth painters attest to how family traditions in art are passed; the same could be said of Charles Willson Peale and his five artist children, Ben Shahn and his three artist children, Max and Jimmy Ernst, A. Stirling and Alexander Calder, Kenneth and Kate Noland, David and Rebecca Smith, Edward and Stuart Davis, A. B. Frost, Sr. and Jr., and many others. Pursuing art at home is not only a means of developing future professional artists, of course; it also brings family members together, as they may work side-by-side or cooperatively on projects. Encouraging children to think creatively has applications in life well beyond the painted canvas.

The reasons that artists beget artists are not difficult to understand. While pursuing art seriously may seem a luxury to some people, the children growing up in this environment generally think of it as normal, especially because home may also serve as the studio. The parents' friends also tend to be artists, which reinforces the sense of normalcy. "When I was young, I thought that everyone grew up to be artists," said March Avery, daughter of painters Milton and Sally Avery.

Learning how to make art may not be forced on these children but, if they show interest—which many invariably do—they are given the best materials with which to work and expert instruction. Some children of artists conclude that their decision to become artists themselves ironically reflects a lack of imagination. "I'm a sucker for people from the Midwest who had to break away from their disapproving parents and come to New York with great hopes of being artists," said Kiki Smith, a sculptor and daughter of sculptor Tony Smith. "Those people really had to work to be artists but, for me, it never seemed all that hard." She noted that much of what she learned as a child came "through osmosis, and all the artist friends, like Barney Newman, who came by the house and talked."

Rather than inheriting the dealers and collectors of her father's work, Smith created her professional connections by herself. Her sculpture is also quite different from that of her father, although it shares many of the same humanistic concerns. Tony Smith, a trained architect who had worked with Frank Lloyd Wright for two years in the 1930s and did not devote himself solely to sculpture until 1960, was a minimalist. His fame rests on monumental plywood or steel sculptures that often start with a triangular base but twist and turn in various directions, frequently suggesting modern-day man. Kiki Smith's interests are less about her father's formal concerns with volume, shape and size and more about the everyday concerns of women—household objects and the shape and structure of their own bodies and internal organs. She is particularly interested in the physical and psychological damage that may be inflicted upon women by others as evidenced by the physical condition of their bodies.

That feminist orientation may have also been a reaction to, as well as a product of, her home environment, since "my father never assumed that I'd be a sculptor like him because I was a girl. I never really had any ambition one way or the other." Deciding on her career was not easy. She had once studied to be a baker at a trade school in Newark, New Jersey. ("I always liked making things—art, food.") Smith also trained as an emergency medical technician, where she learned about the human body at its most vulnerable. It wasn't until she was

24 that Smith decided to be a sculptor and not until age 30 that she became "serious about my work." Unfortunately, her father died when she was 28, so she did not have the benefit of his advice and counsel as the artwork matured.

Some artist-children of artists benefit more from their parents than others. Pieter Brueghel the Younger (1564–1638) was only five when his father, known as the Elder (1525–69) died, while Andrew benefitted from the career and artistic advice of his fathers, N.C. Wyeth, which he in turn passed down to his son Jamie. Sometimes, the pressure of having a renowned parent in the same field may impel certain artistically inclined children to seek out other media. Andrew Wyeth's son Nicholas and Henri Matisse's son Pierre both became art dealers of their parents' work. Of Norman Rockwell's three children, for instance, one became a sculptor and another a writer. Pierre-Auguste Renoir's son, Jean, became a filmmaker, and painter Robert De Niro, Sr.'s son turned to acting. Mark Tansey's father, Richard G. Tansey, is an art historian, one of the coauthors of the college art history text entitled Gardner's *Art Through the Ages*.

Only one of Richard Tansey's four sons went into art—one is an economist, another a banker and the last a student of language—but Mark Tansey's painting seems apt for the child of a scholar. His paintings offer commentaries, or wry observations, on the history of art, especially modernism. His *Action Painting* series, for instance, shows painters working slowly and methodically while miraculously capturing on canvas events that are occurring before their eyes, such as car crashes and space craft launches. Another picture, *Triumph over Mastery II*, depicts a man whitewashing Michelangelo's *Last Judgment* in the Sistine Chapel, flattening the picture plane and eliminating pictorial depth as though to suggest that modernism's "last judgment" of itself as progressive may otherwise be seen as simply destructive.

"Call it a similarity of interest with my father," he said. "My father is someone my art is in dialogue with as well as an example to me. I know that he wanted to be an artist himself." As with Kiki and Tony Smith, there are important differences as well as a "similarity of interest" in the work of the Tanseys. "My artwork presents dilemmas where different theoretical systems collide," Mark Tansey stated. "My system is very different from my father's; it's very different from that of modernism. You can call it a lover's quarrel."

These differences reflect the painter's own life experiences. He worked both at the Whitney Museum of American Art in New York City and for painter Helen Frankenthaler as well as reading the essays of art critics, such as Rosalind Krauss. He also studied art and lived for a time in California, which "takes a freer, less doctrinaire approach to art than New York," where he currently lives. All these experiences are "part of the soup" that helped him achieve his individual voice, reflecting, but not wholly echoing, his father.

Teachers and Other Artists

Of course, not all artists come from artist families. Many, like the "people from the Midwest" whom Kiki Smith finds so appealing, come from backgrounds that offered little support for artistic aspirations. The ideas of art that they inherit and pass on derive from their association with other artists. What makes the history of art more than a chronological listing of artists and the artwork they have created is the ideas and traditions that are passed on—and subtly changed—from one generation to the next. This is a history that is experienced by artists before it is identified and understood by the general public and, for most artists, that experience comes through teachers and other artists.

Teachers. It is not always clear exactly what a teacher develops in a student, as inspiration is rarely a simple matter of cause and effect. In the past, an artist taught his students specific techniques or how-to information, sometimes so they could assist him on his commissioned works (the apprenticeships of the Renaissance era, for instance) or simply to ensure that they would paint (which included mixing pigments and oil) or sculpt in the accepted manner. Even if that is not the teacher's intention nowadays, it is often the case that art students will work in that artist's style for at least a small period of time—art school class exhibits are frequently tributes to their instructors. The reasons for this are not difficult to understand, as the students are in the presence of a working artist, who may refer to heady concepts and whose views about design, composition, color, texture, form and subject matter are more strongly formed than those of his or her students. However, the trend in art classes, programs and schools over the past several decades has been to deemphasize the technical—the how-to stuff—and elevate the conceptual. In effect, the job of today's artists who teach is to inspire students, making them aware of the aesthetic issues to be tackled, but encouraging them to tackle these issues in their own way.

Larry Rivers, one of Hans Hofmann's many students, stated that the elder artist "made art glamorous by including in the same sentence with the names Michelangelo, Rubens, Courbet, and Matisse, the name Rivers. . . . It wasn't that you were a Michelangelo or a Matisse but that you faced somewhat similar problems. What he really did by talking this way was to inspire you to work."* Rivers's paintings and those of Hofmann certainly look quite different and are based on different ideas. "He certainly got me to think a lot," Rivers said. "He said a lot of things I had never thought of before, such as 'Not only do you draw the figure on the page, but you create the space in which the figure exists.' Now, I think that's a very romantic concept. How do you create space? You create the figure and the space around it creates itself, but it sounded very good to me at the time."

One would be hard pressed to identify a stylistic relationship between the American regionalist art of Thomas Hart Benton and the mature work of his student Jackson Pollock, or between the work of Balcomb Greene, founder of the American Abstract Artists group, and his students at Carnegie Tech, Philip Pearlstein and Andy Warhol. Both teachers went beyond the call of duty to encourage their students. Benton demonstrably displayed confidence in the abilities of Pollock, acting supportively as both mentor and parent figure to his turbulent, rebellious student; the two were also united by their desire to show that "real men" could be artists. Greene encouraged his top students to move to New York City, where the most advanced art was being created and exhibited, and he even helped them find an apartment to share.

The influence of Ashcan realist Robert Henri on his student Edward Hopper is not impossible to grasp. In 1935, Hopper himself said that "You must not forget that I was for a time a student of Henri's who encouraged all his students to try to depict the familiar life about them." However, the influence of Henri on Vaclav Vytlacil, one of the members of the American Abstract Artists group, is not easy to identify; and Vytlacil's influence on his student Robert Rauschenberg may be even less evident. Still, the importance of the teacher as conveyer of art wisdom becomes clear if one looks at the line connecting the three artists as representing the most progressive thought in American art during their respective primes for the first six decades of the twentieth century.

Those who currently attempt to teach a specific style often find themselves in battle with iconoclastic students. "Josef Albers was, for me, more a source of aggravation than of inspiration," painter Audrey Flack, who studied with Albers at Yale University in the early 1950s, said. "He was a very rigid man with very rigid ideas. He wanted me, he wanted everyone, to paint squares and, if you didn't, he gave you trouble. I was then an abstract expressionist trying to be a realist. We couldn't even get models to work from. Albers had us all doing squares,

---

*Quoted in *Art Chronicles, 1954–1966* by Frank O'Hara. George Braziller, 1975.

in effect, to make clones of himself." However, the experience of studying with Albers wasn't all negative for Flack. Being in the presence of such an artist was compelling in itself since "he recognized talent, and you knew that he knew." To be identified as having talent by Albers was an inspiration in itself, even though the pursuit of that talent often set up a battle zone in the studio.

One of the immeasurable qualities of an inspiring teacher is a good eye, especially when students are shown how to see (and, therefore, how to create) in a new way. Harry Callahan, who founded and headed the photography department at the Rhode Island School of Design, was legendary for his ability to invigorate the work of his students. Emmet Gowin, a Callahan student during the mid-1960s, credits his teacher with helping to shape his own ideas about art and the world around him. Gowin noted that the "transmission of knowledge was actually very indirect. You were learning in the presence of someone else's thinking, seeing how Callahan identified the task and what his attitude to the task was. He had the kinds of standards for photography that were new to me."

Gowin came to Callahan's first class with a painting and graphic design background, but found his confidence shaken within the first hour. Callahan asked his students to show their photographs to each other. He left the room for a period of time and then returned, walking around the class and looking at various students' work. When he saw Gowin's photographs, he remarked, "You're really going to have to learn how to print" before walking on. "I thought these photographs were the best I could do," Gowin recalled, "but his comment indicated to me that I had to go a lot further than I had in understanding my subject. It was hard to know what he actually meant—was he referring to technical or perceptual problems?—and I think it was wise of him to leave it wide open. His comments were like tarot cards; you wonder if the message was meant for you or for someone else, but you search for applications and generally find them. At other times, he would indicate what the problem was and then say he didn't know how to solve it, leaving me to think about it. I spent a lot of time rethinking and reworking those pictures I had brought in that first day and, a few weeks later, I brought them in to show them, and he told me that they were better."

Other Artists. While beginning artists may often be raw material to be molded and inspired during the time they are studying with a teacher, this changes with time and experience. "Friends eventually take the place of teachers to artists as you mature," Larry Rivers said. By friends, he meant other artists from whom one can hear criticism or take suggestions. Both praise and complaints are usually accepted more readily (and more deeply) coming from fellow artists, because many artists believe that only other artists can truly understand art. "I wouldn't take criticism from a civilian, but I'll take it from another artist," sculptor Bill King noted.

The kind of inspiration that artists offer each other is generally some form of encouragement to keep working. The solitary nature of many artists' careers and the risks of taking a wrong turn in one's work and being perceived as having failed, are more stressful than nonartists generally comprehend. Other artists, who understand the loneliness and risks in this life, offer encouragement for their colleagues that is more meaningful than all the favorable reviews and glamorous art openings.

"One time, I was walking along Madison Avenue," painter Jack Beal said, "during a period when I was on a strange tangent, working in a particularly formalist manner, and I met [painters] Alfred Leslie and Sidney Tillim on the street. Actually, I should say, they almost mugged me right there on the street. They started telling me that I was letting down the cause of representational art, that I had strayed from the path in this work I was doing. It was so touching that they cared enough to mug me."

Beal stated that Alfred Leslie has frequently been a source of inspiration to him, an inspiration to work based on competition: "I'll see something he has done that I've never even tried, and I'll attempt to stretch myself, to pull my work forward to reach that level." On the other hand, sometimes, seeing what some other artist has not done well has led Beal to "try to do it better myself. It's competition in a negative way." Beal's primary source of help, advice and inspiration, however, is his wife, Sondra Freckelton, who is also a painter. "We see each other's work with a clarity that other people couldn't exercise," he said. "We're each other's most severe critics, but we trust each other the most."

Part-Time Artists Who Become Full-Time

Sometimes, it is not at all clear how or where someone becomes inspired to create art. The customary sources of inspiration—family members who are artists, an art teacher or the work of a noted artist, finding delight in certain colors, new technology or a desire to change the world—don't always apply, and this is especially evident with "primitive" and self-taught artists, sometimes called "outsider" artists.

The early history of the United States includes numerous self-taught artists; their lack of education had to do with the absence of art academies or even other artists who were qualified to teach. The dearth of qualified art instructors reflected the fact that there was a very miniscule market for art—it was often viewed as part of the Old World debauchery from which the new nation had broken away. Furthermore, many of those who bought portraits—at the time, the most likely way to earn money as an artist—were more concerned with getting a low price than with the quality of the work.

Limners, or portrait painters, had to learn their craft by trial and error because there weren't teachers who had any greater training. Few of them made an entire living at portraiture, and many worked as house and sign painters, designing family crests and decorating furniture. One of the most renowned self-taught artists of this era, Ralph Earl (1751– 1801), who did make a career of portraiture, lived an itinerant life, moving from New York City to various towns in Connecticut, Massachusetts, and Vermont in search of patrons and to get away from the growing competition. Artists of any promise at all recognized the need to study in Europe, often working at a job to earn the money to pay the passage. Earl himself pursued his art career for seven years in England in the late 1770s and early 1780s—where he was drawn to the work of Thomas Gainsborough, Joshua Reynolds, and Benjamin West—but largely because his Tory sympathies during the Revolutionary War lost him customers.

During the first half of the nineteenth century, schools and artists' associations did open in some of the major cities in the United States, and instructional guides—particularly in watercolors, which were becoming quite popular in England and France as well as in the United States—helped to improve the general level of artistic competence, if not excellence. However, the market for early American primitive art has tended to be more an antiquarian interest (these buyers are as likely to collect colonial furniture as paintings) than the passion of major art collectors; and other artists, critics and historians have largely viewed this artwork with condescension.

Certain largely self-taught artists rise above the condescension. Winslow Homer, a loner whose lack of interest in what other artists were doing required him to slowly and painfully learn for himself what could have been more quickly taught to him in a school, developed into one of this country's most original painters. Anna Mary Robertson "Grandma" Moses (1860–1961) also learned by doing and, unlike Homer, did not even have the experience of seeing the work of major artists in Europe. Too poor to afford wallpaper, Grandma Moses's first "artwork" consisted of painting designs on the walls of her house. She later devoted greater amounts of time to her art in the late 1920s after the death of her husband, in part to overcome her grief and reminisce about her life. Her paintings of rural life did not garner any serious attention for a long time—the fact that she was called "Grandma" revealed the bemusement of the art public—and her first one-person exhibition took place when she was 80.

Hobbies occasionally develop into new careers, especially after retirement. John Kane (1860–1934), a Scottish-born, Pittsburgh house-painter, also painted on the side—interestingly, he used housepaints on his canvases, years before Jackson Pollock startled the art world by doing just that—but was not publicly shown until age 67. Unlike Grandma Moses, however, Kane's highly detailed paintings were taken seriously early on, quickly entering the public collections of major art museums. Morris Hirschfield (1872–1946), another autodidact, was a clothing manufacturer who turned to painting at age 65. James Stewart of Rock Creek, West Virginia, was a coal miner for 30 years. Upon his retirement with black lung disease in 1974, he began to chisel, sand and lacquer pieces of coal into busts of historical and contemporary figures. He soon received commissions from executives of major coal companies to do their portraits, and others purchased his work outright. "I wish I had gotten into this a bit sooner, but I never thought I could make a living at it," Stewart said. "The fellows I used to work with find it hard to connect me with the person they see getting written up in art publications. I never thought of myself as a sculptor but as a coal miner. The people I've known all my life aren't sure if they should look at me differently."

CHAPTER 8

Overcoming Mental Blocks
and Other Obstacles

$\mathcal{T}$HE MYTHICAL VIEW OF ARTISTS HAS placed them in their studios or garrets, waiting for the muse to inspire some great new idea or image. Were that the case, the wait could be a long one, leaving artists with little to do between brainstorms. In fact, most artists rely on good work habits to solve technical, aesthetic or intellectual problems. These include maintaining a regimen of drawing or painting for a certain amount of time every day as well as pursuing certain ideas to their completion in the hope that they might lead to other, new and interesting concepts. In the mostly hands-on profession of art, inspiration comes from doing.

In Search of the Muse

No artist is free from dry periods or mental blocks, when the old ideas seem to lead nowhere and new ones are hard to find. There are really two aspects to this problem. The first is the feeling of having run out of ideas, which tends to be a very temporary condition; the second is a general lack of enthusiasm about creating art itself and losing a sense of what makes art exciting, which can be far more troubling. For artists who have established a market for their work, fear of negative criticism or turning off past collectors may also enter their thinking. "When I'm at an impasse," photographer Sandy Skoglund said, "I try to do whatever feels good. The internal satisfaction has to be the focus." That may be more easily said than done, as some methods work, others don't. Jackson Pollock, who was stung by criticism of his later work, largely gave up painting in the last few years of his life. Italian comic opera composer Gioacchino Antonio Rossini's mental block lasted for the better part of three decades, as he wrote almost nothing of any length or importance for the last half of his life.

Different artists have approached the problem in various ways. Pablo Picasso, for instance, periodically looked for rejuvenation in various media (ceramics, printmaking, sculpture, stage design) and subject matter (copying Old Masters, ancient Greek mythology). Painter Janet Fish "started doing watercolors as a way of loosening up my use of color. I had begun to find that subject matter had come to dominate my painting." Ben Shahn, who by 1950 felt trapped in the socially cons-cious work he had done in the 1930s and 1940s, took a teaching position at Black Mountain College in North Carolina, which proved stimulating to him. "Black Mountain was a very argumentative place. A lot of the abstract expressionists were there," said Shahn's widow, Bernarda Bryson Shahn. "It helped clarify his ideas, and his work also went in a variety of directions after that. He moved from just continuing on with the same subjects that had come out of the Depression—the poor, hungry and homeless people—to more universal themes."

The search for a way out of a dry period may also lead to new ideas for artwork as well as energy for the task. Edward Hopper, who is best known for his paintings of urban life, lived most of the year in New York City but he frequently became restless there, unable to paint. His restlessness led him to travel around the country and to Mexico, subsequently yielding a sizable body of paintings devoted to people on trains and highways, at gas stations and hotels.

Painter Will Barnet, whose career is known for having undergone numerous stylistic changes, has also been prone to dry periods. Born in 1911, Barnet was a realist who focused primarily on social problems in the 1930s. His imagery became increasingly abstract by the early 1940s, and he again returned to realism by the late 1950s. "The dry periods came more during the early years," he stated. "There have been fewer since then. In the early years, they also lasted longer, sometimes up to a year. The problem always was that I wasn't quite sure how to handle my forms. I was searching for something elusive, and it took a while to find the key."

One of the things that helped him find that key was printmaking, first woodblock and later color lithography. It was a natural choice for Barnet, who had worked in the 1930s as a printer and taught graphic art for 45 years at the Art Students League in New York City. "The flatness of the print, the solid blocks of color that you use, especially with the woodcuts, helped me get away from all the gradations of color, helped me get away from the realistic figure, to something more abstract." Barnet's interest in abstraction led to his participation in what was called, in the 1940s and 1950s, the "Indian Space" school of painting, which adopted imagery from the designs of the Mayans, Peruvians and Native American tribes of the Northwest. "It was abstraction that wasn't so dependent on self-expression," he said. "You didn't only deal with yourself but with other, larger cultures."

By the late 1950s, Barnet had again reached a crossroads and was looking for a new key to painting, this time using more realistic, people-oriented subject matter. Like Ben Shahn, Barnet was also searching for a realism that went beyond social problems but he was unsure which themes held enough interest for him. Again, color lithography allowed him to experiment with ideas and techniques that he could take back to the canvas. "With prints, you are still drawing, still composing, still using color, just as in a painting," Barnet said, "but you can change the drawing or composition or colors in the print in a way that you can't with a canvas. The canvas is right there in front of your nose." He has continued to make prints from time to time, to sketch regularly and, until recently, to teach, all of which have provided him with a high degree of artistic stimulation.

Another source of inspiration, or an antidote to a dry period, has come from his fellow artists, seeing what they are doing, listening to the ideas they are pursuing, and talking with them about other artists and their work. "I'm not the kind of person who likes to live in the country all by myself," he said. "I'm a people person. I like to paint people, and I like to be with people. I like living in New York City for that reason."

A student of art history, Barnet also gained inspiration for new ideas from visits to museums, especially the Metropolitan Museum of Art and the Frick Museum in New York. Honoré Daumier and Juan Gris were early sources of inspiration for him—Daumier for his portrayal of the social condition of the poor and oppressed, Gris for his use of color and sense of cubist form—but, later, Barnet gained a new appreciation of the work of Jan Vermeer. "Vermeer could make a universe out of the corner of a room," he said. "I had been thinking about moving inside, from making paintings of people in the street—the old social condition stuff—to paintings of families, my family. A family is an interesting, organic thing. You can watch it start, as it grows and develops, and mark all the important changes that take place along the way. When I saw how well Vermeer could manage interior scenes, I gained the courage to try out what I had been thinking about."

While Barnet has remained interested in the art of the recent and distant past, which he calls "connecting up with art history," as a source of ideas, many other artists feel a bit more detached or want to get away from the art of the past altogether. Photographer Mary Frey noted that she gets "solace and sustenance from looking at the work of artists of the past but, after all, I'm a contemporary artist and I need to find the work of contemporary artists. I think that my work has become part of a dialogue with contemporary art, and so it is more important to me to see what similar or not-so-similar things other artists are doing currently." Noting that a mental block indicates "something that you are trying to avoid," Janet Fish said that a dry period "can lead you to stop working entirely. As they say, when you fall off a horse, you have to get right back on the horse because, the longer you wait, the harder it becomes to get back on the horse. You just have to keep painting. Going to museums can easily become another way to avoid working. It certainly is that way for me."

For many artists, the act of creating a work of art is analogous to following a train of thought, developing and reworking ideas that may or may not come together to form a successful piece. A dry period may arise when artists have not pushed their ideas far enough or when a particular problem has already been solved—leaving artists only to repeat themselves. Janet Fish has found that her response to a problem in her work is to open herself to new ideas and experiences, and to keep working. "Sometimes, I work small when I'm not sure about what I'm doing," she said. "Better a little bad painting than a big bad painting." Fish noted that it is important to distinguish between a dry period, when problems in one's work need to be confronted, and just having a bad day, when nothing seems to go quite right. A particularly rough dry period can lead an artist to "do anything to avoid dealing with the painting." To her mind, the worst thing to do is "indulge in a dry period and let yourself quit working altogether. That way, you lock yourself into a mental block. If you get too polemical, or overly embroiled in a certain narrow idea, you can't go anywhere."

Finding New Inspiration and Creating New Art

Exactly how new styles and concepts in art are born may be the secret of creativity, a power of mind that doesn't become clearer to anyone through knowing that it stems from the right or left side of the brain. Innovation comes through trial and error, experimenting with ideas until something that is both distinct and personal is developed. Artists often develop some sort of moat that effectively distances them from the outside world, and most agree that they must in some way blind themselves to the real world to envision the unseen.

Painter Philip Guston consciously sought to avoid both contemporary and historical art as he prepared himself to start a new work. First, according to his New York art dealer David McKee, Guston would go out to some double feature, picking the trashiest movie he could find so that, by the time he got back to his studio, all the art history he knew and the knowledge of what other artists were doing would be obliterated. Then, he began painting something that he hoped wasn't imitative but fresh.

There are a lot of ways artists prepare themselves to begin a new piece, but they all know the fear Guston had. No one wants to express him- or herself in a work of art only to realize that Matisse did the same thing 70 years earlier. It is increasingly difficult for many artists to get around this problem—a large number of them work in universities and find themselves teaching to students the very stuff they are trying to forget when it's time to create. The more recent emphasis on "quoting" art of the past and "appropriationism" in general by many younger, contemporary artists reflects a new attitude about this concern. To these younger artists, creating in the information age does not always mean creating something original: one takes in data, manipulates it and feeds it back to the world. This reflects a greater faith in the external than the internal world, and it raises questions concerning how artists can create something that is new. The idea of "the new" itself is a modernist concept that many younger, postmodernists reject.

Still, most artists believe that their personal viewpoint is of value and that they can offer more than commentary on past images. Far more than reveling in their sources, artists over the past hundred years have frequently sought to distance themselves from, as well as reject, art that has influenced them. "History . . . is a nightmare from which I am trying to awake," James Joyce wrote, and the Italian futurist F. T. Marinetti proclaimed in a manifesto, "Come on! Set fire to the library shelves! Turn aside the canals to flood the museums! Oh, the joy of seeing the glorious old canvases bobbing adrift on those waters, discolored and shredded!"

Attending double features is one way to block out the rest of the world, but there are many others. "I generally clean the house a few times, or go shopping," noted painter/sculptor Lucas Samaras, "all sorts of stuff to wipe my consciousness clean of what everyone else is doing." "The further I get into my own books, the less capable I become of reading other people's works," author Judith Rossner said. "I read magazines, watch TV. Any stupidity is all right." Painter Larry Rivers also claimed that "I guess that I am guilty of setting up egotistical defenses against intrusions from the outside world from time to time.

Every artist has to make himself a little stupid, a little blind, a little insensitive and a little arrogant—everything we don't want to be." For her part, painter Lois Dodd stated that her recipe is to "get myself some time and space to think, just clear my head of other stuff. Of course, I paint landscapes, and I can generate excitement from just going out into a landscape and looking around. I think it's harder to get excited when you are standing around in your studio."

Within a self-imposed solitude, most artists claim that the first construction, even before the work itself, is their identity that will create the art. The persona or vision is really what the art is about and, within this identity, the artists put their stamp on experiences. This personal voice gives the past a freshness and vitality that moves tradition into innovation.

New art opens one's eyes to the world in a new way—although the line between what is new and what is old is somewhat blurred, because newness is something measured in small degrees. Major breakthroughs are few, and they largely derive from already existing genres, as Picasso's cubism is partially indebted to Cézanne and African art, and Kandinsky's abstract paintings owe much to the fauvists. Artists make a small turn of the dial from what they know, and this moves the new work into its own arena—divorced from, yet carrying on, tradition. Tradition is not a forward-looking entity, and historians only discern it by looking backwards, for instance, identifying how photo-realism derived from pop art, which itself grew out of the principles of dada, many of whose practitioners were greatly influenced by cubism. The approved artists of the nineteenth-century French academies, who denounced the Impressionists, thought of tradition as something to follow but, for most of them, it led nowhere other than obscurity. Artists of the past are silent unless those of the present give them validity through borrowing ideas and expanding on them.

Historians will justifiably show how something that looks new is actually part of a long line of development, but that ignores the fact that the art of our time still looks new to us. What an artist brings to a tradition is the present—a set of ideas, assumptions and circumstances that gives every time period a distinct character—and this finally does wake us up, as James Joyce hoped, from what has gone on before. Contemporary art wakes us up to ourselves. "This history of art is all part of the baggage you take along as an artist," painter Chuck Close said. "I try to purge my work of other people, but there is no sense in reinventing the typewriter when you want to compose a novel. You are an artist because you turn what you have seen and know into something else."

Changing from One Medium to Another

"With painting, you can get a high you find nowhere else," artist Lila Katzen said. "When you're painting, you move in a rhythmic way. There's a lot of give-and-take. With sculpture, on the other hand, you're taking intractable materials and trying to make them into something else. There's so much excruciating work, and it takes so long." So why, then, is Katzen a sculptor rather than a painter? She started out as a painter, studying for three years with Hans Hofmann, turning out abstract expressionist pictures before giving that up in the 1960s for sculptural installations composed of aluminum, plastic, mirrors, fluorescent liquids and ultraviolet lights.

Ultimately, Katzen wanted something more than what the painted canvas could provide. Many artists, in fact, start out in one medium and eventually turn to another as their needs change or their desire to express themselves requires new forms. To most people, art is painting, and most would-be artists enter the field with the desire to learn how to paint. (Far fewer start out with the idea, 'I plan to be a performance artist or a sculptor working with found objects,' or something like that.) Drawing, which more naturally leads to painting than sculpture, for instance, is almost every artist's main introduction to art. Michelangelo jokingly commented that "with my mother's milk, I sucked in the hammer and chisels I use for my statues," although it was really drawing—which led Michelangelo's father to apprentice his son to a painter before Lorenzo de Medici borrowed the young artist for his newly formed sculpture academy—that was his first love.

For Lila Katzen, the evolution from painting to sculpture reflected the sense of dissatisfaction that, with a painting, "you move into it through your eyes and then your mind. I wanted the viewer to have more physical contact with this two-dimensional thing." The transformation did not take place overnight. Her paintings grew in size, sometimes measuring 12-by-12-feet. In order "to get the painting to come out in three-dimensional space," she began using fluorescent paint, placing black lights under the paintings, and creating a painted wooden base on which several painted acrylic sheets were mounted. Still, this sculptural painting did not fully satisfy her, and she stopped painting altogether for a short period of time in order to collect her thoughts. "I realized that I was more in love with the forms and shapes than with the canvas," Katzen stated. "Canvas was only a means to an end, and I could get that physical contact with the viewer more readily with sculpture than through a painting."

George Segal, whose figurative plaster cast sculptures evoke the pathos of everyday life, also studied as a painter and had a number of exhibits of his work during the late 1950s and early 1960s. Like Katzen, he "loved painting, but it was the ideas about what painting should and shouldn't be that were being taught at the time that gave me trouble. There were all these rules and regulations that had to be followed: the surface of the canvas had to remain intact; there could be no illusion of depth; the complete rejection of figuration. I was asked to shut out the validity of what I could see and what I could touch. After a while, the only space I understood was the space between my own body and the canvas."

Ironically, it was the attraction of abstract expressionist painting that impelled Segal to switch from Pratt Art Institute to New York University, where this kind of art was being taught and discussed. When he gradually switched from painting to sculpture, he found the change liberating. "There were strictures to painting that didn't seem to apply to sculpture," he said. "I could use real-world materials in my sculpture, whereas that was impossible in a painting. I could pick up a piece of discarded scrap, turn it over, examine its history, use, associations, shape, and look into my own experience of it, as opposed to following a prescribed idea of what painting is. I have to tip my cap to [Marcel] Duchamp and [John] Cage, who were pioneers in reintroducing the poetry of reality into contemporary art." He added that "my generation broke out of the strictures of art, releasing an explosion of form possibilities." Subsequent artists found themselves thrust into this artistic ferment, frequently looking for a different means of expression than the painted canvas. Painting student William Wegman, for instance, claimed that "painting really seemed dead in the 1960s," and he experimented first with video and later photography, with which he established his reputation.

John Baldessari, who also had started his career as a painter before becoming associated with conceptual art, "became increasingly aware that there was more to art than just painting and sculpture. What I was doing as a painter started to seem elite, as though I was speaking in a private language. Photographic imagery and text was more accessible, because people are used to seeing photographs and text in newspapers." Viewing a photograph in the same way as a painting—"an organization of patches or light, dark and color on a surface"—Baldessari, like Katzen, considers the physical act of painting to be "very pleasurable, about as pleasurable as anything I've ever done, but that sense of pleasure is less important to me than communicating, which I think photography does a little better."

Changes in one's ideas lead to the search for new forms in which to contain or express those ideas. Sometimes, there is a relationship between the new and old work. For example, Reuben Kadish's murals and easel paintings of the 1930s contained heavy, three-dimensional forms, which were not wholly unlike the monumental rough-hewn figures in the sculptures he began to create in the 1950s. A turning point for him occurred during a 10-year period after the Second World War when he operated a dairy farm in Vernon, New York. He stopped painting and began to experiment with sculptural forms, creating figures out of mud and later moving to terra-cotta and bronze.

David Smith, who like Kadish, started as a painter before making his name as a sculptor, always maintained that he was really a painter working in three dimensions. "My student period was involved with painting," he wrote in *Arts* in 1960. "The painting developed into raised levels from the canvas. Gradually the canvas was the base and the painting was a sculpture." He drew his inspiration from painting, or more precisely certain cubist painters, but established his own unique style. The descendant of a pioneer blacksmith, Smith pursued his painting while taking factory jobs as a way to earn a living, such as assembling metal parts at Studebaker or welding in a defense plant during the Second World War. In 1928, however, he first saw pictures of the welded metal sculpture of Julio González and Pablo Picasso in the periodical *Cahiers d'Art* and, in the early 1930s, began to apply his knowledge of welding to creating works of art.

Like welded metal, ceramics was not viewed as a fine art medium until someone trained originally in painting began to make art out of pottery. Peter Voulkos spent a number of years as an abstract expressionist painter, but he also maintained an interest in ceramics based on a pottery class he took at the California College of Arts and Crafts. "Ceramics was a required course for applied arts students—so was belt weaving," Voulkos said. "The college assumed that everyone would go into teaching, and they wanted you to know a little of everything. I was forced to take this clay course, and I fell in love with it." In time, his pursuit of painting fell off, and his abstractly shaped, nonutilitarian ceramic sculptures achieved renown—not only on the West Coast where, during the 1940s and 1950s, an aesthetic grew up that focused on the physical properties of materials rather than on older European distinctions between art and craft, but around the world.

Leaving one principal medium for another doesn't mean never pursuing one's first love again. William Wegman began to draw again and eventually paint—semiabstract landscapes—in the mid-1980s after his photographic model, his dog Man Ray, died. Although still principally a photographer, Wegman's drawings and paintings have been exhibited in a number of galleries and museums. The most notable example of an artist returning to an earlier medium, of course, is Michelangelo, who told various listeners that "painting is not my profession" and had a clearly deficient understanding of frescos, but was still summoned by Pope Julius II in 1508 to paint the Sistine Chapel.

Many artists move back and forth between media throughout their careers. The same freedom they found in opening up new possibilities in art allows them to range over a variety of plastic forms. Peter Voulkos is one who continues to paint now and then, sometimes exhibiting his pictures with the sculpture or without. "I've always vacillated between painting and sculpture," he said. "Working with clay is sort of like working with thick paint—you mix it and push it around."

Artists as Patrons of Other Artists

Most artists have an art collection—usually, of course, it tends to be of their own work, neatly stacked and awaiting buyers. Many artists collect works by others as well, and they do this for a variety of reasons. Sometimes, artists seek to offer their peers encouragement by buying, or swapping for, their artwork; others simply purchase pieces for the same reasons as nonartist collectors. The works that artists collect, however, often has some important relationship to—and, perhaps, even an influence on—their own creations.

Conceptual artist Sol Lewitt, for instance, owns a sizable collection of works by generally like-minded artists that he built by swapping works, intending the trade as a vote of confidence in his colleagues. Norman Rockwell bought paintings from his colleagues when visiting their studios, with the idea of developing a collection of illustration art. Philip Pearlstein and Richard Haas, on the other hand, purchase pieces from art dealers. In fact, neither Pearlstein nor Haas buy paintings; rather, they have bought antiquities (pre-Columbian, Egyptian, Middle Eastern for Pearlstein; Chinese, Egyptian, Etruscan, Greek, Indian and Roman for Haas) as well as folk art (Pearlstein), architectural drawings (Haas) and prints from the Western Hemisphere and the Orient—none of which resemble their own highly detailed paintings.

However, the art that these two painters collect is more than part of their décor—it has become an element in their own work. Objects of American folk art have appeared in some of the more recent Pearlstein paintings. Architectural drawings as well as prints by eighteenth-century Italian artist Piranesi "have influenced me in terms of seeing what others have done," Haas said. He added: "You need the works in your hands, as opposed to seeing a reproduction in a book, to really understand what other artists did. For me, it's really a study collection."

The relationship between the pieces artists acquire and the work they do is frequently one of inspiration or influence. The French Impressionists were all collectors of Japanese prints, whose themes, patterns, and strong colors influenced the paintings they created. Mary Cassatt was led to the theme of mother and child by the Utamaro prints that she collected, and the walls of Monet's house in Giverny were covered with Japanese prints. Paul Gauguin created some paintings in the shape of fans, following the fashion of some Japanese artists, and even Toulouse-Lautrec's stylized monogram was modeled on Japanese insignia.

Large collections aren't for every artist. The post-impressionist French artists known as the Nabis (including Bonnard, Denis, Ranson, Serusier, and Vuillard) each chipped in to buy one painting by their mentor Gauguin, which they shared—perhaps, that is the opposite of collecting. Matisse claimed to have found inspiration in a small canvas by Paul Cézanne entitled *The Bathers*, which he had purchased from a dealer in 1899. Thirty-seven years later, as he donated the picture to the Petit Palais museum in Paris, the artist stated that the Cézanne "has sustained me morally in the critical moments of my venture as an artist: I have drawn from it my faith and my perseverance." Picasso collected various types of artwork, depending upon the kind of work he was doing at the time—including African art during his African-influenced period, and Old Masters later in life.

Today, fewer artists acquire art for the purpose of having an influential work in their possession, largely because there is greater access to public collections. "I never felt that I had to live with anything that needed to be near my eyeball," painter LeRoy Neiman stated. "There are enough museums where you can see whatever you want." That view was echoed by Philip Pearlstein, who noted that "my collecting has more to do with my museum-going, rather than with the work I'm currently doing." An additional reason was offered by photographer Zeke Berman, who pointed out that there is a large number of books of art available: "The difference between reproductions and originals is not that great in photography."

Having important and influential works of art in one's possession is also limited by the escalating prices for art. Haas looks for "what captures my eye and what falls within the range of what I can afford. That unfortunately limits my choices. As soon as I start to get interested in something, prices go up and I can't afford what I've come to like." For that reason, artists—especially younger and lesser-known artists— often rely on trading with their contemporaries, whose work may reflect similar artistic concerns. Trading is certainly an advantage that artists have over nonartist collectors in acquiring works—Zeke Berman noted that with the duplicative medium of photography, "you can trade something and still keep it"—but difficulties may arise. "With trading, you may not get exactly the work you want," said painter Françoise Gilot. "You may find yourself just taking something from an artist in order to be polite." She added that this was not a significant problem for Picasso, with whom she lived for almost 10 years, who, when was owed money by a dealer, frequently took "a painting by another artist in lieu of payment. That way, he got the pieces he really wanted."

Painter Robert Cottingham, who has received works by Chuck Close, Robert Parker, William Steig and Wayne Thiebaud through trades with dealers, noted that one potentially troublesome aspect of swapping with other artists is "the awkwardness. How do you make the initial approach, break the ice? Do you just blurt out that you're interested in trading something of yours for something of theirs? And what if you find out that you covet someone's work but that person doesn't really care for your work nearly as much?"

Another difficulty with trading that particularly affects artists whose works have a strong market is that the Internal Revenue Service treats the value of artwork traded away and received as income, making it subject to a tax. "Trouble with the IRS stopped a lot of people from trading," photographer Joel Meyerowitz said. "They didn't want to report the trade as income because it wasn't really money that could be used to pay the tax with, and they weren't willing to go to jail for it."

For emerging artists, their collections tend to be as good as their contemporaries; with more established artists, as with most nonartist collectors, they are as good as their connoisseurship and wallet. The fact of being an artist doesn't necessarily guarantee a heightened ability to recognize quality in the work of others, but it probably helps. Artists can evaluate how their colleagues of the past and present have solved some of the same problems facing them.

Like many nonartist collectors, Philip Pearlstein relies on specialized art dealers for advice on what antiques to acquire. "You can get stuck with a fake or something that may have been brought to this country illegally," he said. "I don't keep up with all this, and I don't have time to follow the market for antiquities. I prefer to leave this to dealers." On the other hand, the 10,000-or-so-item collection of art and furniture that Andy Warhol amassed was found to contain a hodge-podge of low-, so-so, and high-quality pieces when his estate was sold at Sotheby's in 1988. What became most clear about Warhol after his death was that he had been an inveterate, almost compulsive buyer rather than a pure connoisseur.

While Norman Rockwell did assemble a representative sample of most of the major illustrators' work of his time, he never acquired any major pieces. Much of Picasso's African art collection was also made up of objects of low quality, according to William Rubin, former director of the department of painting and sculpture at New York City's Museum of Modern Art. Part of the reason for this, Rubin claimed, is that Picasso was more a connoisseur of bargains than quality when it came to African art, generally shopping in flea markets.

Artists as Benefactors

"Some of the most generous people in the world are artists," said Rubin Gorewitz, an accountant who has prepared the tax returns and acted as a financial manager for some of the most famous and successful visual artists of the past 30 years, including Jasper Johns, Peter Max and Robert Rauschenberg. Yet, successful artists are rarely thought of as generous benefactors, providing endowments for chairs in college or university departments or underwriting the building of a new wing for a hospital or museum as successful people in other professions have done. Instead, it is believed, visual artists are most generous when they are dead, as the wills of a number of noted, deceased artists (such as Adolph Gottlieb, Keith Haring, Jackson Pollock, Lee Krasner, Robert Mapplethorpe, Mark Rothko, and Andy Warhol) set up foundations in order to make charitable donations to individuals or institutions through the sale of artworks in the estate.

To a degree, the perception of visual artists is that they are recipients rather than the givers of donations. The problem is how publicity is generated and for what purposes. When comedian Bill Cosby donated $20 million to Spelman College in Atlanta in 1988, he also undoubtedly spent x number of thousands of additional dollars for his publicist— the Brokaw Agency in Los Angeles—to trumpet the news. Visual artists are far less likely to use public relations agencies and, when they do, it is usually to announce a new exhibition or the completion of a major commission. When an artist's foundation makes the news, it is more often unwanted attention, such as when the Warhol Foundation was accused of misusing its funds or when the executors of the Rothko estate are brought to trial and charged with fraud.

Most giving by successful visual artists is not posthumous, but it is often unheralded. Many artists, well known and unknown, regularly donate their work for charity auctions that benefits AIDS research, or homeless shelters, or some other philanthropic cause. For this, they receive very little benefit, first, as it is the cause or the event (rather than the individual items sold) that receives public attention and, second, since government regulations only allow artists to deduct the cost of the materials used in artworks they are donating. Giving artworks is often more generous than donating cash, as inflation will cause a dollar to decline in value over time while the worth of a work of art may increase exponentially during that same period. Jack Klein, who was Larry Rivers's landlord for a time, retired and moved to Paris after selling the paintings that the artist gave him in lieu of rent.

Up until 1970, Robert Rauschenberg's generosity frequently consisted of simply handing out cash to people who needed it. "I was doing his taxes one year," Rubin Gorewitz said, "and I told him, based on what he had earned, what he owed the government. He said that was impossible; he said that he didn't have any money left, because he had been giving away so much. He expected a big deduction, not to owe anything to the government." Gorewitz then helped the artist set up a nonprofit foundation, Change, Inc., which systematically provides money to indigent artists, legally permitting Rauschenberg to deduct the amounts spent. About the same time, Gorewitz assisted Jasper Johns in creating Contemporary Performance Arts, a nonprofit foundation that gives money to dancers and other performers. "Art," Gorewitz noted, "is not a career you can always count on to earn money," which is why visual artists may be more willing at times to donate objects rather than cash (they also tend to trade works with other artists rather than purchase them).

Even the most successful visual artist realizes that art is a risky endeavor. During their lives, artists frequently spend a considerable amount of their incomes on materials—sculptors particularly—as well as studio space and other work-related expenses. And yet, the works of art are not necessary, but are purchased for enjoyment. In addition, the vicissitudes of fame in the art world, where artists and styles are popular one season and forgotten the next, may lead noted artists to be cautious about how generous they plan to be while alive. For artists as for everyone else, donations need to be carefully planned. Setting up posthumous foundations to support either the arts or individual artists establishes a mechanism by which works in the estate are sold gradually, in order to maximize prices, and it does not burden the artist or his or her heirs with shortages of cash.

The question of whether or not artists are generous has gained urgency in the wake of funding cutbacks for governmental agencies supporting the arts. Instead of relying on the government to provide financial support to individuals and institutions, which may come with bureaucratic strings attached or that subject the arts to political attack, the argument goes, successful and wealthy artists should pool their cash to establish a private endowment. In effect, they should "give back" to the arts. Some artists and others have suggested that if a national resale royalty law were enacted, providing visual artists with a royalty of 5 percent when their work is resold at a profit, those artists could then donate that sum to a foundation to aid lesser-known artists.

There is a heartfelt logic to this, but it begs an obvious question: Why require artists—as opposed to all other professionals in our society—to be socialists? Why should successful artists share their wealth?

This is a question that would only be asked of artists—visual artists, more specifically—who frequently have known poverty and camaraderie with other struggling artists. Since the nineteenth century, artists have often identified their interests with those of poor people. No one would think to ask the heads of America's larger corporations to set aside a portion of their enormous incomes to help American-based entrepreneurs who are starting their own businesses. Improving the quality of life, which the arts do, is the job of government, and it is by the quality of life that a government and nation are judged.

&

■

Appendix

Correspondence Art Instruction Schools

For many, home study is not only practical but rewarding, providing the student the individual attention of an art instructor. Below are the major correspondence art schools in the United States. For more information on them, contact the National Home Study Council (1601 18th Avenue, N.W., Washington, D.C. 20009, 202/234-5100).

Art Instruction Schools
500 South 4th Street
Minneapolis, MN 55415
(800) 328-7513 or (612) 339-8721

Cartoonerama
Box 263A
Branford, CT 06405
(203) 488-4260

Famous Artists Schools
19 Newtown Turnpike
Westport, CT 06880
(203) 845-2333

Hemphill Schools
510 South Alvarado Street
Los Angeles, CA 90057-2998
(213) 413-6323

International Correspondence Schools
925 Oak Street
Scranton, PA 18515
(717) 342-7701, ext. 341

North Light School
1507 Dana Avenue
Cincinnati, OH 45207
(800) 759-0963

Vermont College of Norwich University
Master of Fine Arts in Visual Art
Adult Center
Montpelier, VT 05602
(800) 336-6974 or (802) 828-8500

Art Instructional Videocassette Publishers and Distributors

The back pages of *The Artists' Magazine, American Artist,* and several other periodicals have advertisements for videos by well- and lesser-known artists working in a variety of fields. In many instances, these are professionally made home movies and sold by the artists themselves; some artists seem to have as large a product line as General Motors. It isn't necessarily wiser to purchase from a publisher or distributor than from the artist as it is the particular artist and his or her technique that is reason for buying the videocassette in the first place. However, this list is largely confined to publishers and distributors.

Art Instruction Associates
2 Briarstone Road
Rockport, MA 01966
(508) 546-6114

Artists InterActive Video Productions
P.O. Box 9615, Dept. A3-92
Berkeley, CA 94709

Artists' Video Productions, Inc.
97 Windward Lane
Bristol, RI 02809
(800) 648-1602

Artquest, Inc.
P.O. Box 88
Chelsea, MI 48118
(800) 200-RT4U

ArtsAmerica, Inc.
Havemeyer Place
Greenwich, CT 06830
(800) 553-5268

Art Video Library
1389 Saratoga Way
Grants Pass, OR 97526
(503) 479-4071

Art Video Productions, Inc.
P.O. Box 941
Woodland Hills, CA 91365-9887
(818) 884-6278

William Blackman Productions
2369 Magda Circle
Thousand Oaks, CA 91360

C & L Productions, Inc.
2001 Brown & Williamson Tower
Louisville, KY 40202
(502) 568-8176

Candlelight Studios
P.O. Box 627
Little River, CA 95456

Centerpoint Distribution, Inc.
434 South First Street
San Jose, CA 95113
(408) 234-4458

Cleda Curtis Art Productions
P.O. Box 269
Oran, MO 63771
(314) 262-2374

Discover Art
P.O. Box 262424
San Diego, CA 92196

Signilar, Inc.
P.O. Box 278
Sanbornton, NH 03269-0278
(603) 934-3222

Sources for Matting and Framing Artwork

Asking for references for professional framers from other artists, collectors, dealers, or museum curators whose framing is appealing is the best approach for any artist. Many of them also advertise in art magazines and will mail brochures of their work.

Mat Cutters

Alto's EZ/Mat, Inc.
607 West Third Avenue
Ellensburg, WA 98926
(800) 225-2497

Borod and McGinnis
3723 Parker Hill Road
Santa Rosa, CA 95404
(707) 525-1618

Cole Engineering
2601 19th Street
Gulfport, MS 39501
(601) 868-9111

Dahle USA
6 Benson Road
Oxford, CT 06483
(203) 264-0505

Excel Hobby Blades Corporation
399 Liberty Street
Little Ferry, NJ 07643
(201) 807-1772

H.F. Esterly/Speed Mat
R.R. 3, Box 890, U.S. Route 1
Wiscasset, ME 04587
(800) 882-7017

Fletcher-Terry Company
65 Spring Lane
Farmington, CT 06053
(203) 677-7331

Gene Green Associates, Inc.
22 Windsor Isle
Longwood, FL 32779
(407) 333-0286

Hunt Manufacturing Company
230 South Broad Street
Philadelphia, PA 19102-4167
(215) 732-7700

Japico Drissler
Feionpapiergros Handel Gmbh & Co.
Insterburger Str. 16
6000 Frankfurt A.M.
Germany
149-69-7932-221

Lion Office Products
401 West Alondra Boulevard
Gardens, CA 90248
(213) 770-8386

Logan Graphic Products
1100 Brown Street
Wauconda, IL 60084
(800) 331-6232

M & M Distributors
P.O. Box 189
Tennent, NJ 07763
(800) 526-2302

Nielsen & Bainbridge
40 Eisenhower Drive
Paramus, NJ 07653
(201) 368-9191

Olfa Products Corporation
6200 S.O.M. Center Road, Suite D10
Cleveland, OH 44139
   or
P.O. Box 747
Plattsburgh, NY 12901
(216) 349-0800

Metal Section Frames

AGF
1551 Adie Road
St. Louis, MO 63043
(314) 991-3311

Alfred Schiftan, Inc.
406 West 31st Street
New York, NY 10001
(212) 532-1984

American Frame
Arrowhead Park
400 Tomahawk Drive
Maumee, OH 43537
(800) 537-0944

American Tombow, Inc.
31115 Via Colinas, Unit 302
Westlake Village, CA 91362
(800) 835-3222

Art Line International, Inc.
20 Wysocki Place
Hackensack, NJ 07601
(201) 342-3305

Borod & McGinnis
3723 Parker Hill Road
Santa Rosa, CA 95404
(707) 525-1618

CM International Mouldings
11015 West Avenue
Kensington, MD 20895
(800) 688-3250

Color Q
2710 Dryden Road
Dayton, OH 45439
(800) 999-1007

Cos-Tom Picture Frame
1121 Bay Boulevard
Chula Vista, CA 92011
(800) 854-6606

Decor Moulding, Ltd.
125 Adams Avenue
Hauppauge, NY 11788
(516) 231-5959

Documounts Framing Service
P.O. Box 26239
Eugene, OR 97402-0464
(800) 769-5639

Sam Flax
39 West 19th Street
New York, NY 10011
(212) 620-3000

Framatic
P.O. Box 4666
Glendale, CA 91222

or
3041 North Coolidge Avenue
Los Angeles, CA 90039
(213) 664-7888

Frame Fit Company
P.O. Box 8926
Philadelphia, PA 19135
(215) 332-0683

FrameMica Company
519 Johnson Avenue
Bohemia, NY 11716
(516) 567-8889

Frames By Mail
11551 Adie Road
St. Louis, MO 63043
(800) 332-2467

Franken Frames
609 West Walnut
Johnson City, TN 37604
(800) 322-5899

Gallery Clips Company
249 A Street
Boston, MA 02210
(617) 482-9347

Gemini Moulding, Inc.
524 South Hicks
Palatine, IL 60067
(708) 359-2005

Giraffe Designs
4510 Bullard Avenue
Bronx, NY 10470
(212) 525-3737

Global Art, Inc.
4550 Airwest, S.E.
Kentwood, MI 49512
(800) 231-9421

Graphik Dimensions, Ltd.
41-23 Haight Street
Flushing, NY 11355
(800) 221-0262

Greco Frame and Supply, Inc.
3813 South Purdue
Oklahoma City, OK 73179
(800) 888-9204

Ivy Industries, Inc.
P.O. Box 7747
Charlottesville, VA 22906
(800) 999-6464

Janow Wholesale Frame & Supply Co.
17 Andover Drive
West Hartford, CT 06110
(800) 225-2669

Larson-Juhl
4320 International Boulevard
Norcross, GA 30093
(404) 925-7492

Marco Picture Frames
3602 North 27th Avenue
Phoenix, AZ 85017
(602) 263-8322

The Mettle Company
P.O. Box 525, Dept. X
Fanwood, NJ 07023
(800) 621-1329

Nelson's Picture Framing Company
1215 Woodmere Street
Traverse City, MI 49684
(616) 946-6868

North American Enclosures
85 Jetson Lane
Central Islip, NY 11722
(800) 645-9209

Piedmont Moulding
P.O. Box 117
Conyers, GA 30207
(404) 483-1066

Roma Moulding
4040 Steeles Avenue West 7
Woodbridge, Ontario L4L 4Y5, Canada
(406) 850-1500

Structural Industries, Inc.
96 New South Road
Hicksville, NY 11801
(800) 645-3993

Tennessee Moulding & Framing Co.
1188 Antioch Pike
Nashville, TN 37211
(800) 821-5483

T.I. Industries/Indiana Moulding
40 West 12th Avenue
P.O. Box 1737
Lexington, NC 27293
(704) 249-4901

Valley Moulding & Frame
10708 Vanowen Street
North Hollywood, CA 91605
(800) 932-7665

Valley Wholesale Supply Corporation
10708 Vanowen Street
North Hollywood, CA 91605
(800) 932-7665

Victor Moulding & Frame
905 Lakeside Drive
Gurnee, IL 60031
(800) 366-9991

Washington Mouldings
11015 West Avenue
Kensington, MD 20895
(301) 946-7311

Other Section Frame Companies

Alto's EZ/Mat, Inc.
607 West Third Avenue
Elensburg, WA 98926
(800) 225-2497
*Mat-cutting handbook and instructional
videocassette, "Mat Cutting Simplified"*

AMCI
5-26 46th Avenue,
P.O. Box 1151
Long Island City, NY 11101
(800) 235-1510
Hand-carved, gold-leaf frames

Art and Framing Center
1121 Bay Boulevard, Suite C
Chula Vista, CA 91911
(800) 477-7024
Mat board

Blue Ridge Moulding & Framing
619 Warwick Street
Roanoke, VA 24105
(800) 272-2583

Denglas
8 Springdale Road
Cherry Hill, NJ 08003
(609) 424-1012
Antireflective glass

Elite Picture Frames
1547 Jayken
Chula Vista, CA 91911
(800) 854-6606
Wood and metal frames

Fetco International, Inc.
403 V.F.W. Drive
Rockland, MA 02370
(617) 871-2000
Frames in exotic woods, brass, ceramics

Frame Fit Co.
(800) 523-3693
http://www.netaxs.com/~framefit
Solid wood frames

FrameWealth, Inc.
R.D. 2, Box 261-7
Otego, NY 13825
(607) 433-2203
Custom frames and moldings

Framing Fabrics International
947 North Cole Avenue
Los Angeles, CA 90038
(800) 832-2742
Silks, linens, suedes

G-M Marketing & Distribution
960-G Melaleuca Avenue
Carlsbad, CA 92009
(619) 929-9164
Baroque-style frames

Genuine Gold Burl, Ltd.
(800) 726-7206
Frames and moldings

Goldleaf Framemakers of Santa Fe
1515 Fifth Street
Santa Fe, NM 87501
(505) 988-5005

Gudbrandsen Frame Company
4565 North Elston Avenue
Chicago, IL 60630
(312) 545-4161
Hardwood moldings

Harvey Fabrics
P.O. Box 668
Oyster Bay, NY 11711
(800) 221-1096
Fabrics for framing

Imperial Picture Frames
P.O. Box 598
Imperial Beach, CA 91933
(800) 423-2620
Wood and plastic frames

Innerspace/Innerseal
43 East Lancaster Avenue
Paoli, PA 19301
(215) 644-9293
*Sealers and spacers forming a barrier
between molding and work*

Kandu Industries, Inc.
1825 Industrial Park Drive
Grand Haven, MI 49417
(800) 747-0728
Ready-made frames

La Marche Moulding
20780 Leapwood Avenue
Carson, CA 90746
(213) 515-0475

Masterviewer Art & Frame Supply
1730 Dairy Ashford
Houston, TX 77077
(800) 735-8790
Rotating mat board sample holder

Matline, Inc.
P.O. Box 7121
Fairfax Station
Fairfax, VA 22039
(703) 978-4521
Ruling tools for cutting mats

New World Frames Co., Inc.
7 Krit Court
Keene, NH 03431
(603) 352-2401

PB & H Moulding Corporation
124 Pickard Drive East
Syracuse, NY 13211
(315) 455-5602
Handcrafted wood mouldings

Picture Framing Magazine
P.O. Box 420
Manalapan, NJ 07726
*Instructional videocassette "Conservation
Framing"*

Pres-On Merchandising Corporation
1020 South Westgate Drive
Addison, IL 60101
(708) 543-9370
Adhesive-coated mounting board

Pro-Craft
P.O. Box 81757
Cleveland, OH 44181
(800) 662-1000
Solid wood frames

Specialty Tapes
1405 16th Street
Racine, WI 53403
(414) 634-6688
Pressure-sensitive tapes for framing

Sprayaway, Inc.
484 Vista Avenue
Addison, IL 60101-4468
(708) 628-3000
Antistatic glass cleaners, adhesives

Talas
213 West 35th Street
New York, NY 10001
Conservation materials

Tennessee Moulding & Framing Co.
1188 Antioch Pike
Nashville, TN 37211
(800) 821-5483

Ten Plus, Inc.
9949 Taber Place
Santa Fe Springs, CA 90670
(213) 944-8899

Valley Moulding & Frame
10708 Vanowen Street
North Hollywood, CA 91605
(800) 524-1413 (CA); (800) 932-7665 (U.S.)

Viratec True Vue
1315 North Branch Street
Chicago, IL 60622
(312) 943-4200
Ultraviolet filtering glazing for framing

Warehouse Framers
507 Bishop Street, N.W.
Atlanta, GA 30318
(800) 227-2467
Sectional and custom frames

Wholesale Distributors Association
1901 Oakcrest Avenue, #3
St. Paul, MN 55113-2677
(800) 735-3025

The Williamson Company
206 North Summit, P.O. Box 477
Wayne City, IL 62895
(618) 895-2157
Baroque gold-leaf frames

Wolsey Company
15110 East Nelson Avenue
City of Industry, CA 91747
(818) 336-4575

Mat Board

A/N/W-Crestwood Paper Company
Division of Willmann Paper Company
315 Hudson Street
New York, NY 10013
(212) 989-2700

American Cardboard Company
3201 Fox Street
Philadelphia, PA 19129
(800) 523-3200

Archival Products, L.A.
4129 Sepulveda Boulevard
Culver City, CA 90230
(213) 391-3883; (213) 395-1465

Art Advantage/Eagle Mats
Box 550, Wind Cave Road
Hot Springs, SD 57747
(800) 228-0850

Art and Framing Center
1121 Bay Boulevard, Suite C
Chula Vista, CA 91911
(800) 477-7024

Bee Paper Company
321 Hamburg Turnpike
P.O. Box 2366
Wayne, NJ 07470
(201) 942-0260

Charrette
31 Olympia Avenue
Woburn, MA 01888
(800) 424-2467

The Columbia Corporation
Route 295
Chatham, NY 12037
(800) 833-1804

Crescent Cardboard Company
100 West Willow Road
Wheeling, IL 60090
(800) 323-1055

Gemini Moulding Company
524 South Hicks
Palatine, IL 60067
(708) 359-2005

Hartman Plastics, Inc.
R.D. #4 368B Poplar Road
Honey Brook, PA 19344
(215) 273-7113

Hunt Manufacturing Company
230 South Broad Street
Philadelphia, PA 19102-4167
(215) 732-7700

Larson-Juhl
4320 International Boulevard
Norcross, GA 30093
(404) 925-7492

Letraset USA
40 Eisenhower Drive
Paramus, NJ 07653
(201) 845-6100

Lineco, Inc.
P.O. Box 2604
Holyoke, MA 01041-0101
(800) 322-7775

Miller Cardboard Company
75 Wooster Street
New York, NY 10012
(212) 226-0833

Monsanto Company
800 North Lindbergh Boulevard
St. Louis, MO 63137
(314) 694-1000

Moore Push-Pin Company
1300 East Mermaid Lane
Wyndmoor, PA 19118
(215) 233-5700

Nielsen & Bainbridge
40 Eisenhower Drive
Paramus, NJ 07653
(201) 368-9191

Parsons Paper Division
84 Sargeant Street, P.O. Box 309
Holyoke, MA 01041
(413) 532-3222

Peterboro Cardboards, Ltd.
P.O. Box 476, 259 Landsdowne St. East
Peterborough, Ontario K9J 6Z6, Canada
(705) 742-0471

Re Use It Poster Board
P.O. Box 1450
Norcross, GA 30091
(800) 826-0343

Rising Paper Company
295 Park Street
Housatonic, MA 01236
(413) 274-3345

Rupaco Paper Corporation
110 Newfield, Raritan Center
P.O. Box 6564
Edison, NJ 08818
(908) 417-9266

Salwen Paper Company
151 Fieldcrest Avenue
Carson, NJ 08837
(908) 225-4000

Savage Universal Corporation
144 East 39th Street
New York, NY 10016
(212) 986-5752
   or
800 West Fairmont Drive
Tempe, AZ 85282
(602) 967-5882

Scratch-Art Company
P.O. Box 303
Avon, MA 02322
(508) 583-8085

Strathmore Paper Company
South Broad Street
Westfield, MA 01085
(413) 568-9111

Stu-Art
2045 Grand Avenue
Baldwin, NY 11510
(516) 546-5151

Wyndstone Papers
2001-A South Calumet Avenue
Chicago, IL 60616
(312) 943-3916

Custom Framers
The House of H. Heydenryk, Jr., Inc.
417 East 76th Street
New York, NY 10021

Julius Lowy Frame & Restoring
   Company, Inc.
223 East 80th Street
New York, NY 10021
   or
28 West End Avenue
New York, NY 10023

Eli Wilner & Company, Inc.
1525 York Avenue
New York, NY 10028

Mail Order Art Supply Companies

As the number of artists continues to grow in this country, so does the volume of services, including the ability to purchase art materials through the mail. There are many companies offering single product lines, such as projectors or easels (not included in this listing), but among the largest companies selling a range of merchandise to artists are:

Aiko's Art Materials Import
714 North Wabash
Chicago, IL 60611
Specializes in Japanese handmade paper,
and other Oriental art supplies

Aldy Graphic Supply, Inc.
1115 Hennepin Avenue
Minneapolis, MN 55403
(800) 289-2539
Products for printers and designers

Alvin and Company, Inc.
P.O. Box 188AA
Windsor, CT 06095
(203) 243-8991
Drafting, art and engineering supplies

Armstrong Products
P.O. Box 979
Guthrie, OK 73044
(405) 282-7584
Panels used in making booths for art fairs

Art Express
P.O. Box 21662
Columbia, SC 29221
(800) 535-5908
General art supplies

Art Mart
P.O. Box 1824
Aptos, CA 95001-1824
(800) 688-5798
Winsor & Newton paints, brushes, and
papers

Art Supply Warehouse
360 Main Avenue
Norwalk, CT 06851
(800) 243-5038
General art supplies

Arthur Brown and Bros., Inc.
58-95 Maurice Avenue
Maspeth, NY 11378
(800) 772-0619
General art supplies

Artisan/Santa Fe, Inc.
717 Canyon Road
Santa Fe, NM 87501
(800) 331-6375
General fine art supplies

Artists' Connection
600 Route One South
Iselin, NJ 08830
(800) 851-9333
General art supplies

ArtQuick Corporation
P.O. Box 565
Lincoln, MA 01773

Binders Discount Art Center
P.O. Box 53097
Atlanta, GA 30335
(800) 877-3242
General art supplies

Dick Blick
P.O. Box 1267
Galesburg, IL 61401
(800) 447-8192 (placing an order)
(800) 933-2542 (product information)
General art supplies

Cartoon Colour Company, Inc.
9024 Lindblade Street
Culver City, CA 90232
(213) 838-8467
Materials for cartoonists

Cerulean Blue Ltd.
Box 21168
Seattle, WA 98111
(206) 323-8600
Materials for fiber artists

Cheap Joe's Art Stuff
347 Industrial Park Drive
Boone, NC 28607
(800) 227-2788
General art supplies

Cheap Paint
11 Prince Street
New York, NY 10012-3578
(800) 932-9375
Artists paints

Chroma, Inc.
205 Bucky Drive
Lititz, PA 7543
(717) 626-8866; (800) 257-8278
Acrylic paints

Daler-Rowney
Two Corporate Drive
Cranbury, NJ 08512-9584
(609) 655-5252
General fine art supplies

David Davis—Classic Art Materials
D.D. Catalog Corp.
148 Mercer Street, Dept. 4
New York, NY 10012
(212) 343-9040; (800) 999-8519
General fine art supplies

Designs Plus
P.O. Box 1927
Santa Rosa, CA 95402
(800) 253-7224
Storage systems for art

Dixie Art Supplies
2612 Jefferson Highway
New Orleans, LA 70121
(800) 783-2612
General fine art supplies

Fidelity Products Co.
5601 International Pkwy., P.O. Box 155
Minneapolis, MN 55440-0155
(800) 328-3034
Graphic arts supplies

Flax Artist Materials
1699 Market Street
San Francisco, CA 94103
(415) 552-2355
General art supplies

Fletcher Lee & Co.
P.O. Box 007
Elk Grove, IL 60009-0007
(800) HOT-BUYS
Artists paints

General Pencil Co.
67 Fleet Street
Jersey City, NJ 07306
(201) 653-5351
or

P.O. Box 5311, 3160 Bay Road
Redwood City, CA 94063
(415) 369-4889
Drawing implements, erasers

Graphic Chemical & Ink Co.
728 North Yale Ave., Box 27, Dept. AA
Villa Park, IL 60181
(800) 465-7382
Printmaking supplies

Graphic Media Co.
Dept. A, 13916 Cordary Avenue
Hawthorne, CA 90250
Graphic art supplies

Gwartzman's
448 Spadina Avenue
Toronto, Ontario M5T 2C8, Canada
(416) 922-5429

The Italian Art Store
84 Maple Avenue
Morristown, NJ 07960
(973) 644-2717
Fine art supplies

Jerry's Artarama
117 South Second Street
New Hyde Park, NY 11040
(800) 827-8478
General art supplies

Kolinsky
43 Parkside Drive
East Hanover, NJ 07936
(800) 322-5254
Watercolor brushes

Joe Kubert Art Supplies
37A Myrtle Avenue
Dover, NJ 07801
(201) 328-3266
General art supplies

Leo Uhlfelder Co.
420 South Fulton Avenue
Mount Vernon, NY 10553
Fine art supplies

Tom Lynch Watercolors, Inc.
P.O. Box 1418
Arlington, IL 60005
Watercolor supplies

T.G. Miller's Sons Paper Co.
330 East State Street
Ithaca, NY 14850
(800) 724-3113
General art supplies

Montoya Art Studios, Inc.
435 Southern Boulevard
West Palm Beach, FL 33405-2605
(407) 832-4401
Supplies for sculptors

New York Central Art Supply
Dept. AA-10, 62 Third Avenue
New York, NY 10003
General art supplies

norArt
Harstrup Associates, Inc.
51 Storer Avenue
Pelham, NY 10803
(914) 738-7168
http://www.mediatekk.com/web/
    harstrup
Artists paints

Nova Color
5894 Blackwelder Street
Culver City, CA 90232
(213) 870-6000
Artists paints

Oriental Art Supply
P.O. Box 6596
Huntington Beach, CA 92615
(714) 962-5189

S.C. Ott's
714 Greenville Boulevard
Greenville, NC 27858
(800) 365-3289
General art supplies

Paragona Art Products
P.O. Box 3324
Santa Monica, CA 90408
(800) 991-5899
General art supplies

Pearl Paint
P.O. Box 946
Smithtown, NY 11787
(212) 431-5420; (800) PEARL-91
General art supplies

Perma Colors Division
226 East Tremont
Charlotte, NC 28203
(704) 333-9201; (800) 365-2656
Fine art supplies

John Pike Art Products
P.O. Box 171
Endwell, NY 13761
(800) 882-0417
General art supplies

S&S Worldwide
Mill Street
Colchester, CT 06415
(203) 537-3451
Materials for fine artists and craftspeople

Sax Arts & Crafts
P.O. Box 51710/Dept. A2
New Berlin, WI 53151
(414) 784-6880
General art supplies

Selwyn Textile Co., Inc.
134 West 29th Street
New York, NY 10001
(800) 223-3032
Linen and cotton canvases

Sisyphus Art Supply
(800) 872-2545
Stretcher bars and canvases

Daniel Smith
4130 First Avenue South
Seattle, WA 98134-2302
(800) 426-6740
General art supplies

Stretch-Art
141 East 162 Street
Gardena, CA 90248
(800) 942-8212
http://www.stretchart.com
Linen and cotton canvases

Stu-Art
2045 Grand Avenue
Baldwin, NY 11510
(516) 546-5151
Mats, frames and shrink-wraps

Testrite Instrument Co., Inc.
135 AA Monroe Street
Newark, NJ 07105
Easels, light boxes, exhibition lights, projectors

Triangle Art Center
P.O. Box 8079
Princeton, NJ 08543
(609) 883-3600
General art supplies

Tricon Colors
16 Leliarts Lane
Elmwood, NJ 07407
(201) 794-3800

Tubes in Time
P.O. Box 369
New Oxford, PA 17350
(717) 624-8993
Cardboard mailing tubes

United Art Education Supply
Box 9219
Ft. Wayne, IN 46899
(800) 322-3247
Fine art materials; elementary school art supplies

Utrecht
33 35th Street
Brooklyn, NY 11232
(718) 768-2525; (800) 223-9132
General art supplies

Wallis Pastel
(503) 244-1138
Pastels

Williamsburg
R.R. 1, Box 465E
East Meredith, NY 13757
(800) 293-9399
Artists paints

Windberg Enterprises, Inc.
8601 Cross Park Drive, Suite 200
Austin, TX 78754
(800) 531-5181
Art panels

Yuemei
E.A.C., Inc., 1033 Farmington Avenue
Farmington, CT 06032
(800) 414-9141
Chinese papers

Artists Who Make Art Supplies for Other Artists

"Part of my responsibility as an artist is to get the materials I feel I need, not just what is readily available," painter Larry Bell said. For that reason, Bell calls on painter Stefan Watson at Watson Paper Company in Albuquerque, New Mexico, for the specialized handmade papers he uses in his works on paper. A small but growing number of artists like Watson have moved from making materials for themselves to producing art supplies for other artists. They include:

Robert Doak & Associates
89 Bridge Street
Brooklyn, NY 11201
(718) 237-0146
Pastels, watercolor concentrates, oil paints, resins, conservation materials, linen and cotton duck

Gamblin Artists Colors
P.O. Box 625
Portland, OR 97207
(503) 228-9763
Artist- and student-grade oil paints, etching inks

Guerra Paints & Pigments
510 East 13th Street
New York, NY 10009
(212) 529-0628
Pigment colors, powders and concentrates, resins, additives, thickeners, binders, oil paints

Larry Horowitz
Box 120, Croton Heights Road
Yorktown Heights, NY 10598
(914) 962-2383
Pastels

Lapis Arts
1295 South Dahlia Street
Denver, CO 80222
(303) 298-7804
Oil paints

Keith Lebenzon
6200 S.W. Roundhill Way
Portland, OR 97221
(503) 292-4252
Brushes

Carl Plansky
315 Berry Street
Brooklyn, NY 11211
or
266 Elizabeth Street
New York, NY 10012
(212) 219-9535
Oil paints

R&F Encaustics
110 Prince Street
New York, NY 10012
(914) 331-3112; (800) 206-8088
Encaustic paints, oil paint sticks

Watson Paper Company
1719 Fifth Street
Albuquerque, NM 87102
(505) 242-9351

William & Arthur
12-18 Commerce Street
Brooklyn, NY 11031
Oil paints

Certain art stores also are known for stocking materials that include custom brushes, crayons, inks, paints, papers, pastels, pigments, and resins made by artists as well as other top-quality speciality items manufacturered in the United States or abroad:

Artisans Santa Fe
717 Canyon Road
Santa Fe, NM 87501
(505) 988-2179; (800) 331-6375

New York Central Art Supply
62 Third Avenue
New York, NY 10003
(212) 477-0400

Savoir Faire
P.O. Box 2021
Sausalito, CA 94966
(415) 332-4660

Art Workshops

Thousands of workshops are offered throughout the year and around the country, for artists of most media and all levels of skill. Many are arranged by the instructors themselves, while inns and schools hold most of the others. The March issues of *American Artist* magazine and *The Artist's Magazine* provide comprehensive listings of who is offering what where and when. Below are a number of the largest workshop sponsors (rather than workshops offered by individual artists), where one may write for information.

Domestic Workshops

Alabama
American Society of Portrait Painters
P.O. Box 230216
Montgomery, AL 36123-0216
(800) 622-7672

Arizona
Scottsdale Artists' School, Inc.
P.O. Box 8527
Suite 201
Scottsdale, AZ 85252-8527
(602) 990-1422

California
Artist Workshop
2230 Pennsylvania Avenue
Fairfield, CA 94533
(707) 425-1560

Artists Workshop Tours Agency
606 Myra Avenue
Chula Vista, CA 91910
(619) 585-8071

Cambria Pines Lodge Workshops
2905 Burton Drive
Cambria, CA 93428
(805) 927-4200

Central Coast Studio Workshops
Suite C, 365 Quintana Road
Morro Bay, CA 93442
(805) 772-4198

CSU Summer Arts
Humboldt State University
Arcata, CA 95521
(707) 826-5401

D'Pharr Painting Workshops
8527 MacDuff Court
Stockton, CA 95209
(209) 477-1562

Hillcrest Art Center
800 Hillcrest
Cambria, CA 93428
(805) 927-1537

Ladybug Art Gallery & Workshop Studio
462 Rose Street
Bishop, CA 93514
(619) 873-3600

Lighthouse Art Center Workshops
575 Highway U.S. 101 South
Crescent City, CA 95531
(707) 464-4137

Mendocino Art Center
P.O. Box 765
Mendocino, CA 95460
(707) 937-5818

Merced College Watercolor Workshop
3600 M Street
Merced, CA 95348
(209) 384-6223

Palos Verdes Art Center Master Series
    Workshops
5504 West Crestridge Road
Rancho Palos Verdes, CA 90274
(310) 541-2479

Redwood Coast Art Workshops
Lighthouse Art Center
575 U.S. Highway 101 South
Crescent City, CA 95531
(707) 464-4137

San Diego Artists' School Workshops
P.O. Box 803
Jamul, CA 91935
(619) 697-9114

Colorado
Anderson Ranch Arts Center Workshops
P.O. Box 5598, 5263 Owl Creek Road
Snowmass Village, CO 81615
(303) 923-3181

Artists of the Rockies Workshops
Westcliffe Centre for the Arts
P.O. Box 930
Westcliffe, CO 81252
(719) 783-2296

Blackhawk Mountain School of Art
Box 5324
Estes Park, CO 80517
(800) 477-2272

Colorado Watercolor Workshops
3305 Brenner Place
Colorado Springs, CO 80917
(719) 591-0380

Higher Elevations Artists Workshop
P.O. Box 457
Lake City, CO 81235
(212) 246-4405

Loveland Academy of Fine Arts
205 12th Street, S.W.
Loveland, CO 80537
(800) 762-5232

Schalew Corporation Workshops
346 South Karval Drive
Pueblo West, CO 81007-2721
(719) 547-0329

Upper Edge Gallery Workshops
303 East Main
Aspen, CO 81611
(303) 544-0803

Connecticut
Brookfield Craft Center Workshops
P.O. Box 122
Brookfield, CT 06804
(203) 775-4526

Rudman Watercolor Workshops
274 Quarry Road
Stamford, CT 06903
(203) 322-1448

Florida
Armory Arts Center Master Artist
    Workshops
1703 South Lake Avenue
West Palm Beach, FL 33401
(561) 832-1776

Gainesville Fine Arts Association
P.O. Box 4323
Gainesville, FL 32613-4323

Hilton Leech Studio Watercolor
    Workshops
P.O. Box 15766
4433 Riverwood Avenue
Sarasota, FL 34277-1766
(941) 924-5770

Palm Beach Photographic Workshops
600 Fairway Drive
Deerfield Beach, FL 33432
(407) 391-7557

Katherine Rowland Workshops
P.O. Box 35187
Sarasota, FL 34242
(813) 349-1714

Visual Arts Center of Northwest Florida
  Workshops
19 East 4th Street
Panama City, FL 32401
(904) 769-4451

Georgia
Atlanta College of Art Workshops
1280 Peachtree Street, N.E.
Atlanta, GA 30309
(404) 898-1169

Illinois
Artists Book Works Workshops
1422 West Irving Park Road
Chicago, IL 60613
(312) 348-4469

Indiana
Art Barn
695 North 400 East
Valparaiso, IN 46383
(219) 462-8520

Louisiana
New Orleans Watercolor Workshops
8809 Tanglewild Place
New Orleans, LA 70123
(504) 737-5281

Maine
Eastport Arts Center
P.O. Box 153
Eastport, ME 04631
(207) 853-2955

Maine Coast Art Workshops
P.O. Box 236
Port Clyde, ME 04855
(207) 372-8200

Rock Gardens Inn
P.O. Box 178
Sebasco Estates, ME 04565
(207) 389-1339

Round Top Center for the Arts
Box 1316, Business Route 1
Damariscotta, ME 04543
(207) 563-1507

Sebasco Art Workshops
Rock Gardens Inn
Sebasco Estates, ME 04565
(207) 389-1339

Maryland
Haystack Mountain Workshops
408 Washington Street
Cumberland, MD 21502
(301) 777-0003 or (800) 286-9718

Massachusetts
Cape Cod School of Art
P.O. Box 948
Provincetown, MA 02657-0948
(508) 487-0101

Copley Society of Boston
158 Newberry Street
Boston, MA 02116
(617) 536-5049

North Shore Arts Association
197 Rear East Main Street
Gloucester, MA 01930
(508) 283-1857

Patuxent Art Workshops
12220 Shadetree Lane
Laurel, MD 20708
(301) 725-0386
Workshops take place on Cape Cod, MA

Rockport Art Association
The Old Tavern on Main Street
Rockport, MA 01966
(508) 546-6604

Seaward Inn Painting Holidays
Seaward Inn, Marmion Way
Rockport, MA 01966
(508) 546-3471

Michigan
Creative Art Workshops
6850 Brookeshire Drive
West Bloomfield, MI 48322
(313) 669-4736; (800) 750-7010

The Depot Watercolor Workshops
420 Rail Street
Negaunee, MI 49866
(906) 475-4067

Helga's Palette
P.O. Box 736
Sault Ste. Marie, MI 49783
(906) 632-3437 or (941) 983-0119

Kalamazoo Institute of Arts
314 South Park Street
Kalamazoo, MI 49007
(616) 349-7775

Northern Michigan Art Workshops
720 South Elmwood, Suite 3
Traverse City, MI 49684
(616) 941-9488

Minnesota
Atelier North School of Classical
    Realism
1066 Highway 61 East
Two Harbors, MN 55616
(218) 834-2059

Bloomington Art Center
10206 Penn Avenue South
Bloomington, MN 55431
(612) 948-8746

Grand Marais Art Colony
P.O. Box 626
Grand Marais, MN 55604
(800) 385-9585

Minnesota River School
190 South River Ridge Circle
Burnsville, MN 55337
(800) 205-2489

Missouri
Artists Unlimited Fourth Annual Workshop
Contact: Sandra Luck
9804 East 76th Terrace
Raytown, MO 64138-1709
(816) 353-1422

Montana
Beartooth School of Wildlife Art
Box 103
Big Timber, MT 59011
(406) 932-5228

Nebraska
Art Workshops
6741 Kansas Avenue
Omaha, NE 68104-1035
(402) 571-6299

Autumn Art Workshops
Route 2, Box 79
Oshkosh, NE 69154
(308) 772-4365

New Jersey
Cinnaminson Art Workshops
1316 Sylvania Avenue
Cinnaminson, NJ 08077
(609) 829-3485

New Mexico
Carrizo Art School
Drawer A
Ruidoso, NM 88345
(800) 687-2787

Casa Feliz Workshops
137 Bent Street
Taos, NM 87571
(505) 758-9790

Cloudcroft Summer Workshops
213 East Fir Avenue
Muleshoe, TX 79347
(806) 272-3889
Workshops take place in Cloudcroft, NM

Fechin Institute Art Workshops
P.O. Box 220
San Cristobal, NM 87564
(505) 776-2622

Flyfishing and Painting Workshop
P.O. Box 574
Santa Fe, NM 87504-0574
(888) 833-3383

Mountain Majesty Workshops
P.O. Box 66
High Rolls, NM 88325
(800) 682-2547

New Mexico Artists' Association
2801 Rodeo Road, Suite 239B
Santa FE, NM 87505
(505) 982-5639

Plum Tree Workshops
Box A-1
Pilar, NM 87531
(800) 373-6028

Rio Grande Artes Workshops
Holy Cross Retreat
P.O. Box 158
Mesilla Park, NM 88047
(505) 524-3688

Taos Institute of Arts
P.O. Box 1389
Taos, NM 87571
(505) 758-2793

Trillium Workshops
31 Walmer Road, Unit 1
Toronoto, Ontario M5R 2W7, Canada
(800) 263-1505
Workshops take place in Santa Fe, NM

Valdes Santa Fe Art Workshops
1006 Marquez Place
Santa Fe, NM 87501
(505) 982-0017

New York
Arts Guild of Old Forge, Inc.
Arts Center, Rte. 28 at Whistle Creek
Old Forge, NY 13420
(315) 369-6411

Drawing Academy of the Atlantic
180 Varick Street
New York, NY 10014
(212) 206-7444

Fabrizio Art Studios
1556 Third Avenue
New York, NY 10128
(212) 289-1466

Hudson River Valley Art Workshop
Greenville Arms
P.O. Box 659
Greenville, NY 12083-0659
(518) 966-5219
(800) 877-5219

Manhattan Graphics Center
476 Broadway
New York, NY 10013
(212) 219-8783

New York Academy of Art
419 Lafayette Street
New York, NY 10003
(212) 505-5300

Omega Institute
R.D. 2, Box 377
Rhinebeck, NY 12572
(914) 338-6030

Pastel Society of America
15 Gramercy Park South
New York, NY 10003
(212) 533-6931

Pearl Art & Craft Workshops
2411 Hempstead Turnpike
East Meadow, NY 11554
(516) 731-3700

R & F Encaustics
110 Prince Street
Kingston, NY 12401
(800) 206-8088

Skidmore College Summer Six Art
    Program
Saratoga Springs, NY 12866
(518) 581-5000, ext. 2372

Woodstock School of Art
P.O. Box 338
Woodstock, NY 12498
(914) 679-2388

North Carolina
Penland School Summer Workshops
Penland, NC 28765
(704) 765-2359

North Dakota
International Music Camp Summer
    School of Art
1725 11th Street, S.W.
Minot, ND 58701
(701) 263-4211

Ohio
Artist's Studio Workshops
North Light Art School
1507 Dana Avenue
Cincinnati, OH 45207
(800) 825-0963

Ohio Institute of Photography Workshops
2029 Edgefield Road
Dayton, OH 45439
(513) 294-6155

Six Steps to Success
Color Q, Inc.
2710 Dryden Road
Dayton, OH 45439
(800) 999-1007

Oklahoma
Bartlesville Art Association Workshops
P.O. Box 3211
Bartlesville, OK 74006
(918) 333-4134

Oklahoma Art Workshops
6953 South 66th East Avenue
Tulsa, OK 74133
(918) 492-8863

Oregon
A.I.M. Workshops & Painting Trips
P.O. Box 279
Jacksonville, OR 97530
(541) 899-1179

Art in the Mountains Workshops
19715 Sunshine Way
Bend, OR 97702
(503) 382-0988

Joseph Art School
P.O. Box 106
Joseph, OR 97846
(800) 459-3605

Oregon School of Arts and Crafts
8245 Southwest Barnes Road
Portland, OR 97225
(503) 297-5544

Pennsylvania
Handcrafter Gallery and Studio
112 School Lane
Telford, PA 18969
(215) 721-9505

Pine Knob Inn
Box 275
Canadensis, PA 18325
(717) 595-2532

Pocono Pines Gallery and Workshops
Pocono Pines, PA 18350
(717) 646-3937

South Carolina
Hilton Head Art League Workshops
P.O. Box 7753
Hilton Head Island, SC 29938
(800) 995-4068

Tennessee
Farmhouse Artist, Inc.
P.O. Box 6
Walland, TN 37886
(615) 982-7479

Texas
Artists and Craftsmen Associated
2917 Swiss Avenue
Dallas, TX 75204
(214) 368-5829

Bayou Oaks Artist Colony
Contact: Judy Courtwright
Route 1, Box 211
Angleton, TX 77515
(409) 848-1888

Cowboy Artists of America Museum
P.O. Box 1716
Kerrville, TX 78029
(210) 896-2553

Hill Country Arts Foundation
Jeaneane B. Duncan-Edith McAshan
    Visual Arts Center
P.O. Box 176
Ingram, TX 78025
(210) 367-5120

Mossy Brake Workshops
Mossy Brake Art Gallery
Route 2, Box 66B
Uncertain, TX 75661
(903) 789-3288

Prude Ranch School of Art Workshops
Box 3451
Ruidoso, NM 88345
Workshops take place in Ft. Davis, TX

Vermont
Art Workshops of Vermont
Box 57
Chittenden, VT 05737
(800) 445-2100

Pine Mountain Studio
Route 313, Battenkill Road
Arlington, VT 05250
(802) 375-6038

Plein-Air Painting Workshops
New Horizon Studios
1034 Woodstream Terrace
Seabrook, MD 20706
(301) 794-5706

Sketch Vermont Art Workshops
Gallery on the Green
One The Green
Woodstock, VT 05091
(800) 9-ARTIST

Virginia
American Academy of Equine Art
P.O. Box 1315
Middleburg, VA 22117
(864) 486-4667

Art Farm Workshops
Route 5, Box 85
Lexington, VA 24450
(703) 463-7961

Art League
105 North Union Street
Alexandria, VA 22314
(703) 683-2323

Shenandoah Valley Art Center
P.O. Box 907
Waynesboro, VA 22980
(703) 949-7662

Thistledown Farm Workshops
Route 2, Box 259
Hot Springs, VA 24445
(703) 962-1801

Webster's World
6644 Barrett Road
Falls Church, VA 22042
(703) 698-1920

Washington
Academy of Realist Art
5004 Sixth Avenue, N.W., Suite B
Seattle, WA 98107
(206) 784-4268

Coupeville Arts Center
Palettes Plus II Workshops
P.O. Box 171
Coupeville, WA 98239
(360) 678-3396

Creative Colored Pencil Workshops
1620 Melrose
Seattle, WA 98122
(206) 622-8661

Santa Fe Intensive Drawing & Pastel
    Workshop
c/o The Academy of Realist Art
5004 Sixth Avenue, N.W., Suite B
Seattle, WA 98107
(206) 784-4268

Wisconsin
Dillman's Creative Arts Foundation, Inc.
Dillman's Sand Lake Lodge, Inc.
P.O. Box 98F
Lac du Flambeau, WI 54538
(715) 588-3143

Peninsula Art School Workshops
Box 304
Fish Creek, WI 54212
(414) 868-3455

Foreign Workshops

Bermuda
Hudson River Valley Art Workshops
P.O. Box 659
Greenville, NY 12083-0659
(518) 966-5219

Canada
John Abott College
P.O. Box C.P. 2000
Ste. Anne de Bellevue, Quebec H9X 3L9
Canada
(514) 457-3063

Arts Mont-Tremblant
C.P./P.O. Box 448
Mont-Tremblant, Quebec J0T 1Z0
(613) 345-6058

Federation of Canadian Artists
952 Richards
Vancouver, British Columbia V6B 3C1
Canada
(604) 274-2838

Holland College Centre of Creative Arts
50 Burns Avenue
Charlotte, Prince Edward Island C1E 1H7
Canada
(902) 566-9310

Island Lake Lodge
Box 3023
Collingwood, Ontario L9Y 3Z2
Canada
(705) 444-2331

Island Mount Arts Workshops
Box 65
Wells, British Columbia V0K 2R0
Canada

Metchosin International Summer
    School of the Arts
3505 Richmond Road
Victoria, British Columbia V8P 4P7
Canada
(604) 598-1695

Prince Edward Island Art and Nature
    Workshops
Box 2000, Dept. 152
Charlottetown, Prince Edward Island
    C1A 7N8
Canada

Strathgartney Country Inn
Bonshaw R.R. 3
Prince Edward Island C0A 1C0
Canada
(902) 675-4711

Trillium Workshops
92 Lakeshore Road East, Unit B2
Mississauga, Ontario L5G 1E3
Canada
(800) 263-1505

White Rock Summer School of the Arts
Box 150, 106–1656 Martin Drive
White Rock, British Columbia V4A 6E7
Canada
(604) 536-1122

England

Academy of Realist Art
5004 Sixth Avenue, N.W.
Seattle, WA 98107
(206) 784-4268

Artscape Painting Holidays
40/41 The Vintners
Temple Farm Industrial Estate
Southend-on-Sea, Essex SS2 5RZ
England

Mounts Bay Art Centre
Trevatha, Faugan Lane
Newlyn, Penzance, Cornwall TR18 5DJ
England
0736-66284

Summer School of Painting & Drawing
Henlian Mill, Llangynyw
Welshpool, Powys
Wales SY21 8EN
Great Britain
0938-810269; 0702-617900

France

A.I.M. Workshops & Painting Trips
P.O. Box 271
Jacksonville, OR 97530-0279
(541) 899-1179

Art Trek
P.O. Box 1103
Bolinas, CA 94924
(415) 868-9558

En Plain Air School of Painting
12 Rue d'Orchampt
75018 Paris
France
(011 331) 42-54-10-35; (301) 961-1062

Provence-Calvisson Art Workshops
30420 Calvisson
France

South of France Painting Workshops
24 Rue de la Ville
34320 Fontas
France
(33) 67-25-20-76

Greece

Aegean Workshops, Artists International, Inc.
148 Black Point Road
Niantic, CT 06357
(860) 739-0378

Apelles Art International Workshops
P.O. Box 99537
Raleigh, NC 27624-9537
(800) 274-2544

Art School of the Aegean
P.O. Box 1375
Sarasota, FL 34230-1375
(941) 351-5597

Guatemala
Art Workshops in La Antigua Guatemala
4758 Lundale Avenue South
Minneapolis, MN 55409-2304
(612) 825-0747

Italy
Art Workshop International
463 West Street
New York, NY 10014
(212) 691-1159

Artsmart
41 Lincoln Terrace
Harrington Park, NJ 07640
(201) 768-1151

Florence Academy of Art
Via delle Casine, 21/r
50122 Florence
Italy
(011) 39-55-24-54-44

Grand Marais Art Colony Workshops
P.O. Box 626
Grand Marais, MN 55604
(800) 385-9585

La Romita School of Art, Inc.
1712 Old Town, N.W.
Albuquerque, NM 87104
(505) 243-1924

Paint in Italy
Studio 309, 41 Union Square
New York, NY 10003
(212) 486-1462

Mexico
Acapulco Art Workshops
2882 West Long Circle
Littleton, CO 80120
(303) 738-8824

Amistad (Friendship) Workshops
1342 Neans Drive
Austin, TX 78758

Taller Fernando Sandoval
Hidalgo No. 1212
Centro, Oaxaca, CP 68000
Mexico

Puerto Rico
Tropical Workshops in Puerto Rico
c/o Galleria San Juan
204 Boulevarde del Valle
San Juan, Puerto Rico 00901
(809) 722-1808

Tour Agencies

Artists Workshop Tours Agency
606 Myra Avenue
Chula Vista, CA 92010
(619) 585-8071

Creative Art Workshops
6850 Brookeshire Drive
West Bloomfield, MI 48322
(313) 669-4736

Friends of the Arts & Sciences
Leech Studio
4433 Riverwood Avenue
P.O. Box 15766
Sarasota, FL 34277-1766
(813) 923-3031

Webster's World
6644 Barrett Road
Falls Church, VA 22042
(800) 344-7843

Art Publications

A number of magazines and journals are published for artists that include news in the field, trends and opinions, listings of upcoming juried art shows, art workshops and other opportunities, technical information and career advice as well as feature articles. Among these are:

American Artist
One Color Court
Marion, OH 43305
(800) 347-6969
$24.95 a year

Art Calendar
P.O. Box 1040
Sterling, VA 22066
(703) 430-6610
$29 a year

ARTnews
P.O. 2083
Knoxville, IA 50197-2083
(800) 284-4625
$32.95 a year

The Artist's Magazine
P.O. Box 2120
Harlan, IA 51593
(800) 333-0444
$24 a year

Art Now Gallery Guide
Art Now, Inc.
P.O. Box 888
Vineland, NJ 08360
(201) 322-8333
$35 a year

Art Paper
Visual Art Information Service, #206
2402 University Avenue West
St. Paul, MN 55114
(612) 645-5542
$20 a year

Sunshine Artists USA
1700 Sunset Drive
Longwood, FL 32750
(407) 323-5927
$22.50 a year

Fairs and Festivals in the Northeast
Fairs and Festivals in the Southeast
Arts Extension Service, Division of
    Continuing Education
604 Goodell
University of Massachusetts
Amherst, MA 01003
(413) 545-2360
$7.50 apiece; $13.00 for the pair

ACTS Facts
Arts, Crafts and Theater Safety
181 Thompson Street, #23
New York, NY 10012
(212) 777-0062
$10 a year

Art Hazards News
Center for Safety in the Arts
5 Beekman Street, #1030
New York, NY 10038
(212) 227-6220
$21 annually

Institute Items
Art & Craft Materials Institute
100 Boylston Street, #1050
Boston, MA 02116
(617) 426-6400
*$20 a year (for individual artists); $50 a
    year (for companies)*

Index

Allworth Books

Allworth Press publishes quality books to help individuals and small businesses. Titles include:

The Artist's Resource Handbook, Revised Edition
by Daniel Grant (softcover, 6 × 9, 248 pages, $18.95)

The Business of Being an Artist, Revised Edition
by Daniel Grant (softcover, 6 × 9, 272 pages, $18.95)

Artists Communities by the Alliance of Artists' Communities
(softcover, 6¾ × 10, 224 pages, $16.95)

The Fine Artist's Guide to Marketing and Self-Promotion
by Julius Vitali (softcover, 6 × 9, 224 pages, $18.95)

Arts and the Internet by V. A. Shiva
(softcover, 6 × 9, 208 pages, $18.95)

Fine Art Publicity: The Complete Guide for Galleries and Artists by Susan Abbott and Barbara Webb
(softcover, 8½ × 11, 190 pages, $22.95)

The Artist's Complete Health and Safety Guide, Second Edition
by Monona Rossol (softcover, 6 × 9, 344 pages, $19.95)

Legal Guide for the Visual Artist, Third Edition
by Tad Crawford (softcover, 8½ × 11, 256 pages, $19.95)

Licensing Art & Design, Revised Edition
by Caryn R. Leland (softcover, 6 × 9, 128 pages, $16.95)

Business and Legal Forms for Fine Artists, Revised Edition
by Tad Crawford (softcover, 8½ × 11, 144 pages, $16.95)

The Laws of Fésole: Principles of Drawing and Painting from the Tuscan Masters by John Ruskin, introduction by Bill Beckley
(softcover, 6 × 9, 224 pages, $18.95)

Lectures on Art by John Ruskin, introduction by Bill Beckley
(softcover, 6 × 9, 256 pages, $18.95)

Please write to request our free catalog. If you wish to order a book, send your check or money order to Allworth Press, 10 East 23rd Street, New York, NY 10010. Include $5 for shipping and handling for the first book ordered and $1 for each additional book. Ten dollars plus $1 for each additional book if ordering from Canada. New York State residents must add sales tax.

If you wish to see our catalog on the World Wide Web, you can find us at Millennium Production's Art and Technology Web site:
http://www.arts-online.com/allworth/home.html
or at **allworth.com**